Intergroup Communication

Language as SOCIAL ACTION

Howard Giles,
General Editor

Vol. 2

PETER LANG
New York • Washington, D.C./Baltimore • Bern
Frankfurt am Main • Berlin • Brussels • Vienna • Oxford

Intergroup Communication
MULTIPLE PERSPECTIVES

JAKE HARWOOD & HOWARD GILES,
Editors

PETER LANG
New York • Washington, D.C./Baltimore • Bern
Frankfurt am Main • Berlin • Brussels • Vienna • Oxford

Library of Congress Cataloging-in-Publication Data

Intergroup communication: multiple perspectives /
edited by Jake Harwood, Howard Giles.
p. cm. — (Language as social action; v. 2)
Includes bibliographical references and index.
1. Intergroup relations. 2. Social groups.
3. Communication—Social aspects. 4. Group identity.
I. Harwood, Jake. II. Giles, Howard. III. Series.
HM716.I56   302.3—dc22   2004011677
ISBN 0-8204-6739-1
ISSN 1529-2436

Bibliographic information published by **Die Deutsche Bibliothek**.
Die Deutsche Bibliothek lists this publication in the "Deutsche
Nationalbibliografie"; detailed bibliographic data is available
on the Internet at http://dnb.ddb.de/.

Cover design by Sophie Boorsch Appel

The paper in this book meets the guidelines for permanence and durability
of the Committee on Production Guidelines for Book Longevity
of the Council of Library Resources.

© 2005 Peter Lang Publishing, Inc., New York
275 Seventh Avenue, 28th Floor, New York, NY 10001
www.peterlangusa.com

Printed in the United States of America

To our families—the ultimate ingroup

Lori, Chloe, and Jonah
J.H.

Jane and Robbie
H.G.

CONTENTS

*Part 2. Communicating Identity Across
Communication Contexts*

Part 3. Epilogue

1
Intergroup Theory and Communication Processes

Jake Harwood
Howard Giles
Nicholas A. Palomares

While the study of stereotypes, prejudice, and discrimination has flourished among social psychologists in recent years (Brewer & Gaertner, 2003), communication scholars have been slower to address intergroup issues, at least until recently, despite their relevance to society. The current book is intended to stimulate more research and theory examining the key role of communication in intergroup relations. Messages about groups and the exchange of messages between groups constitute a fundamental part of the intergroup landscape, and it is time for communication researchers to play more of a pivotal role in providing an understanding of group-based injustice (Harwood, in press; Lambert, 1980).

The study of intergroup processes in social psychology can be traced to the early twentieth century (e.g., Katz & Braly, 1933; Lippmann, 1922), and notable landmarks can be identified in subsequent years (e.g., Allport, 1954; Sherif, Harvey, White, Hood, & Sherif, 1961; Tajfel & Turner, 1986). In Europe, work on intergroup issues was largely sparked by the development of social identity theory (SIT) by Tajfel and his colleagues at the University of Bristol in the early 1970s (Tajfel, 1978). SIT remains a powerful influence on the field to this day. Mainstream social psychology books and journals are paying increasing attention to intergroup issues, specifically SIT (e.g., in the form of *Annual Review of Psychology* chapters, dedicated journals such as *Group Processes and Intergroup Relations*, handbooks [e.g., Brown & Gaertner, 2003] and numerous articles in journals such as the *Journal of Personality and Social Psychology*). In addition, a number of books have been published in recent years examining SIT from a psychological perspective (e.g., Abrams & Hogg, 1999; Capozza & Brown, 2000; Hogg & Abrams, 2001; Robinson, 1996).

The early research on SIT included some of the first to examine language and communication processes in intergroup contexts (e.g., Bourhis, Giles, & Tajfel, 1973; Giles, 1977, 1978), including Giles's work on speech (now communication) accommodation theory (CAT), which is outlined in more detail later. Thus, the tradition of research on intergroup communication processes is long-standing. However, the study of intergroup communication never achieved recognition as a distinct area in its own right.

Intergroup communication research is currently growing. Researchers are increasingly examining the ways in which group memberships shape and are shaped by communication (e.g., Clément, 1996; Giles & Coupland, 1991; Gudykunst, 1986, 1998). This growth can be attributed in part to the relevance of intergroup issues to so many domains within communication. At this point, we see a need for a book that integrates the diverse work pertaining to these issues, drawing on both communication and social psychological work (and with contributors from both disciplines). We believe this book will set the stage for a growth in intergroup communication work over the next decade, as well as establish the area as more distinct and recognizable within the communication field. The recent founding of a division of intergroup communication in the International Communication Association is a promising development in this regard. This chapter provides an argument that intergroup communication is a distinct theoretical and empirical domain by describing its conceptual bases, illustrating its omnipresence, and discussing the central theoretical paradigms within the area. Throughout this chapter, we use real world examples to make clear the significance and relevance of intergroup communication as an important field of inquiry.

What is Intergroup Communication?

Intergroup communication occurs when either party in a social interaction defines self or other in terms of group memberships. From its early stages, SIT noted that people could understand the self in terms of *personal identity* (a perception of self as a unique individual with particular traits, preferences, etc.) and *social identity* (a perception of self as a member of particular groups, along with the associations relevant to those groups). Examples of such group memberships include age groups, nationalities, sexual orientations, cultures, religions, academic, sporting, and political groups, to name just a few. Intergroup communication occurs when social identity (rather than personal identity) is salient for at least one participant. This definition highlights three important issues.

First, intergroup communication is not communication that occurs between groups. Rather, it occurs when the transmission or reception of messages is influenced by the group memberships of the individuals involved. To this extent, it is important to distinguish between group communication and intergroup communication, although one can certainly take an intergroup perspective on group communication (Hogg & Tindale, this volume).

Second, not all individuals have to perceive an interaction through an intergroup lens in order for intergroup communication to occur. An example of this is a recent interaction at one of our campuses where a group of white students shouted the slur "A.I." (standing for Asian Invasion) at a group of Asian American students walking down the street in the university community. Such an interaction is clearly intergroup in nature, however it is defined as such merely by one side's characterization of the other's identity. For the Asian American students in the encounter, other identities (gender, sorority house, student) might have been more salient until the point at which their ethnic categorization was made salient by the other.

Third, the definition makes clear that self- and other-categorizations are linked. Drawing on the previous example, the students' explicit categorization of the others as "Asian" invokes an implicit self-categorization of themselves as *not* Asian (and given the salience of ethnicity, presumably as white). This categorization then becomes relevant for all parties in the situation. Hence, when intergroup communication occurs, self- and other-categorization, group salience, and social (group) identification are likely concomitants. Social identifications often have linguistic manifestations, as in the use of Ebonics or Spanglish, adolescent jargon, or ethnophaulisms such as those mentioned above (Mullen & Leader, in press).

Given the large literature on "interpersonal communication" generated by communication scholars in recent years (Knapp & Daly, 2002), it is useful to distinguish intergroup from interpersonal communication. While at times the distinction between intergroup and interpersonal communication has been drawn along a single continuum, we are more engaged by models that view communication as having the potential to be high or low on both intergroup and interpersonal dimensions (Giles & Hewstone, 1982; Gudykunst & Lim, 1986; Stephenson, 1981). This allows the theoretical possibility for four quadrants in a space defined by two (theoretically orthogonal, if correlated in practice) continua.

In the first quadrant, interpersonal and intergroup salience are both high. These are situations in which people deal with each other as individuals, while also considering group differences. An interaction in which a son discloses that he is gay to his father might be an example of this. Their relational history would likely mean that interpersonal salience would be high—the father is likely to deal with the son as the unique individual who he has always known. At the same time, the categorization of the son based on sexuality will be salient and each individual's understanding of the category "gay" will factor into the conversation.

The second quadrant includes communicative behaviors based on high interpersonal salience and low intergroup salience. For example, two old friends talking about an incident from the past might well be dealing with each other almost entirely in terms of their unique personal characteristics and relational history, with social group memberships playing little role.

The third quadrant demonstrates the ability for interactions to be highly defined in terms of group memberships with little interpersonal influence. This quadrant is illustrated in the earlier example. The "Asian Invaders" were defined purely by their ethnicity, and there was no incorporation of interpersonal elements in the interaction (let alone their diverse Asian nationalities and cultures). This quadrant is characteristically associated with negative behaviors; however, positive behaviors are also possible here (at the extreme, for instance, nurturing behaviors toward an infant are almost entirely category-driven, and are overwhelmingly positive [S. Wright, personal communication, June 15, 2004]).

The fourth quadrant covers situations low in interpersonal and intergroup salience. Examples of these sorts of interactions occur when individuals are inebriated, unable to use interpersonal or intergroup features of their interactions, or simply are not motivated to consider such information. Mindless interactions with service personnel might sometimes fit into this category, but in general we suspect that such communication is rare when substance abuse is not involved.

These categories provide a useful heuristic for considering communicative events, and raise some more general points about intergroup communication. First, the degree to which encounters are intergroup and interpersonal are, in practice, negatively correlated. That is, as encounters become highly intergroup in nature, the consideration of interpersonal features is often reduced. It appears to be difficult to engage someone simultaneously in terms of their unique personal characteristics and their group memberships, although it is certainly not impossible (consider, for instance, a thrilling discussion of cultural differences between a husband and wife in a multicultural marriage). Certain scholars from the self-categorization tradition argue that dealing with others at high levels of personal and social categorization is actually impossible, and they emphasize the inherent conflict between these two levels of categorization (Oakes, Haslam, & Turner, 1994). We adopt a somewhat more liberal attitude, accepting that, at times, both personal and social categorizations may be salient, while still acknowledging a tendency for one to suppress the other.

Second, these dimensions tend to be associated with experienced affect. Encounters high in group salience tend to be dissatisfying, low in intimacy, and high in conflict (Harwood, Hewstone, Paolini, & Voci, in press; Islam & Hewstone, 1993; Williams & Giles, 1996). Likewise, we tend to associate strongly interpersonal interactions as positive events (caring, loving, etc.). However, we would caution that intergroup encounters can be rewarding and satisfying events (e.g., the married couple above), and interpersonal encounters can obviously be conflict-ridden (e.g., an adolescent discussing with her parents the restrictions they intend to impose upon her). Hence, we would caution against a simplistic association of intergroup as bad and interpersonal as good. In this context, it is worth noting the lack of attention paid to communication processes in the intergroup contact literature (cf. Brown, Maras, Masser, Vivian, & Hewstone, 2001; Reid & Giles, in press). A huge volume of research in the past 50 years has attempted to understand the ways in which contact between members of different groups can influence intergroup attitudes (Brewer & Gaertner, 2003). However, while this work concerns a fundamentally communicative event (contact between an ingroup and outgroup member), the event itself has been treated as a black box. Most contact research focuses on a few structural aspects of the encounter (often manipulated *a priori* by the investigator: e.g., cooperation, status, task focus—Brewer & Gaertner, 2003), and its outcomes. We see tremendous potential in examinations of the specific communicative dynamics of intergroup contact.

Third, we note the ubiquity of group salience. While "purely" interpersonal communication is a theoretical possibility, in fact many interpersonal encounters can be usefully understood and explained in intergroup terms. Communication within intimate relationships can be infused with group identities (Harwood, Soliz, & Lin, in press; Wright, Aron, & Tropp, 2002); indeed, heterosexual marriage is inherently an intergroup (gender-wise) institution, and interaction in marriage is often infused with gender roles, stereotypes, and identifications (Tannen, 2003). Even communication between individuals from the *same* group can become infused with intergroup issues if shared identifications become salient and influence communication (e.g., two fraternity members talking about their house or about non-Greeks).

Fourth, encounters between individuals are not rigidly classified into one of these quadrants. Indeed, one interaction of even a few short minutes could shift from one quadrant to another and back again in complex trajectories, as well as be subjectively construed by the participants in very different ways.

Interestingly, of course, communication also plays an important role in *constructing* the nature of group memberships and group categories (e.g., Potter & Wetherell, 1998). This role of communication has been given less attention in the literature, however it is fundamental, especially as it relates to dimensions of group identity (Abrams, O'Connor, & Giles, 2003). Theoretical developments such as self-categorization theory have illustrated the importance of understanding how and when particular group categorizations become salient, but largely from a socio-psychological standpoint. We would urge more attention to the communicative determinants of group categorization and category salience, as well as attention to the negotiability of such categorizations (Harwood, Raman, & Hewstone, 2005). Likewise, communication theorists seem well positioned to examine the ways in which some individuals exist on the margins or boundaries between groups. For instance, Hajek et al. (this volume) discuss bisexuals' difficult position as not heterosexual, but also not accepted in the gay community. Likewise, Ryan et al. (this volume) talk about the difficult situation of blind people who can at times see things (e.g., with peripheral vision). These liminal identities raise questions for others in the environment about the legitimacy of an identity and encourage difficult attributions (e.g., she's not *really* blind, gay, etc.). Such issues tie into questions of authenticity that are currently important in, for instance, sociolinguistics (e.g., Coupland, 2003).

Social Identity Theory and Its Legacy

We now describe a major theory of intergroup relations, social identity theory (SIT), and the subsequent developments that have extended this work into the communication literature. The theory originated in the early 1970s as an attempt to understand how psychological and sociological processes interact to produce micro and macro intergroup dynamics (Tajfel, 1978; Tajfel & Turner, 1986). It suggests that maintaining psychological distinctiveness between the ingroup and the outgroup is functional for individuals. In some manifestations, the motivation for maintaining positive distinctiveness has been described in terms of self-esteem (individual or collective), uncertainty reduction, or positive identity (Abrams & Hogg, 1999). Regardless of the specific motivational mechanism, the fact that people seek to view their ingroups as better than, and distinct from, outgroups is clear from the literature. Hence, individuals categorize their social worlds, categorize themselves into ingroups and others into outgroups, and engage in social comparisons between those groups. To the extent that the ingroup membership is valued and salient, the individual can be said to have a social identification with that group.

When one's social identity is positive, all is well. However, when one's social identity is not positive (i.e., comparisons with the outgroup yield negative results), then individuals are motivated to seek alternatives. Three strategies for remedying a negative social identity are suggested by SIT and feature significantly in most chapters in this volume. First, group members can leave their current group and *as-*

similate to an outgroup that has a positive comparison among other groups (social mobility). Mobility allows an individual to transition between groups making their ingroup and outgroup comparisons more favorable, which results in a new, more positive social identity. An example of assimilation is seen in Asian individuals who wish to alter the physical characteristics of their eyelids through surgery. This surgery offers a way for Asian individuals to assimilate to Caucasians through physical appearance. A similar example occurs when former gang members remove their associations with gangs by erasing gang-associated tattoos. Converging toward the dress style, dialect, non-verbals and discourse structures of another group are other examples of this strategy.

An alternative approach to improving a negative social identity is *social creativity*. This actually encompasses a set of strategies, including making in*tra*group comparisons, redefining the negative dimensions of comparison to be more positive, and creating new dimensions of comparison. These social creativity strategies achieve a positive social identity by changing aspects of the ingroup-outgroup comparisons. Examples include groups using a once low-prestige language or dialect (e.g., Québécois French) or a once derogatory word (e.g., *nigger/nigga, queer, dyke, etc.*) as an expression of ingroup camaraderie. Groups might also seek alternative points of comparison, for example, by comparing themselves with alternative outgroups (e.g., older adults might compare themselves with even older people to obtain positive comparisons, rather than seeking negative comparisons with those who are younger—Coupland, Coupland, & Giles, 1991).

The third strategy for converting a negative social identity into a positive one is *social competition*. With this strategy, individuals in groups resort to a direct struggle for a positive social identity. Examples are political activity, marches, vigils, protests, and the like. The existence of political lobbies in Washington, DC (and other national capitals) such as the American Association for Retired Persons and the National Association for the Advancement of Colored People provides evidence of this kind of activity. Once again, this has clear communicative parameters.

SIT posits that the choice of which strategy to pursue depends on the perception of alternatives to the status quo. If boundaries between groups are open (i.e., it is feasible to change group memberships), then mobility is an option; if they are closed, then it is not (Giles & Johnson, 1981). However, even if mobility is an option, other factors might preclude it. For instance, individuals who are highly identified with their groups are unlikely to engage in mobility. At the other extreme, social competition strategies are only likely in situations in which the intergroup status quo is perceived as unstable or illegitimate. Subordinate groups who perceive their position in the social hierarchy to be appropriate and inevitable will not engage in large scale campaigns for a change in the hierarchy. Thus, it is possible to examine the individual and collective level intergroup situation and reach conclusions about likely responses to negative social identity. Extensive recent reviews of SIT are available (Capozza & Brown, 2000; Robinson, 1996).

Communication theory has been influenced by SIT in a number of ways. Communication accommodation theory (CAT) included features of SIT as it was sequentially refined (for a history of its development, see Gallois, Ogay, and Giles, 2004), and CAT is invoked to good interpretive effect in many chapters in this volume. CAT focuses particularly on the ways in which language is used in interpersonal interaction to establish social identities and achieve intergroup comparisons (Gallois, Giles, Jones, Cargile, & Ota, 1995; Giles & Powesland, 1975; Shepard, Giles, & LePoire, 2001). For instance, individuals might emphasize their accents or even switch languages to emphasize their relative group identities. CAT focuses on the fundamental importance of language, accent, and dialect to individuals' social identities. More recent work has focused on the multiple complex ways in which group memberships can influence mutual adaptation and accommodation in intergroup encounters (Coupland, Coupland, Giles, & Henwood, 1988). For instance, particular attention has been given to the ways in which individuals might accommodate toward stereotypes of other groups, or specific context- and group-related power dynamics (Hummert & Ryan, 2001).

Building on CAT, ethnolinguistic identity theory (ELIT) (Giles & Johnson, 1987) discusses the socio-psychological processes underlying specific language strategies adopted by ethnolinguistic group members in social interaction. A particular focus of ELIT is on the extent to which an encounter is defined as interethnic, and behavior is shaped by that definition (Sachdev & Bourhis, this volume). One of the central concepts in ELIT is *group vitality* (or ethnolinguistic vitality) (Bourhis, Giles, & Rosenthal, 1981; Giles, Bourhis, & Taylor, 1977). This concept refers to the "strength" of a particular language group, with particular emphasis on the demographic numbers and concentration of a language's speakers, the language's status, and the level of institutional support (e.g., through the media) for the language (Harwood, Giles, & Bourhis, 1994). This concept has had considerable impact in terms of geolinguistics (McConnell, 1991), second language learning (e.g., Evans, 1996) and language planning (Landry & Allard, 1994), with a particular focus on the ways in which perceptions of vitality are associated with language maintenance and ethnic solidarity. As with CAT, uses of the vitality construct have extended beyond language groups to the examination of age groups and others (e.g., Harwood, Giles, Clément, Pierson, & Fox, 1994).

Recently, self-categorization theory (SCT) has emerged as a powerful and insightful development of the SIT tradition, and a number of chapters herein invoke this theory. SCT focuses on the cognitive bases of categorization and identification more than SIT, and, hence, it is centered on the psychological origins of group processes. SCT theorists treat categorization as a fundamental and functional cognitive process. In other words, they refute the notion promulgated elsewhere that stereotypes are inherently negative or are a result of cognitive errors or shortcuts, noting instead that if collective identities are salient in a given situation, then cognitively speaking stereotypes are the most appropriate categorical device to apply. In other words, while the *content* of specific stereotypes is objectionable to some people, their use in a given context might be functional and rational.

Other perspectives on intergroup relations have also been influential, and underlie various chapters in this book (e.g., Fiske & Taylor, 1991; Hecht et al., 2002; Sherif, 1966; van Dijk, 1987). Social cognition research has been a dominant force in stereotyping research in the United States particularly. This work has influenced both the examination of stereotypes from a communication perspective (e.g., Hummert, Garstka, Ryan, & Bonnesen, 2004) and the examination of cognitive representations of communication (e.g., Harwood, McKee, & Lin, 2000). Work on discursive psychology has been influential in the examination of discourses surrounding group memberships (Potter & Wetherell, 1998). Recently, the boundaries between these traditions have been blurring, given the increasing focus on cognitive mechanisms in the (broadly speaking) social identity literature and a growing interest in context and sociological level variables among social cognition researchers. This is also apparent in the communication literature where most intergroup communication scholars draw upon social cognition and social identity work, as well as maintain a broader perspective on the importance of language in constituting and maintaining categories. However, SIT is at the heart of the current book, and, hence, we have given it more attention at the outset.

The Current Book

The perspectives outlined above have directly influenced some communication research, and other work in the field can be understood using these perspectives as lenses, even when the impetus for the work came from other theories. The chapters of this book reflect two complementary approaches to the relationship between communication and intergroup relations.

In the first part of the book we focus on specific intergroup contexts. Thus, we have chapters examining communication within and between cultural, disability, age, sex and sexuality, and language groups. This "contextual" focus is useful because it draws attention to the similarities and differences between various intergroup contexts. All contexts share dynamics in terms of identity processes, stereotyping, status hierarchies, and intergroup discrimination. However, each has its own unique features. For example, age is a continuum that we (somewhat arbitrarily) divide into groups, whereas sex is generally understood as a categorical variable. Similarly, sexuality is a largely concealable identity (Cameron & Kulick, 2003), whereas concealment is considerably more difficult with many (but not all) cultural and disability identities (Gallois, 2004). Some of these contexts offer paradigm examples of negative attitudes and prejudice, whereas some other contexts offer situations in which the disadvantaged group can be evaluated quite "positively" (e.g., the "women are wonderful" effect: Eagly & Mladinic, 1994). Indeed, whereas many intergroup contexts are characterized by a lack of contact and negative intergroup communication, sex offers a situation of institutionally supported contact in the form of marriage, to the extent that intragroup contact (in the form of homosexual marriage) is actively condemned by many in

the United States. Thus, considering the different contexts of intergroup communication can make us aware of the unique complexities
of specific contexts and the fact that theories that work well in one
context might fall apart in another.

The second part of the book derives its structure from the traditional levels of inquiry within communication, although aspects of
both sections of the book are interlaced (for example, with respect to
gender relations in male-dominated workplaces, see Boggs and Giles,
1999). With the exception of "interpersonal communication" research
(covered in Part 1), we examine how work at other levels can be understood from an intergroup perspective. Thus, there are chapters on
small group, organizational, mass, and Internet communication. The
consideration of *levels* of communication allows us to provide clear
guidance to researchers in those areas as to how an intergroup approach can enhance their research. Also, these chapters make clearer
the ways in which other areas of communication might be usefully
informed by an intergroup perspective, although there is clearly not
space in this text to cover them all. For instance, recent work has
demonstrated the utility of intergroup theory for understanding
health communication (Harwood & Sparks, 2003), police-community
relations (Giles, 2002), family communication (Harwood, Hewstone,
et al., in press; Soliz & Harwood, 2003), instructional communication
(Edwards & Harwood, 2003), intercultural communication training
(Cargile & Giles, 1996), stigma (Abrams & Giles, 2004), terrorism
(Sparks, in press), and undoubtedly others. We hope that these chapters encourage scholars to explore the role of intergroup processes in
other communication areas (e.g., visual, political, and legal communication).

Wherever possible, we have encouraged authors in this volume to
reach out to other methodological and ideological traditions other
than their own, and we believe this emerges as a valued feature of this
collection (e.g., Hecht et al.); indeed, some vivid rapprochements are
offered as by Paulsen et al. in their melding of neopositivism on the
one hand, with critical discourse analysis on the other. Although we
have worked with authors on draft iterations of their chapters, we
have not imposed standardized sections nor recommended content
coverage. Rather, we have avoided homogeny for the sake of diverse
approaches from scholars renowned for their expertise in different

intergroup arenas. Indeed, it is *their* reading of their area, whether it be an overview of past accomplishments in more traditional spheres or articulating research agendas in developing areas (Paulsen et al.) that has excited us. Eclecticism also abounds across the chapters to the extent that different intergroup situations have been examined together that are not usually reviewed in the same context (Hajek et al.; Williams & Garrett), new models and propositions are formulated for the first time (Harwood & Roy; Ryan et al.), social policy is highlighted (Sachdev & Bourhis), and attention is directed primarily toward new vistas of intergroup communication research (Hogg & Tindale; Paulsen et al.; Postmes & Baym). This book closes with an epilogue that draws closer links between self-categorization theory and the communication discipline.

The area of intergroup communication is in its early development, but it is an area that can grow and develop quickly. Huge volumes of research on communication exist, and much of that work pertains to intergroup issues—whether it was explicitly designed to address intergroup issues or not. Likewise, a very substantial body of work on intergroup social psychology exists, and quite a bit of that work pertains to communication processes, whether or not that was the original intent of the authors. We hope this book helps illustrate some of the links between these two literatures, to the mutual benefit of each. Ultimately, the goal of intergroup research is to understand and ameliorate situations of prejudice and discrimination. These can range from a minor snub that is attributed to group membership to genocide. No book is going to solve these problems, however we hope to provide some insight into the ways in which human communication processes contribute to intergroup problems and may provide some salves for those human divides. Eliminating or ignoring group differences is not our desired outcome. Communication scholars' role here is rather to understand how group differences can be represented in messages that are inclusive and embrace diversity, which support group identifications while not denying others' affiliations, and which foster positive social identities while disaffirming prejudice and discrimination. Such lofty goals offer the promise for the field of communication to leave an important legacy for human civilization.

References

Abrams, D., & Hogg, M. A. (Eds.) (1999). *Social identity and social cognition.* Oxford, UK: Blackwell.

Abrams, J. R., & Giles, H. (2004). An intergroup approach to communicating stigma. In S. H. Ng, C. N. Candlin, & C. Y. Chiu (Eds.), *Language matters: Communication, culture, and identity* (pp. 27–62). Hong Kong: City University of Hong Kong Press.

Abrams, J. R., O'Connor, J., & Giles, H. (2003). Identity and intergroup communication. In W. B. Gudykunst (Ed.), *Cross-cultural and intercultural communication* (pp. 209–224). Thousand Oaks, CA: Sage.

Allport, G. W. (1954). *The nature of prejudice.* Reading, MA: Addison-Wesley.

Boggs, C., & Giles, H. (1999). "The canary in the cage": The nonaccommodation cycle in the gendered workplace. *International Journal of Applied Linguistics, 22,* 223–245.

Bourhis, R. Y., Giles, H., & Rosenthal, D. (1981). Notes on the construction of a "Subjective Vitality Questionnaire" for ethnolinguistic groups. *Journal of Multilingual and Multicultural Development, 2,* 144–155.

Bourhis, R. Y., Giles, H., & Tajfel, H. (1973). Language as a determinant of Welsh identity. *European Journal of Social Psychology, 3,* 447–460.

Brewer, M. B., & Gaertner, S. L. (2003). Toward reduction of prejudice: Intergroup contact and social categorization. In R. Brown & S. L. Gaertner (Eds.), *Blackwell handbook of social psychology: Intergroup processes* (pp. 451–472). Malden, MA: Blackwell.

Brown, R., & Gaertner, S. L. (2003). *Blackwell handbook of social psychology: Intergroup Processes.* Malden, MA: Blackwell.

Brown, R., Maras, P., Masser, B., Vivian, J., & Hewstone, M. (2001). Life on the ocean wave: Testing some intergroup hypotheses in a naturalistic setting. *Group Processes and Intergroup Relations, 4,* 81–97.

Cameron, D., & Kulick, D. (2003). *Language and sexuality.* Cambridge: Cambridge University Press.

Capozza, D., & Brown, R. (Eds.) (2000). *Social identity processes: Trends in theory and research.* Thousand Oaks, CA: Sage.

Cargile, A., & Giles, H. (1996). Intercultural communication training: A critical review and new theoretical perspective. *Communication Yearbook, 19,* 385–423.

Clément, R. (Ed.). (1996). The social psychology of intergroup communication [Special Issue]. *Journal of Language and Social Psychology, 15* (3).

Coupland, N. (2003). Sociolinguistic authenticities. *Journal of Sociolinguistics, 7,* 417–456.

Coupland, N., Coupland, J., & Giles, H. (1991). *Language, society and the elderly: Discourse, identity and ageing.* Oxford, UK: Blackwell.

Coupland, N., Coupland, J., Giles, H., & Henwood, K. (1988). Accommodating the elderly: Invoking and extending a theory. *Language in Society, 17,* 1–41.

Eagly, A. H., & Mladinic, A. (1994). Are people prejudiced against women? Some answers from research on attitudes, gender stereotypes and judgments of competence. In W. Stroebe & M. Hewstone (Eds.), *European review of social psychology* (Vol. 5, pp. 1–35). New York: Wiley.

Edwards, C. C., & Harwood, J. (2003). Social identity in the classroom: An examination of age identification between students and instructors. *Communication Education, 52,* 60–65.

Evans, C. (1996). Ethnolinguistic vitality, prejudice, and family language transmission. *Bilingual Research Journal, 2,* 177–207.

Fiske, S. T., & Taylor, S. E. (1991). *Social cognition* (2nd ed.). New York: McGraw-Hill.

Gallois, C. (2004). Communicating disability: Stereotypes, identity and motivation. In S. H. Ng, C. N. Candlin, & C. Y. Chiu (Eds.), *Language matters: Communication, culture, and identity* (pp. 355–374). Hong Kong: City University of Hong Kong Press.

Gallois, C., Giles, H., Jones, E., Cargile, A. C., & Ota, H. (1995). Accommodating intercultural encounters: Elaborations and extensions. In R. Wiseman (Ed.), *Intercultural communication theory* (pp. 115–147). Thousand Oaks, CA: Sage.

Gallois, C., Ogay, T., & Giles, H. (2004). Communication accommodation theory: A look back and a look ahead. In W. B. Gudykunst (Ed.), *Theorizing about intercultural communication* (pp. 121–148). Thousand Oaks, CA: Sage.

Giles, H. (Ed.). (1977). *Language, ethnicity and intergroup relations.* London: Academic.

Giles, H. (1978). Linguistic differentiation between ethnic groups. In H. Tajfel (Ed.), *Differentiation between social groups* (pp. 361–393). London: Academic.

Giles, H. (Ed.) (2002). *Law enforcement, communication, and community.* Amsterdam: Benjamins.

Giles, H., Bourhis, R. Y., & Taylor, D. M. (1977). Towards a theory of language in ethnic group relations. In H. Giles (Ed.), *Language, ethnicity, and intergroup relations* (pp. 307–348). London: Academic Press.

Giles, H., & Coupland, N. (1991). *Language: Contexts and consequences.* Pacific Grove, CA: Brooks/Cole.

Giles, H., & Hewstone, M. (1982). Cognitive structures, speech, and social situations. *Language Sciences, 4,* 187–219.

Giles, H., & Johnson, P. (1981). The role of language in ethnic group relations. In J. C. Turner and H. Giles (Eds.), *Intergroup behavior* (pp. 199–243). Oxford, Blackwell.

Giles, H., & Johnson, P. (1987). Ethnolinguistic identity theory: A social psychological approach to language maintenance. *International Journal of the Sociology of Language, 68,* 66–99.

Giles, H., & Powesland, P. F. (1975). *Speech style and social evaluation.* London: Academic.

Gudykunst, W. B. (Ed.). (1986). *Intergroup communication.* London: Edward Arnold.

Gudykunst, W. B. (1998). *Bridging differences: Effective intergroup communication.* Thousand Oaks, CA: Sage.

Gudykunst, W. B., & Lim, T. S. (1986). A perspective for the study of intergroup communication. In W. B. Gudykunst (Ed.), *Intergroup communication* (pp. 1–9). London: Edward Arnold.

Harwood, J. (in press). Communication as social identity. In G. Shepherd, J. St. John, & T. Striphas (Eds.), *Communication as…: Stances on theory.* Thousand Oaks, CA: Sage.

Harwood, J., Giles, H., & Bourhis, R. Y. (1994). The genesis of vitality theory: Historical patterns and discoursal dimensions. *International Journal of the Sociology of*

Language, 108, 167–206.

Harwood, J., Giles, H., Clément, R., Pierson, H., & Fox, S. (1994). Perceived vitality of age categories in California and Hong Kong. *Journal of Multilingual and Multicultural Development, 15,* 311–318.

Harwood, J., Hewstone, M., Paolini, S., & Voci, A. (in press). Grandparent-grandchild contact and attitudes towards older adults: Moderator and mediator effects. *Personality and Social Psychology Bulletin.*

Harwood, J., McKee, J., & Lin, M. C. (2000). Younger and older adults' schematic representations of intergenerational communication. *Communication Monographs, 67,* 20–41.

Harwood, J., Raman, P., & Hewstone, M. (2005). *The communication dynamics of group salience.* Unpublished manuscript, University of Arizona.

Harwood, J., Soliz, J., & Lin, M. C. (in press). Communication accommodation theory: An intergroup approach to family communication. In D. O. Braithwaite & L. Baxter (Eds.), *Family communication theories.* Newbury Park, CA: Sage.

Harwood, J., & Sparks, L. S. (2003). An intergroup communication approach to cancer. *Health Communication, 15,* 145–160.

Hecht, M. L., Faulkner, S. L., Meyer, C. R., Niles, T. A., Golden, D., & Cutler, M. (2002). Looking through Northern Exposure at Jewish American identity and the communication theory of identity. *Journal of Communication, 52,* 852–870.

Hogg, M. A., & Abrams, D. (2001). *Intergroup relations.* Philadelphia: Psychology Press.

Hummert, M. L., Garstka, T. A., Ryan, E. B., & Bonnesen, J. L. (2004). The role of age stereotypes in interpersonal communication. In J. F. Nussbaum & J. Coupland (Eds.), *Handbook of communication and aging research* (pp. 91–121). Mahwah, NJ: Erlbaum.

Hummert, M. L., & Ryan, E. B. (2001). Patronizing. In W. P. Robinson & H. Giles (Eds.), *The new handbook of language and social psychology* (pp. 253–270). Chichester, UK: Wiley.

Islam, M. R., & Hewstone, M. (1993). Dimensions of contact as predictors of intergroup anxiety, perceived outgroup variability, and outgroup attitude: An integrative model. *Personality and Social Psychology Bulletin, 19,* 700–710.

Katz, D., & Braly, K. (1933). Racial stereotypes of one hundred college students. *Journal of Abnormal and Social Psychology, 28,* 280–290.

Knapp, M. L., & Daly, J. A. (Eds.) (2002). *Handbook of interpersonal communication* (3rd ed.). Thousand Oaks, CA: Sage.

Lambert, W. C. (1980). The social psychology of language: A perspective for the 1980s. In H. Giles, W. P. Robinson, & P. M. Smith (Eds.), *Language: Social psychological perspectives* (pp. 415–424). Oxford: Pergamon.

Landry, R., & Allard, R. (1994). The Acadians of New Brunswick: Demolinguistic realities and the vitality of the French language. *International Journal of the Sociology of Language, 105–106,* 181–215.

Lippmann, W. (1922). *Public opinion.* New York: Harcourt, Brace, Jovanovich.

McConnell, G. D. (1991). *A macro-sociolinguistic analysis of language vitality.* Sainte-Foy, Quebec: Laval University Press.

Mullen, B., & Leader, T. (in press). Linguistic factors: Antilocutions, ethnonyms, ethnophaulism, and other varieties of hate speech. In J. Dovidio, P. Glick, & L. Rudman (Eds.), *On the nature of prejudice.* Malden, MA: Blackwell.

Oakes, P. J., Haslam, S. A., & Turner, J. C. (1994). *Stereotyping and social reality.* Oxford: Blackwell.

Potter, J., & Wetherell, M. (1998). Social representations, discourse analysis, and racism. In U. Flick (Ed.), *The psychology of the social* (pp. 138–155). New York: Cambridge University Press.

Reid, S., & Giles, H. (Eds.). (in press). Communication and intergroup contact [Special Issue]. *Group Processes and Intergroup Relations.*

Robinson, W. P. (Ed.) (1996). *Social groups and identities: Developing the legacy of Henri Tajfel.* Oxford: Butterworth-Heinemann.

Shepard, C., Giles, H., & LePoire, B. A. (2001). Communication accommodation theory. In W. P. Robinson & H. Giles (Eds.), *The new handbook of language and social psychology* (pp. 33–56). Chichester, UK: Wiley.

Sherif, M. (1966). *In common predicament: Social psychology of intergroup conflict and cooperation.* Boston: Houghton-Mifflin.

Sherif, M., Harvey, O. J., White, B. J., Hood, W. R., & Sherif, C. W. (1961). *Intergroup conflict and cooperation: The Robber's Cave experiment.* Norman, OK: University of Oklahoma Press.

Soliz, J., & Harwood, J. (2003). Perceptions of communication in a family relationship and the reduction of intergroup prejudice. *Journal of Applied Communication Research, 31,* 320–345.

Sparks, L. (in press). Social identity and mass-mediated representations of terrorist groups: An intergroup communication approach to terrorism. In H. D. O'Hair, R. Heath, & G. Ledlow (Eds.), *Communication, communities and terrorism.* Westport, CT: Praeger.

Stephenson, G. M. (1981). Intergroup bargaining and negotiation. In J. C. Turner & H. Giles (Eds.), *Intergroup behavior* (pp. 168–198). Chicago: University of Chicago Press.

Tajfel, H. (Ed.) (1978). *Differentiation between social groups: Studies in the social psychology of intergroup relations.* London: Academic Press.

Tajfel, H., & Turner, J. C. (1986). The social identity theory of intergroup behavior. In S. Worchel, & W. Austin (Eds.), *Psychology of intergroup relations* (pp. 7–24). Chicago: Nelson-Hall.

Tannen, D. (2003). Gender and family interaction. In J. Holmes & M. Meyerhoff (Eds.), *The handbook of language and gender* (pp. 179–201). Malden, MA: Blackwell.

Van Dijk, T. A. (1987). *Communicating racism: Ethnic prejudice in thought and talk.* Newbury Park, CA: Sage.

Williams, A., & Giles, H. (1996). Intergenerational conversations: Young adults' retrospective accounts. *Human Communication Research, 23,* 220–250.

Wright, S. C., Aron, A., & Tropp, L. R. (2002). Including others (and groups) in the self: Self-expansion and intergroup relations. In J. P. Forgas & K. Williams (Eds.), *The social self: Cognitive, interpersonal and intergroup perspectives* (pp. 342–363). Philadelphia: Psychology Press.

PART 1

Communicating Identity Within and Between Social Groups

2

Culture: Intersections of Intergroup and Identity Theories

Michael L. Hecht
Ronald L. Jackson II
Margaret J. Pitts

Culture is a central organizing principle of human activity. How, why, when, and where we do what we do is motivated, at least in part, by the rules, perspectives, and ideals of the culture(s) in which we live. Often, when communication scholars write about culture, they explore its functions, definitions, and effects (Baldwin, Faulkner, Hecht, & Lindsley, in press). In the multifaceted, interdisciplinary conversation on culture, we are introduced to concepts such as Hofstede's (2001) dimensions of cultural variability (individualism/collectivism, masculinity/femininity, power distance, and uncertainty avoidance). Additionally, concepts like intercultural personhood, ingroup/outgroup perspectives, as well as accommodation, acculturation, and assimilation emerge. In this chapter, our goal is to present culture from an intergroup perspective, to explore how it is understudied as an identity construct in intergroup communication research, and to present some new directions for integrating culture into intergroup research. To accomplish this, we will first offer our definition of culture, and then summarize research that employs at least one of the three leading culture-related intergroup approaches—social identity, communication accommodation, and ethnolinguistic identity theories—while noting some of the voids or gaps in these paradigms. Then, we discuss the communication theory of identity and the cultural contracts theory as frameworks that seek to address the absence of identity as a central construct in the previously mentioned mainstream cultural conceptualizations.

Defining Culture

By any definition, culture is a pervasive influence on communication and social relations. Culture provides our norms, values, and practices; it defines our communities and our relationships. Yet, for something so pervasive and consequential, culture is difficult to define. Like two hands cupping water, culture shapes how we see the world, how we behave, and who we are. As long as the cup retains the water, we can see it, know it, and experience it. Similarly, when we are aware of culture, we can define and understand it. However, the water soon leaks out of the cup and we are left with empty hands, wondering what the "cupping/water" was. Like the cup, we can define culture in many ways and through many experiences, but in looking back, we are often left with the feeling that those definitions do not adequately describe all that culture is. If we focus too much on a type of entity (e.g., nation state) we miss the nuances of diasporic experiences and the pervasive effects of socio-economics. If we accent only worldviews, then we leave little room for intracultural variances and multicultural perspectives. If, instead, we look at functions or psychological states, we wind up with laundry lists that expand with each new investigation.

Culture has been defined in many ways. Baldwin et al. (in press) analyzed more than 300 definitions of culture and identified seven overlapping themes:

- Structure/Pattern: Definitions that look at culture in terms of a system or framework of elements (e.g., ideas, behavior, symbols, or any combination of these or other elements)
- Function: Definitions that see culture as a tool to achieve some end
- Process: Definitions that focus on the ongoing social construction of culture
- Product: Definitions of culture in terms of artifacts
- Refinement: Definitions that frame culture as an orientation toward a higher intellect or morality
- Power/Ideology: Definitions that focus on group-based power
- Group membership: Definitions that speak of culture in terms of a place or group of people or that focus on belonging to such a place or group

These last two themes, power/ideology and group membership, are the most recent ones, and it is to the latter that we turn our attention in this chapter. From an intergroup perspective, we place group membership in a hierarchically superordinate position, and view structures, patterns, functions, processes, products, refinement, and power/ideology through the lens of group membership. In so doing, we are able to answer questions such as how a sense of belonging creates (process) systems (structure) that achieve specific outcomes (function), how group membership is marked by objects (product), how groups develop a finer sense of self over time (refinement), and how groups are hierarchically organized and develop their own ideology (power/ideology). Thus, the intergroup perspective provides a framework for defining culture through the theme of group membership. As we will see, there is an irony to this effect because, in a very real sense, the construct of culture is itself undernourished within the intergroup perspective.

Three Intergroup Perspectives

Perhaps in reaction to the elusiveness of *culture*, the intergroup perspective on culture emerged. The intergroup perspective examines the roles that language and discourse play in creating membership and the dynamics of hierarchies that exist between and among groups. This tradition provides a stable orientation to studies of culture by focusing on membership in groups and shifting our view to what many believe is the very essence of culture—membership and community. It is important to note, however, that in adopting this perspective, the overriding interest is in the group. Thus, unless we see group values as implicitly and inextricably linked to cultural values, such a perspective might neglect other cultural constructs.

Intergroup research, specifically social identity theory, quickly spread across disciplines and branched into related, but more distinct, theories of language and identity. On the heels of social identity theory, one branch took on a communication focus, feeding into communication accommodation theory which, thereafter, examined more of the roles of verbal and nonverbal communication shifts during intergroup encounters (Giles, Mulac, Bradac, & Johnson, 1987). A second branch morphed into ethnolinguistic identity theory, focusing on macro language issues in intergroup relations (Giles & Johnson, 1987).

Social Identity Theory

The intergroup perspective has an important grounding in Tajfel and Turner's (1986) social identity theory (SIT). An underlying concept of SIT is that in certain situations when group or social identity becomes salient (e.g., intercultural encounters), a person will behave not according to her or his individual belief system, but in terms of the belief system held by the larger identity group. Such a reaction has a significant effect on satisfaction with intercultural communication. These encounters are often deeply rooted in group-based stereotypes, resulting in dissatisfactory, and sometimes harmful, intergroup interactions. Essentially, when a particular social identity becomes salient, ingroup behaviors tend to become stereotypical and normative, while perceptions of the outgroup become stereotypic, often rendering the intergroup interaction discriminatory and competitive (Hogg, Terry, & White, 1995). Further, individuals are seen as motivated to achieve or maintain a positive cultural identity, so they might rely on language and behaviors rooted in these stereotypes to dissociate themselves from the other group. Relatedly, Leets (2001) points to social identity as "the most powerful theoretical construct to explain perceptions of racist speech" (p. 676).

Of particular importance in today's multicultural and transnational environment is the role of social identity in relocation. Thus, SIT can be usefully applied to the intercultural area of cross-national adjustment and adaptation. As national borders become more permeable, understanding the role of identity and identity salience in the process of cross-cultural adjustment from an intergroup perspective is important. For example, in these intercultural encounters, nationality often becomes the most salient social category for interactants, providing the basis for intergroup comparison and behaviors. International relocation is often marked by anxiety due to the lost sense of identity, and may be followed by attempts to reclaim one's identity and reduce anxiety (Piontkowski, Florack, Hoelker, & Obdrzálek, 2000). For example, overseas students often experience an increase in national identity salience, and as a result, they often seek out conationals who can support their identity and create home-culture enclaves (Kosmitzki, 1996; Wilkinson, 1998). Berry's (1999) acculturation strategies provide a heuristic model that allows us to understand the relationship between social identity and international or domestic acculturation. Berry suggests that persons who have either permanently or temporarily relocated to a new country, as well as ethnic groups that form pockets in a dominant majority culture, engage in one of four acculturation strategies: integration with, separation from, assimilation to the dominant majority, or social marginalization. Current research in this area suggests the strength of ingroup identity will affect group members' acculturation strategies as well as their psychosocial well-being. For example, research indicates that a strong national or ethnic identity (e.g., separationist attitude) is related to psychological wellness in cultural contexts wherein there exists dominant and nondominant groups, whereas a strong dominant-group identity among nondominant group members (e.g., assimilationist attitude) is related to decreased social difficulties (Ward & Rana-Deuba, 1999, 2000). Thus, ethnic or cultural identity maintenance appears to be related to psychological health, while assimilation is related to social well-being. Though variables such as expected outcome, similarity, and ingroup bias may affect the acculturation *attitude* held by the dominant group (Piontkowski et al., 2000), adapting to the dominant majority group culture may be only one of the viable options for non-dominant group members. These individuals do not necessarily view cultural maintenance and adaptation as mutually exclusive options (Verkuyten & Thijs, 2002).

When people from different cultures are engaged in communication, misunderstandings, stereotypic communication, and even racist speech can occur if interactants rely on inaccurate or stereotyped assumptions. While intergroup communication is not inherently bad (in fact, it is often quite rewarding), uncertainty is often produced. This has led to another application of SIT, research examining uncertainty reduction within intergroup encounters. Gudykunst and Hammer (1988), for example, argue interactants reduce uncertainty in intergroup encounters by predicting and explaining the behavior of an outgroup member. These predictions and explanations are often derived from the social identity processes of ingroup identification and intergroup comparisons, or from the prototypicality of the other's cultural behavior. Specifically, they suggest that intergroup encounters marked by a highly salient social identity and positive intergroup comparisons result in high levels of uncertainty reduction and more effective communication. What is not taken into account with this particular extension of uncertainty reduction theory are power and the social histories represented in people from different cultures, which can serve to obstruct communication. Therefore, we must also ask, how are people "organized socially according to local conception of cultural identities, and thus how resources, both material and social, are distributed across people who engage such identities or are made sense of according to such categories" (Cooks, 2001, p. 347).

Applying a social identity perspective to intergroup encounters between people who have or perceive different cultural histories can offer insight into the likelihood of interaction between cultural groups, their motivation to communicate and desire to understand one another, and the impact that the depth and significance of their socio-political histories will have. Gallois' (2003) recent presidential address to the International Communication Association, discusses groups who, at this time, are not able to achieve effective intercultural communication because their social identities are embedded in centuries of antagonistic intergroup interactions. Communication scholars must consider the socio-political histories that influence and inform social identity. Although intercultural communication scholars frequently take ameliorating cultural relations as their overriding purpose, applying an intergroup frame, specifically SIT, to this field of inquiry reminds us that groups might not be motivated to communicate, or might only be motivated to communicate in a harmful manner (Gallois, 2003). Further, as the following discussion on communication accommodation theory shows, people might strategically communicate in such a way as to create intergroup *miscommunication*.

Communication Accommodation Theory

Communication accommodation theory (CAT) is primarily concerned with the motivation and social consequences underlying a person's change in communication styles (Giles, 1973; Giles et al., 1987), a concept similar to code-switching (Li, 2001). Particularly interesting is its application to culture and communication wherein scholars can look at language convergence, divergence, and maintenance between identity and cultural groups. For example, we can apply CAT to the intercultural communication context in order to identify possible group differences as marked through verbal and nonverbal communication strategies, such as converging and diverging speech.

Whereas SIT helps intercultural communication scholars explain likelihood, motivation, and outcome of intercultural encounters, CAT offers insight into the specific communication strategies that people use to express their social identities and intergroup attitudes. Moreover, SIT tells us that people desire to maintain their identity, and differentiate from the outgroup, but CAT shows *how* people communicate that distance. CAT shows that, depending on the relative social positioning between two groups and the desired outcome of the interaction, individuals will choose to accommodate to the communication of the outgroup in ways that distinguish them from that group (divergence), or in ways that reduce dissimilarity (convergence) or remain at the same level of difference (maintain). As such, group members can express social approval or disapproval of another person or group, as well as express values, attitudes, and intentions associated with their own social group through communication shifts toward or away from the other person (Giles, Bourhis, & Taylor, 1977). For example, nonconverging speech can be especially powerful for ethnic and national groups trying to maintain their social identity, as they can use this linguistic device as a symbolic tactic for maintaining their group distinctiveness while rejecting outgroup norms (Fishman, 1999; Giles & Coupland, 1991; Liebkind, 1999). Thus, identity maintenance strategies through communication accommodation and non-accommodation can serve to foster *or* hinder the development of intergroup understanding (Tong, Hong, Lee, & Chiu, 1999).

Intercultural communication is often marked by difficulties that can be attributed to, in part, a lack of shared conversational rules (Gudykunst, 1991). Gumperz (1992) argues, for example, that in bilingual encounters, it is not an issue of comprehension, but rather a lack of understanding or practice with a particular communicative style that can lead to ineffective communication. Recently, scholars have implemented CAT to explore the role of communication practices specific to language and culture, such as backchannel responses (Heinz, 2003), and the use of cooperative and intrusive interruptions (Li, 2001) in communication encounters between persons of different cultural backgrounds. Such investigations help to identify the degree to which persons involved in an intergroup encounter coordinate or disassociate through their communicative style. If an identity group is threatened by an outgroup, members are likely to perceive encounters in intergroup terms and strategically use language in order to create or maintain a positive social identity (Abrams, O'Connor, & Giles, 2002). For example, ingroup members might positively distinguish themselves through linguistic means by emphasizing national accent, dialect, or language (Bourhis & Giles, 1977; Giles & Coupland, 1991). However, when social identities are not salient in the intergroup encounter, both groups might converge to one language style in order to achieve effective communication. Moreover, speakers can simultaneously diverge and converge making an effort to accommodate the communication needs of the outgroup while maintaining allegiance to one's ingroup. One can also "over-accommodate" wherein group members go too far in converging and give the appearance of being inauthentic or trying too hard, something that Hecht, Jackson, and Ribeau (2003) label the "accommodative dilemma."

Contextual factors surrounding the intergroup encounter, including immediate and past experiences, significantly influence the strength and direction of communication accommodations (Giles, 1973). Moreover, the strength with which a person holds a group identity, as well as the relative power held by the other interactant, will impact an individual's proclivity to converge or diverge within ingroup or intergroup encounters (Li, 2001).

Ethnolinguistic Identity Theory

One final intergroup approach to culture and communication is ethnolinguistic identity theory (ELIT). ELIT is a natural progression from SIT and CAT, as it provides even more focus on the socio-contextual variables present in an intergroup encounter among people with specific cultural histories and ethnic backgrounds. Early versions of ELIT (Giles et al., 1977) emphasized the importance of three structural variables that influence the vitality of ethnolinguistic groups: status, demographics, and institutional support. Group vitality is the strength with which a particular social context supports the existence of a particular identity group (Giles & Coupland, 1991). Groups are only able to maintain their social identity to the extent that the surrounding social context can achieve consensus as to what that identity is and permits its survival (Noels & Clément, 1996). Groups with strong vitality (often dominant majority groups) are likely to thrive as a social unit in the intergroup context, while groups with low vitality could eventually cease to exist as distinct groups (Giles et al., 1977; Harwood, Giles, & Bourhis, 1994). However, groups low in ethnolinguistic vitality, but with a group perception of high vitality or strong identity, might engage in ethnic or ethnolinguistic revival (Liebkind, 1999), such as the Québécois nationalist revival in the 1960s (Bourhis & Marshall, 1999). Ethnolinguistic revival or survival is strongly related to group boundaries and multiple group memberships, because ethnolingustic identity is strengthened when group boundaries are impermeable and there are few alternatives for other group memberships (Liebkind, 1999).

Utilizing ELIT as an intergroup frame to investigate communication between groups demands a direct focus on power, structures of hierarchy, and status in a community that SIT and CAT do not necessitate. ELIT exposes structures in the intergroup encounter that implicate who ought to accommodate to whom, when, and to what extent. This is especially apparent in multilingual, multicultural contexts. Ethnic vitality, for example, influences the willingness of a nondominant group member to communicate in a second language held by the dominant majority. Clément, Baker, & MacIntyre (2003) summarize the body of literature on ethnolinguistic vitality and willingness to communicate as "the language of the highest vitality group is the one that predominates, whether from the point of view of interpersonal situations or in terms of collective language shifts" (p. 193).

Culture in the Intergroup Approach
Each of the three intergroup approaches previously discussed are prominent paradigms in the intergroup literature. In none, however, is culture prominently located. In fact, one may argue, as we suggest above, that the construct of culture is incompletely conceptualized or developed within intergroup theory. This may be desirable. Perhaps intergroup theory is not about culture. Baldwin et al. (in press) do not share this view and neither do we. We believe that intergroup theory provides an excellent framework for understanding culture.

Fortman and Giles (in press) provide a framework for an intergroup approach to culture. They argue that "clearly, culture is dependent on group membership." Moreover, they note that culture is a group-driven experience, and that an intergroup approach "offers a unique perspective on the function and impact of group membership in relation to the assessment of culture as a scientific variable." Intergroup theory uniquely positions researchers to describe how people identify themselves, their cognitive representations of their own and others' groups, and how people communicate within and across group lines. Further, Fortman and Giles argue that intergroup theory is uniquely situated to explain the fluid and flexible nature of culture by describing people's multiple group memberships and identities.

However, culture is not isomorphic with the intergroup perspective. As Fortman and Giles (in press) note, culture can be viewed as the process through which groups operate, but also as input (independent variable) or outcome (dependent variable) of group processes. Thus, from their perspective, the intergroup approach differentiates culture and groups. They pose the problematic question, "when do we designate a group a 'culture'?" Moreover, the very quality of intergroup theory that allows it to provide a unique perspective on cultural fluidity, the presence of multiple group memberships within a culture, also provides a way of contrasting and integrating culture and group. The vehicle Fortman and Giles suggest is the construct of "vibrancy"—that is, the degree and type of association with the specific group as well as the overall culture. Conceptualizing a 2 x 2 matrix (high/low, group/culture), they suggest that culture and groups overlap and intersect, but might not be isomorphic. In other words, person A might identify strongly with occupation, but not with national or ethnic culture. Conversely, person B might identify strongly with both occupation and nation. The cell of the matrix would influence which interactions are seen as intergroup and which are not. Persons A and B, for example, might perceive an ingroup experience when talking about work, but an intergroup experience when discussing the effects of international trade on their industry.

Thus, it would appear that intergroup theory has much to contribute to the study of culture and, in turn, a consideration of culture can enrich the theory. One area of mutual interest and focus is the study of identity. Two recent theoretic conceptualizations accounting for cultural and co-cultural identity shifting and maintenance demonstrate this promise.

Identity and Culture

One outcome of the intergroup research just presented was the realization that identities are multilayered and complex, as is their influence on intergroup communication. Hecht's (e.g., 1993) communication theory of identity (CTI) and Jackson's (e.g., 2002) cultural contracts theory (CCT) were developed in response to the lack of direct cultural and identity links in previous intergroup theories. The CTI defines the individual, relational, interactional, and communal layers of identity and, in doing so, situates identity, interpersonal communication, and community in juxtaposition to each other. The theory is concerned with how individuals and communities define their identities as well as how those identities are nested in relationships and expressed through communication. Particularly salient is the process of identity management in which individuals must balance the competing demands of multiple identities and means of expression, their own social relationships, social groups, and personal relationships (Shin & Jackson, 2003). This process of management can be seen as a form of negotiation, a process with which CCT is concerned. CCT suggests people co-develop cultural contracts in order to establish ground rules for interaction. The development of cultural contracts between interactants is largely based on core symbols, meanings, and labels through which individuals make sense of reality. The final section of this chapter presents these communication-centered approaches to identity with a specific focus on culture.

Communication Theory of Identity
Many of the constructs in the intergroup approach (e.g., CAT's convergence, maintenance, and divergence) refer to interaction at the dyadic level. Consequently, when these terms are used among intergroup researchers, they signify identities that are activated at primarily *social* cognitive levels. Yet, Hecht's (e.g., 1993) communication theory of identity (CTI) suggests it is critical to explore the individual, roles, social interaction, and relationships, and the collectivity as layers of identity because all exist simultaneously during interaction with others. Using this approach, individuals are able to reflect on ways identities are externalized *and* internalized. Identity is formed, maintained, and modified in a communicative process and, thus, reflects communication (Hecht, 1993; Hecht et al., 2003).

Moreover, Hecht et al. (2003) posit two ways through which communication is internalized as identity. First, symbolic meanings of social phenomena are created and exchanged through social interaction. Identity is formed when some relevant symbolic meanings are attached to and organized in an individual in various situations through social interaction. Social interaction is internalized as identity when one forms symbolic meanings and associates these meanings with self. Second, when people place themselves in socially recognizable categories, they confirm or validate whether these categories are relevant to them through social interaction. Thus, identity is formed and reformed by categorization through social interaction.

Identity, in turn, is manifested in social interaction through expectations and motivations (Hecht, 1993). Specific identities entail specific expectations, and these expectations influence the person's communication. Hence, identity is externalized to social interaction through expectations attached to identities.

Four layers of identity. In light of the direct relation between identity and communication, the theory posits various loci of identity involving not only an individual but social interaction (Hecht, 1993; Hecht et al., 2003). In American culture, identity tends to be regarded as a separate entity within the individual (Carbaugh, 1989). It is seen as a cognitive schema by which one understands and interprets the social world (Markus & Sentis, 1982). However, social interaction is also a locus of identity because identity is a social process, existing in the social world between and among people and residing in social interaction (Burke & Reitzes, 1981; Pearce, 1989). Hecht (1993) embraced both the individual and social interaction as the loci of identity, positing four layers where identity resides. These four aspects of an individual's identity sometimes match each other but sometimes are contradictory. Following are the basic notions of the four layers and relationships among them (Hecht 1993; Hecht et al., 2003).

A *personal layer* refers to the individual as a locus of identity. Identity is stored in a personal layer as self-concept, self-image, self-cognitions, feelings about self, or spiritual sense of self-being. Identity as a personal layer provides "understanding [of] how individuals define themselves in general as well as in particular situations" (Hecht et al., 2003, p. 236).

The *enactment layer* places communication at the locus of identity wherein the self is seen as a performance, as expressed. Thus, identity is enacted through communication.

Next is the *relational layer* in which relationship is the locus of identity. Identity is a product, jointly negotiated and mutually formed in relationships through communication. The relational layer has three levels. First, an individual constitutes his or her identities in terms of other people through social interaction. How other people view an individual and the ascriptions they make influences the person's identity. Second, an individual identifies himself or herself through his or her relationships with others, such as marital partners, co-workers, and friends (e.g., I am a husband, accountant, friend). Third, a relationship itself is a unit of identity. Thus, a couple as a unit, for instance, can establish an identity.

Finally, the *communal layer* conceptualizes identity as existing within a group. Group members usually share characteristics and collective memories upon which a common group identity is established. Thus, the communal characteristics of a group function to form the group identity.

Interpenetration of layers. The four layers of identity are not separate from each other. They are interpenetrated. While they can be seen as functioning independently of each other for analytical purposes, they actually and necessarily work together. Thus, analyses are enriched when layers are considered two at a time, three at a time, or all four at once. In some situations, each or some of the layers might be dialectically related (i.e., contradictory or exclusive of each other). In other situations, some or all of the layers are integrated. The communal layer might focus a researcher on the rituals or norms handed down to new members, norms that might trouble more acculturated members. For example, the portrayal of Jewish American identity on the television show *Northern Exposure*, which conflated this identity with being from New York, angered Jewish Americans who face this ascription in their daily lives (e.g., Midwesterners who others assume are not Jewish) (Hecht et al., 2002). At this level of analysis, the layers are sensitizing constructs for social research.

However, the layers are not only research or analytical perspectives, but are also the ways people have of conceptualizing their own identity. People who see themselves as invested in what they do (e.g., "I am a politician") are emphasizing the enacted level, while those whose self-concept is tied to their image as a relational partner (e.g., "I am a spouse") are more concerned with the relationship level. Here, the layers act as organizing principles for social life. Similarly, gang membership, religious affiliation, and corporate memberships all emphasize the communal level. Moreover, the layers can be similar or different from each other. A friend can ascribe an identity that is different from one's personal identity. These continuities and discontinuities have been called "identity gaps" and were found to have profound effects on social interaction and outcomes (Jung & Hecht, in press). Therefore, the layers are useful to researchers and are also part of the lived experience of social actors. Essentially, the purpose of layers, as explicated in the CTI, is to help individuals make sense of the world around them. However, this sense making often is dyadic or communal and, as such, negotiated. For example, Jewish Americans, like members of other stigmatized groups, face the difficult question of when to disclose their identity and when to closet it (Hecht & Faulkner, 2000). Cultural contracts theory (CCT) was developed to explicate these negotiation processes.

Cultural Contracts Theory

CCT conceptualizes the *negotiation of cultural identity* as a process in which people consider the gain, loss, or exchange of their agency or their power to define their own worldview (e.g., Jackson, 2002). Intercultural research has taught us that while culture is shared, personal identities are the proprieties of individuals. Hence, when discussing the negotiation of cultural identities, we are referring to a negotiation process during which tension arises because one's identity or worldview is socially co-constructed, yet still "owned" by the individual person. This negotiation takes place through core symbols, meanings, and labels attributed to individual identity and through which individuals understand reality. When one's core symbols, meanings, or labels are in direct conflict with someone else's, that incompatibility spawns conflict that might or might not be resolved. If two or more cultural interactants wish to resolve such a misalignment of perspectives, then they will undergo a process of identity negotiation during which their own existing cultural contracts will be renegotiated.

Everyone has either implicitly or explicitly "signed" or agreed to at least one *cultural contract* or set of interpretations one uses as a guide for what they value or believe and how they will behave. A cultural contract is simply a way one has agreed to see and relate to the world. Human beings have many cultural contracts. An individual might have a cultural contract for relating to students in the class-room, another for relating to family, and another for relating to a church pastor. *Cultural contracts* are the end products of each identity negotiation, thus, every "signed" or agreed-upon cultural contract has a direct impact on one's identity (Jackson, 2002).

Negotiation is an important metaphor to describe the process of identity recognition, relational coordination, and value exchange via interaction. It suggests that identities are not simply conceded while communicating; rather, there is an attempt to hold onto aspects that define who one is. As with any negotiation, one can either choose to abide by an existing contractual arrangement or sign another contract. Although the concept of identity negotiation is simple, it is not always clear what is being negotiated, especially since identities are nonmate-rial. The cultural contracts paradigm was introduced to make sense of this ambiguity.

Cultural contracts are necessary because when people interact, their identities will overlap to a greater or lesser extent, and contracts are needed to preserve, protect, and define the boundaries and pa-rameters around which the self develops. The situation is complex because the individuals' identities are played out in juxtaposition to each other and within cultural contacts. What happens if both interac-tants see themselves as "leader?" What if there are cultural differences in their definitions of leadership? What if both want to enact their identities in response to another? These similarities and differences between identities must be dealt with through interaction as people co-orient to each other. This co-orientation process can be seen as an "identity negotiation" involving varying degrees of cooperation and flexibility, and the resulting agreement is a "contract" that specifies the rules and conditions for mutual identity management. The theory posits that identities are negotiated via cultural contracts at every stage of relationship development, irrespective of context, from initial interaction to relational termination. Moreover, these negotiations, in every instance, impinge on one's own self-definition and are subject to change at any given time by free will or the application of social, psy-chological, or political force. It is crucial to have such a paradigm that allows for the flexibility of behavior and free choice that characterizes all human interaction. CCT is as much a process-driven approach as it is a typological one.

Cultural contract types. At some point in our lives, many of us decide to accept and abide by the cultural values, norms, beliefs, and communication patterns of a given culture as a template for how to behave; hence, we all have cultural contracts reflective of our world-view. This worldview shifts over time and during critical incidents with relational partners. The effect on identities, whether it is a shifting or solidifying move, depends upon the significance of the initiating incident and nature of the identity negotiation process.

At least one of three cultural contract types is likely to emerge during identity negotiation: ready-to-sign, quasi-completed, and co-created cultural contracts. *Ready-to-sign cultural contracts* are pre-negotiated, and no further negotiation is allowed (Jackson & Simpson, 2003). These contracts are designed to promote assimilation or maintain one's own worldview, and thus relational coordination might not be the goal. Those who seek to introduce a ready-to-sign contract are often firmly entrenched in their own perspective and are not interested in others' worldviews. Essentially, they take their cultural understandings into every encounter and have no interest in learning about other cultural traditions, values, norms, and beliefs. Cultures, languages, and norms survive in part through their insularity, and the world is too complex to negotiate identity in every encounter.

As the most rigid of the contract types, the *ready-to-sign cultural contract* is the type that dominant groups often "hold in their pocket." Dominant groups almost instantaneously, and often subconsciously present ready-to-sign contracts to marginalized group members. For example, the reason that language forms like Ebonics have not reached full political legitimacy is because of the North American ready-to-sign contract that refuses to recognize the standards, structure, and function of Ebonics. With English as the lingua franca of the United States, there is concern that other language variations or languages will be validated and contest English as the appropriate standard of American speech (Barker et al., 2001). With dominant groups, signing other contract types is rarely the goal of interaction or relational coordination. At the same time, *non*dominant groups might also hold non-negotiable or ready-to-sign cultural contracts in situations or encounters they feel they can control, such as those that are primarily social rather than political or economic.

Quasi-completed cultural contracts are partly pre-negotiated and partly agreements to relationally coordinate one's identities with those of another. Although ready-to-sign contracts are likely to be the most common type of contract signed by dominant groups, quasi-completed contracts are perhaps the most common type of cultural contract signed by nondominant groups. One distinguishing characteristic of the quasi-completed contracts is that they represent ordinarily short-term or temporary episodes of identity shifting. People code-switch every day when they go to work, school, or participate in formal public events and activities. Signers of the quasi-completed contract are usually not ready to fully co-create and not necessarily ruling out maintaining their own worldview. These persons "straddle the fence" in terms of their commitment to relationally coordinate. They would rather maintain some measure of comfort with their environments and worldview. Arguably, some quasi-completed contacts are "signed" as self-protection in order to avoid stress. For nondominant groups, however, such contracts are often contaminated by prejudice and discrimination. For example, some African Americans try to "talk proper" on the telephone by changing their tonality and inflection to "sound White" in order to avoid racially-biased treatment such as linguistic profiling (Ford, 1998; Rickford & Rickford, 2000).

Finally, *co-created cultural contracts* are fully negotiable with two parameters being personal preferences or requirements. Co-created cultural contracts are the ideal kinds of social agreements we would like to have with cultural others because they provide the optimal means of relational coordination across cultures and signal that the relationship is fully negotiable and open to differences. If a cultural contract is co-created, there is full acknowledgment and appreciation of cultural differences. Cultural differences are not ignored, yet do not become the only reason the two relational partners are together. Signing this type of contract indicates openness to and embrace of other worldviews. The emphasis is truly on mutual satisfaction rather than obligation to one another or each other's respective cultures. At the same time, co-created contracts are behavioral. That is, mere talk about harmony and cohesiveness does not constitute a co-created contract; one must also demonstrate the unconditional appreciation of the other person. The co-created contract stipulations for a Black-White romantic relationship in the US, for example, typically must include acknowledgment and appreciation of the cultural ancestries, values, norms, beliefs, practices, and patterns that govern their behaviors as individuals and as partners.

Naturally, many marginalized group members tend to seek relationships where co-created cultural contracts can be signed. With a strong emphasis on being real, genuine, positive, unique, caring, and committed to community, many seek relationships where these features are present and consistent facets of interaction. Although identities shift, mature, and are negotiable, the co-created contract discards pretenses and creates safe spaces for relational growth. It allows for ultimate trust and openness while facilitating the unpacking of all the social, emotional, and psychological "baggage" we all carry as human beings, some of which is directed toward one another through enacted prejudices.

Quasi-completed and co-created cultural contracts are most common among marginalized group members. As Jackson (1999) suggests, only marginalized groups are *obligated* to negotiate quasi-completed or co-created contracts. They have no choice if they are to be successful. The vacillation that characterizes quasi-completed contracts is the hallmark of marginalization. However, dominant group members may also sign such contracts as sympathizers, allies, and anti-establishment activists. The basic concepts and assumptions of the cultural contracts approach can be applied in the other intergroup contexts presented in this book. We present the theory as one vehicle for understanding the profound nature of human interaction processes concerning the construction and negotiation of identity.

Conclusion

Our purpose in this chapter was to provide an overview of culture as seen from a variety of theoretical positions stemming from an intergroup perspective. Returning to our previous analogy, defining and investigating culture is as difficult, and often as fleeting, as cupping water. The hands that cup the water also provide its shape, just as those who investigate culture provide its definition. While culture has a deep influence on communication, identity, and social relationships across varied contexts, it is difficult, if not impossible, to hold it steady enough to investigate its intricacies. We have argued that culture shapes how we see the world, how we behave, and who we are. Therefore, an understanding of the impact culture has on our daily lives is most important. Although we have suggested such an investigation is a difficult endeavor, we have outlined three intergroup theories that help us to understand culture from an intergroup communication perspective (social identity, communication accommodation, and ethnolinguistic identity theories), and we have offered two communication-centered theories of culture and identity (communication theory of identity and cultural contracts theory). These frameworks and approaches toward culture are the hands that shape our understanding of culture. While each pair of hands offers unique insight into the cultural underpinnings especially salient in intergroup encounters, acknowledging the communicative and intergroup nuances that each one highlights offers intergroup and intercultural communication scholars a deeper understanding of the critical role culture plays in everyday interactions.

By offering several modes for exploring culture as an intergroup phenomenon, it is our hope that scholars will shift their focus on culture from the traditional fixed categories approach (e.g., geographical, biological, national categories) to an approach that takes as its focus group membership, specifically those seen in identity groups and speech communities. Such an approach would offer studies of culture a firm grounding by focusing on how people identify with groups, how others identify people as members of groups, as well as how groups define themselves and are defined by others. This move shifts our view to the very essence of culture-membership, identity, and community, a move we hope will motivate current and future intergroup scholars with an interest in culture to embrace social and personal identities while maintaining a grasp on our historical and traditional notions of culture.

References

Abrams, J., O'Connor, J., & Giles, H. (2002). Identity and intergroup communication. In W. B. Gudykunst & B. Mody (Eds.), *Handbook of international and intercultural communication* (2nd ed., pp. 225–240). Thousand Oaks, CA: Sage.

Baldwin, J. R., Faulkner, S. L., Hecht, M. L., & Lindsley, S. L. (in press). *Defining culture*. Mahwah, NJ: Erlbaum.

Barker, V., Giles, H., Noels, K. A., Duck, J., Hecht, M. L., & Clément, R. (2001). The

English-Only movement: A communication analysis of changing perceptions of language vitality. *Journal of Communication, 51,* 3–37.

Berry, J. W. (1999). Intercultural relations in plural societies. *Canadian Psychology, 40,* 12–21.

Bourhis, R. Y., & Giles, H. (1977). The language of intergroup distinctiveness. In H. Giles (Ed.), *Language, ethnicity, and intergroup relations* (pp. 119–135). London: Academic Press.

Bourhis, R. Y., & Marshall, D. E. (1999). The United States and Canada. In J. A Fishman (Ed.), *Handbook of language and ethnic identity* (pp. 244–264). Oxford: Oxford University Press.

Burke, P. J., & Reitzes, D. C. (1981). The link between identity and role performance. *Social Psychology Quarterly, 44,* 83–92.

Carbaugh, D. (1989). *Talking American: Cultural discourses on Donahue.* Norwood, NJ: Ablex.

Clément, R., Baker, S. C., & MacIntyre, P. D. (2003). Willingness to communicate in a second language: The effects of context, norms, and vitality. *Journal of Language and Social Psychology, 22,* 190–209.

Cooks, L. (2001). From distance and uncertainty to research and pedagogy in the borderlands: Implications for the future of intercultural communication. *Communication Theory, 11,* 339–351.

Fishman, J. A. (1999). Sociolinguistics. In J. A. Fishman (Ed.), *Handbook of language and ethnic identity* (pp. 152–162). Oxford: Oxford University Press.

Ford, B. (1998). Talkin' proper. *American Quarterly, 50,* 125–129.

Fortman, J., & Giles, H. (in press). Communicating culture. In J. R. Baldwin, S. L. Faulkner, M. L. Hecht, & S. L. Lindsley (Eds.), *[Re]conceptualizing culture across the disciplines.* Mahwah, NJ: Erlbaum.

Gallois, C. (2003). Reconciliation through communication in intercultural encounters: Potential or peril. *Journal of Communication, 53,* 5–15.

Giles, H. (1973). Accent mobility: A model and some data. *Anthropological Linguistics, 15,* 87–105.

Giles, H., Bourhis, R. Y., & Taylor, D. M. (1977). Towards a theory of language in ethnic group relations. In H. Giles (Ed.), *Language, ethnicity, and intergroup relations* (pp. 307–348). London: Academic Press.

Giles, H., & Coupland, N. (1991). *Language: Contexts and consequences.* Pacific Grove, CA: Brooks/Cole.

Giles, H., & Johnson, P. (1987). Ethnolinguistic identity theory: A social psychological approach to language maintenance. *International Journal of the Sociology of Language, 68,* 69–99.

Giles, H., Mulac, A., Bradac, J. J., & Johnson, P. (1987). Speech accommodation theory: The first decade and beyond. *Communication Yearbook, 10,* 13–48.

Gudykunst, W. B. (1991). *Bridging differences: Effective intergroup communication.* Newbury Park, CA: Sage.

Gudykunst, W. B., & Hammer, M. R. (1988). The influence of social identity and intimacy of interethnic relationships on uncertainty reduction processes. *Human Communication Research, 14,* 569–601.

Gumperz, J. J. (1992). Interviewing in intercultural situations. In P. Drew & J. Heritage (Eds.), *Talk at work: Interaction in institutional settings* (pp. 301–327). Cambridge: Cambridge University Press.

Harwood, J., Giles, H., & Bourhis, R. Y. (1994). The genesis of vitality theory: Historical patterns and discoursal dimensions. *International Journal of the Sociology of Language, 108,* 167–206.

Hecht, M. L. (1993). 2002: A research odyssey toward the development of a communication theory of identity. *Communication Monographs, 60,* 76–82.

Hecht, M. L., & Faulkner, S. L. (2000). Sometimes Jewish, sometimes not: The closeting of Jewish American identity. *Communication Studies, 51,* 372–387.

Hecht, M. L., Faulkner, S. L., Meyer, C. R., Niles, T. A., Golden, D., & Cutler, M. (2002). Looking through Northern Exposure at Jewish American identity and the communication theory of identity. *Journal of Communication, 52,* 852–870.

Hecht, M. L., Jackson, R. L., & Ribeau, S. A. (2003). *African American communication.* Mahwah, NJ: Erlbaum.

Heinz, B. (2003). Backchannel responses as strategic responses in bilingual speakers' conversations. *Journal of Pragmatics, 35,* 1113–1142.

Hofstede, G. (2001). *Culture's consequences: Comparing values, behaviors, institutions and organizations across nations* (2nd ed.). Thousand Oaks, CA: Sage.

Hogg, M., Terry, D., & White, K. (1995). A tale of two theories: A critical comparison of identity theory with social identity theory. *Social Psychology Quarterly, 58,* 255–269.

Jackson, R. L. (1999). *The negotiation of cultural identity.* Westport, CT: Praeger.

Jackson, R. L. (2002). Exploring African American identity negotiation in the academy: Toward a transformative vision of African American communication scholarship. *Howard Journal of Communication, 12,* 43–57.

Jackson, R. L., & Simpson, K. (2003). White positionalities and cultural contracts: Critiquing entitlement, theorizing and exploring the negotiation of white identities In W. Starosta & Chen, G. M. (Eds.), *Ferment in the intercultural field* (pp. 319–326). Thousand Oaks, CA: Sage.

Jung, E., & Hecht, M. L. (in press). Elaborating the communication theory of identity: Identity gaps and communication outcomes. *Communication Studies.*

Kosmitzki, C. (1996). The reaffirmation of cultural identity in cross-cultural encounters. *Personality and Social Psychology Bulletin, 22,* 238–248.

Leets, L. (2001). Explaining perceptions of racist speech. *Communication Research, 28,* 676–706.

Li, H. Z. (2001). Cooperative and intrusive interruptions in inter- and intracultural dyadic discourse. *Journal of Language and Social Psychology, 20,* 259–284.

Liebkind, K. (1999). Social psychology. In J. A. Fishman (Ed.), *Handbook of language and ethnic identity* (pp. 140–151). Oxford: Oxford University Press.

Markus, H., & Sentis, K. (1982). The self in information processing. In J. Suls (Ed.), *Psychological perspectives on the self* (Vol. 1., pp. 41–70). Hillsdale, NJ: Erlbaum.

Noels, K. A., & Clément, R. (1996). Communicating across cultures: Social determinants and acculturative consequences. *Canadian Journal of Behavioral Science, 28,* 214–228.

Pearce, W. B. (1989). *Communication and human condition*. Carbondale, IL: Southern Illinois University Press.

Piontkowski, U., Florack, A., Hoelker, P., & Obdrzálek, P. (2000). Predicting acculturation attitudes of dominant and non-dominant groups. *International Journal of Intercultural Relations, 24*, 1–26.

Rickford, J., & Rickford, R. (2000). *Spoken soul: The story of Black English*. New York: Wiley.

Shin, C. I., & Jackson, R. L. (2003). A review of identity research in communication theory: Re-conceptualizing cultural identity. In W. Starosta & G. M. Chen (Eds.), *Ferment in the intercultural field* (pp. 268–312). Thousand Oaks: Sage.

Tajfel, H., & Turner, J. (1986). The social identity theory of intergroup behavior. In S. Worchel & W. Austin (Eds.), *Psychology of intergroup relations* (2nd ed., pp. 7–24). Chicago: Nelson Hall.

Tong, Y.-Y., Hong, Y.-Y., Lee, S-L., & Chiu, C-Y. (1999). Language as a carrier of social identity. *International Journal of Intercultural Relations, 23*, 281–296.

Verkuyten, M., & Thijs, J. (2002). Multiculturalism among minority and majority adolescents in the Netherlands. *International Journal of Intercultural Relations, 26*, 91–108.

Ward, C., & Rana-Deuba, A. (1999). Acculturation and adaptation revisited. *Journal of Cross-Cultural Psychology, 30*, 422–442.

Ward, C., & Rana-Deuba, A. (2000). Home and host culture influences on sojourner adjustment. *International Journal of Intercultural Relations, 24*, 291–306.

Wilkinson, S. (1998). Study abroad from the participants' perspective: A challenge to common beliefs. *Foreign Language Annals, 31*, 23–39.

3

Female, Straight, Male, Gay, and Worlds Betwixt and Between: An Intergroup Approach to Sexual and Gender Identities

Christopher Hajek
Jessica R. Abrams
Tamar Murachver

Major strides have been made in the past two decades to address identities based on gender (for reviews, see Maccoby, 1998; Ruble & Martin, 1997), and even more recently, identities developed around sexual orientation (see Abrams & Giles, 2004; Cox & Gallois, 1996; Hajek & Giles, 2002). That notwithstanding, work is needed that examines these identities from an intergroup perspective. This chapter attempts to answer that call, drawing on intergroup approaches such as social identity (SIT: Tajfel & Turner, 1986) and self-categorization (Turner, Hogg, Oakes, Reicher, & Wetherell, 1987) theories to address systematically communication between and within groups defined by sexuality and gender. Following a discussion of sexual identity labels, we use mechanisms at the core of these theories to explain discrimination against gay and lesbian individuals by members of the heterosexual majority. We then consider intragroup dynamics, taking as examples group identities formed around physical characteristics, special interest organizations, and bisexuality.

In subsequent sections of this chapter, we examine the relationships among concepts of masculinity and femininity, and sexual and gender identities, exploring how they contribute to perceptions and evaluations of group members. We also draw upon communication accommodation theory (CAT: e.g., Giles, Coupland, & Coupland, 1991) and concepts from social constructionism to explain how individuals and groups create and are influenced by gender identities. Finally, we discuss the implications of these dynamics for other inter-group contexts as well as directions for future research. Importantly, we acknowledge that our theoretical undertaking is complicated by the diversity, invisibility, and dynamic nature of gay and gender identities, not to mention the dynamic nature of the labels associated with these identities. Similarly, we acknowledge our largely Western perspective on these identities and their labels, and that the social construction of some gender and sexual identities can vary by culture in ways too numerous to address here (see Broido, 2000).

Lesbian and Gay Identity Development: The Role of Labels and Self-Categorization

Examining sexual identity from a social identity perspective, Cox and Gallois (1996) acknowledge that most models of homosexual identity development adopt a *purely* psychological perspective, noting the dif-ferent stages of homosexual identity acceptance. These authors state that while such models are useful, they do not explain how individu-als negotiate their identity development within the broader social context. They contend that studying gay and lesbian identity devel-opment from a *social* psychological perspective accounts for these in-fluential social factors, such as the condemnation of gay people by the heterosexual majority. In her discussion of homosexual identity and communication, Dobinson (1999, p. 267) remarks that "the specifics of my own identity, and how I define it, will often be secondary to the identity and definitions that society imposes on me. Whether I call myself *bisexual*, *lesbian*, *dyke*, or *queer*, I will be subject to the same pat-terns of discrimination simply for not following the heterosexual norm."

Social psychological theory provides several useful frameworks for understanding the integral relationship between identity devel-opment and intergroup relations between heterosexuals and gays. Although Cox and Gallois (1996) have applied social identity theory to homosexual identity *development*, we wish to tease apart concep-tions of sexual and gender identities by examining their relationships to communication. In so doing, and as noted repeatedly throughout this book, our approach considers group identity as being related to self-categorization and self-stereotyping (Turner, 1982, 1985). According to Brown and Turner (1981), when individuals engage in self-stereotyping, they react to themselves and others not as unique individuals, but instead as members of a group who share common characteristics and have similar needs, goals, and norms. Self-categorization among lesbians and gay men, for example, is reflected in their "coming out" as members of a distinct group (Rust, 1993a). In her examination of bisexual and lesbian women who have come out, Oswald (2000, p. 69) reported the experience of one of her participants that epitomizes self-categorization: "My sister will mention queer stuff to me. I think that's the main change. My family talks about [queer] issues to me. And they relate to me as one of this group of people...it feels really good." Both theorists and practitioners view coming out as a critical step toward achieving a positive sexual minority identity (Miller & Boon, 2000; Moorhead, 1999). Not surprisingly, in their investigation of reasons for coming out, Boon and Miller (1999) found the drive to be "true" to one's identity a primary motivator.

Labels, or the terms individuals use to define themselves, are also a communicative manifestation of self-stereotyping (Chapman & Brannock, 1987). By adopting a particular label, individuals acknowledge they share certain attributes. With regard to sexuality, Paul (1984, p. 56) writes that "the meaning of sexual labels—one's summing up of one's sexual and affectional experiences and interests—is a personal process and also a declaration to the social organization of one's standing within it." Individuals define themselves as "gay," "queer," "lesbian," "homosexual," "transsexual," or "transgender," each label indicating group membership, carrying different identity connotations. For example, Faderman (1991) argues that women who came to lesbianism through radical feminism do not consider lesbianism a sexual identity. Instead, lesbian-feminism is a *political* choice to call attention to, and take a stand against, male power. In Paul's (1985) reflection on labels, he explains that while some are pejorative, and associated with social sex-role, others are political in content, diverging from the simple consideration of erotic desire. With regard to her own sexuality, Dobinson (1999) declares that she has assumed four different sexuality labels: "lesbian," "bisexual," "dyke," and "queer." She describes how she moved from dyke, a label that implies being brash and assertive about same-sex desire, to queer, an identity not "defined or definable" (p. 265). In addition to identity being fluid and malleable, Donovan (1992) contends that identity often changes according to context. In his study of the use of the labels "homosexual," "gay," and "lesbian," he found that the same individuals use different labels in certain contexts. For example, one of his participants reported that "homosexual" was an appropriate term to use in technical or legal contexts, yet in informal social contexts he used the word "gay."

Heterosexuals often adopt labels that sexual minorities use to define themselves; however, such labels are usually used in a derogatory fashion. For instance, the word "gay" is a common pejorative among young people, as are other gay identity labels (Thurlow, 2001). Additionally, Valentine (1998) suggests that name-calling, or "naming," is central to questions of identity and power. According to this scholar, "abusive naming practices are indexical of social attitudes and mark delineations, whether latent or explicit, of ingroup and outgroup" (p. 3). With this in mind, naming others can be considered (from a CAT perspective) an intergroup act of divergence that carries implications for lesbian and gay identity negotiation, including how they compare themselves to one another, as well as to those in the heterosexual mainstream. Furthermore, heterosexuals' derogatory use of terms such as the word "gay" with one another (on an ingroup basis) may similarly aid in the negotiation of a heterosexual identity closely linked with conceptions of masculinity.

Social Identity Theory and a
Threatened Gay and Lesbian Identity

Despite some accounts of an increasing social acceptance of gay people in Western society (Wood, 1998), members of this group continue to live as minorities in a largely heterosexual social system, and they face the consequences of negative attitudes held by the (heterosexual) majority (Herek & Glunt, 1993; Kite & Whitley, 1996; for a review, see Schwanberg, 1993). Gay people are frequently disowned by their families, fall victim to hate crimes, and are often verbally harassed. Studies have indicated that heterosexuals possess more negative attitudes toward homosexuals of their own gender (e.g., Herek, 1988; Kite & Whitley, 1996), and that heterosexual participants have maintained increased physical distance from a gay target (Wolfgang &

Wolfgang, 1971). Additionally, heterosexual participants have reported feelings of anxiety (Cuenot & Fugita, 1982) or have engaged in reactive behaviors upon being approached by a gay person in a given context (Gray, Russell, & Blockley, 1991).

In terms of SIT (Tajfel & Turner, 1986), some heterosexuals might seek positive distinctiveness through comparisons with gay people who, in general, possess lower social status than do heterosexuals in mainstream society. Some male heterosexuals, for example, might seek positive distinctiveness through comparisons with gay men in order to validate or affirm their "male" identity, given the importance and strict regulation of masculinity in Western societies in general, and in the US in particular. Similarly, and consistent with SIT, some homophobic heterosexuals of either gender might fear the "psychological proximity" of homosexuality and, therefore, might discriminate against gay men or lesbians in order to psychologically distance themselves from their own homosexual feelings (e.g., Adams, Wright, & Lohr, 1996). We argue here that such negative, communicated attitudes of heterosexuals toward gay people threaten the stability of gay social identity and may, therefore, compromise gay individuals' self-esteem. This instability can, in turn, contribute to many gay individuals' adoption of one or more communicative coping strategies that fall within the purview of SIT to cope with a negative social identity (see Harwood, Giles, & Palomares, this volume).

The first of these strategies is *individual mobility*, in which individuals will attempt to leave their present group and join a more positively distinct group. Gay men and lesbians' adoption of this strategy is complicated by issues surrounding the degree to which an individual can, or desires to be, "open" regarding his or her identity. Gay identity is, arguably, not a matter of personal choice. As a result, gay men and lesbians are unlikely to employ this strategy over time to escape a threatened social identity (i.e., attempt to become heterosexual). However, one might consider gay identity to have permeable boundaries compared to race or gender in that gay men can "pass" as heterosexual. Factors that determine whether someone will attempt to pass as heterosexual include the degree to which that person identifies with the group—those identifying to a mild degree perhaps being more inclined to pass as heterosexual. Additionally, a gay or lesbian person might be more likely to pass as heterosexual in social contexts in which sexual orientation is not likely to become salient (e.g., on a part-time job with limited opportunities for sustained and in-depth, social interaction). However, such "passing" can come at the price of emotional and communicative problems associated with the denial of one's true nature. This notion is supported by research indicating that the lack of self-disclosure pertaining to identity-related trauma is associated with the experience of physical and emotional distress (e.g., Pennebaker, Barger, & Tiebout, 1989). Unsuccessful attempts on the part of gay men and lesbians to leave their group, or a likely inability or unwillingness to do so, may result in their adoption of one or more of the strategies discussed below.

Next, and consistent with the SIT *social creativity* strategy, is the possibility that gay men and lesbians can change negative values assigned to the ingroup into more positive ones (Tajfel & Turner, 1986). For instance, self-categorizing with the label "queer" can be understood as a strategic way of denying the derogatory use of that term to the outgroup. Similarly, gay men can transform the negative social value placed on gay sex by celebrating it, for instance, in pride parade displays of sexuality. The collective function of these is evidenced by these events being annual commemorations of the Stonewall riots of 1969 (in which gay men revolted against police oppression) that were in and of themselves reactions to a threatened social identity. This emphasis on sex and sexuality is, of course, particularly salient as an intergroup strategy, given that sexual orientation is the central distinguishing element between gay and straight people.

Social creativity can also be seen in gays' intergroup comparisons. When comparison with the heterosexual majority does not yield positive distinctiveness, they might change the comparison outgroup. That is, the ingroup (gay men) will cease or avoid using the high-status outgroup (e.g., heterosexuals) as a comparative frame of reference. Given the enhanced appearance-consciousness in much of gay male culture—a phenomenon not shown to occur among lesbians—younger gay men often compare themselves to older (and often less physically "attractive") gay men to gain positive distinctiveness (Hajek & Giles, 2002). The adoption of this strategy enables younger gay men to self-enhance and regain self-esteem without questioning the status quo of heterosexual cultural domination. Such social comparisons are not new among gay men. Writers have noted decades of social comparative phenomena within gay male culture in the form of subgroups positioning themselves against one another. For example, Rofes (1998) has stated that gay people in general have, at different times, targeted gay hippies, early gay libbers, overly masculine or muscular gay men, effeminate gay men, and drag queens, to name a few.

The final SIT strategy in which gay and lesbian people may engage to achieve positive distinctiveness is direct *competition* with the outgroup (heterosexuals), a situation that is likely to foster intergroup antagonism. Gay groups, in pursuit of legal sanctions that validate and legitimate gay identity, often engage in social competition with mainstream heterosexual society in the form of political action and social protest. For example, gay activist groups routinely protest their exclusion from legal, socially-sanctioned relationships that provide long-term financial and emotional security.

Intergroup Communication *Within* Groups Defined by Sexual Orientation

Intergroup dynamics between gay individuals and the heterosexual majority, and between gay age groups, are but two of the several intergroup contexts on which we have set our sights. However, before delving into the remainder of these worlds gay, lesbian, and betwixt and between, we will provide a brief discussion of the increasingly familiar "gay, lesbian, bisexual, transgender" (GLBT) identity that fuels our rationale for examining the remaining sexual identity subgroups in turn.

The term "gay, lesbian, bisexual, and transgender" (GLBT) emerged in the 1990s as an umbrella term to identify sexual minorities. Today, most gay and lesbian organizations in the US include bisexuality and transgender. Interestingly, the air of inclusion inherent in the GLBT label has done little to engender a sense of community among GLBT individuals. This is especially apparent in the case of transgendered people, who lack common ground with many gays and lesbians. This might be caused, in part, by transgendered individuals' not having formed an adequate group definition or mutual understanding among even their own members (Moorhead, 1999). Furthermore, unlike homosexuals, who define themselves in terms of sexuality, transgendered people are more concerned with gender identity (Valentine, 2003), making it difficult for them to be included in mainstream gay and lesbian politics. In effect, then, although the term GLBT continues to gain ground as a unifying *label*, the reality is that the groups comprising it often share intergroup relationships. These relationships are contrary to Gaertner's common ingroup identity model (Gaertner et al., 1999), which predicts that the formation of a superordinate identity can help reduce intergroup conflict. The adoption of a common group identity is based on a sense of entitativity (e.g., common fate, similarity, salience, and boundedness), and various factions of the GLBT "community" do not perceive such entitativity. This view is exemplified in one gay columnist's sarcastic response to a bisexual woman who questioned lesbian and gay values, the columnist writing, "Pardon me if I don't join the bisexual brigade at the GLBTQRSTUVWXYZ parade" (Dan Savage, April 3, 2004).

Given this seeming lack of entitativity, in the following paragraphs we will explore communicative phenomena of labeling, self-categorization, and identity formation that occur between subgroups defined by sexual orientation.

The "Bear" Movement

One gay male group-based identity that represents divergence from the appearance-conscious ideals of much of gay male culture, and that illustrates the self-stereotyping that these identities involve, is the "bear" movement. The most common definition of a "bear" is a gay man who is large, hairy, and has facial hair. However, many men that do not embody these physical characteristics self-stereotype as bears, opening the possibility that being a bear is as much a state of mind as it is the possession of a certain body type. The fluidity of this boundary indicates that some sexual identities might serve social functions that extend beyond their primary descriptions. The brochure for "Bears Ventura," a California bear organization, states that being a bear involves "a sense of comfort with our natural masculinity and bodies that is not slavish to the vogues of male attractiveness that is so common in gay circles and the culture at large." This description exemplifies the complexity of sexual orientation identities, as well as self-stereotyping that is intended to counter the ideals of the perceived mainstream "gay" identity.

The North American Man/Boy Love Association
Another group that diverges from mainstream gay culture is the North American Man/Boy Love Association (NAMBLA), an organization comprised of members that seek support for free sexual expression between gay male adults and children. NAMBLA was an active group within the International Lesbian and Gay Association (ILGA) prior to the more visible gay and lesbian movement of the 1990s. However, realizing that NAMBLA was hindering the lesbian and gay movement, ILGA expelled NAMBLA less than a year after it was granted consultative status to the United Nations Economic and Social Council in 1993. Such boundary management might originate from the fear that an extreme faction such as NAMBLA could be perceived as representative of the gay and lesbian movement, thus making the latter appear to be more extreme than it actually is. Lesbian and gay civil rights activists who supported the ouster buttressed this explanation by noting that NAMBLA was not part of the gay and lesbian "community," and that they thoroughly rejected NAMBLA's efforts to insinuate that pedophilia was an issue related to gay and lesbian civil rights (Tsang, as cited in Gamson, 1997).

Bisexuals
As our preceding discussions have indicated, whereas identity labels might appear to be restrictive or even unnecessary to some (Horowitz & Newcomb, 2001), they serve important boundary functions within groups defined by sexual orientation. This notion is key to any discussion of bisexuality—another sexual identity with negotiated boundaries. Paul (1985) contends that because sexuality is often dichotomized as being either homosexual or heterosexual, bisexuals are caught between two sexual categories. As a result, they lack a clear social identity, a strong political voice, and substantial recognition from the academic community. A lack of group vitality (Harwood, Giles, & Bourhis, 1994) makes it difficult for bisexuals to mobilize collectively.

Despite bisexuals being considered a sexual minority, they have long faced prejudice from gays and lesbians. For instance, Rust (1993a) argues that many models of sexual identity formation fail to recognize bisexuality as a legitimate sexual identity. She explains that because many models are linear, with a complete homosexual identity at the end of a continuum, bisexuality is considered to be merely a transitional identity. According to MacDonald (1981), perceiving bisexuality in this manner reinforces the heterosexual/homosexual dichotomy, and suggests that bisexuals are denying their "true" gay identity. Thus, bisexuals face skepticism from many gays and lesbians who might subscribe to the belief that bisexuals can easily merge or pass as heterosexual when convenient (e.g., when prejudice occurs), but also bask in any victories that punish or end homosexual discrimination (Paul, 1984).

Lesbians are thought to be particularly antagonistic toward bisexuals (Rust, 1993b). Faderman (1991) writes that the tension between bisexual women and lesbians began in the early 1970s, shortly after the lesbian feminist movement diverged from the feminist movement. Lesbians were concerned about bisexual women's commitment to lesbian and gay liberation and were wary of bisexual women's closer relationships with *two* dominant outgroups—men and heterosexuals (Rust, 1993b). Despite this schism between groups, if the bisexual movement maintains its momentum, it will likely gain status as a legitimate sexual identity, and the tension between the groups might diminish.

"Masculine" and "Feminine" Gay Men

Sexual orientation and gender identities are linked in interesting ways. Relevant to our following discussion of gender identity is the intergroup divide between gay men who are "masculine" and "feminine." Taywaditep (2001) reports that many gay men hold anti-effeminacy attitudes. He explains that prior to the gay liberation movement in the early 1970s, gender nonconformity, in the form of camp and drag, was appreciated and celebrated by gay men. However, a goal of the gay movement was to replace the "limp-wristed swish" gay male stereotype (Taywaditep, 2001, p. 9). The answer was "The Butch Shift" (Fernbach, cited in Humphries, 1985), whereby gay men adopted a hyper-masculine appearance and marginalized effeminate gay men, a pattern still common today. This marginalization is evident in sexual and romantic rejection, low self-esteem, and poor psychological adjustment (Bailey, Kim, Hills, & Linsenmeier, 1997). For example, sexual rejection is evident in the phrase "no fems" found in gay male personal ads. More generally, evidence indicates that homosexuality per se violates traditional gender roles (Kurdek, 1988; Madon, 1997), which results in negative attitudes toward gays and lesbians. Whitley and Egisdottir (2000) argue that "dislike of lesbians and gay men should be particularly strong among people who hold traditional gender-role attitudes because homosexuality poses an especially strong threat to their system of gender beliefs" (p. 949). In a recent investigation of the relationship between gender and perceptions of male homosexuality, sex of the participant and whether the target person appeared feminine or masculine were the most important factors in perceiving someone as being homosexual (Wong, McCreary, Carpenter, Engle, & Korchynsky, 1999). The authors explain that men who violate gender-related expectations are judged even more harshly than are women.

The above sections have explored identities based on sexual orientation. Having examined language use and theoretical mechanisms at the core of communication within and between groups formed around these identities, we now turn to an exploration of gender identity.

Gender Identity and Social Interaction

In this section, we describe how gender is actively created through social interaction, much like some of the above-mentioned sexual identities. Our focus is on how gender is performed in different contexts, and how identification shapes communication. In particular, we explore the role of communication accommodation (Giles, Coupland, & Coupland, 1991) in these social interaction processes.

The Conceptualization of Gender

How gender is conceptualized influences how it is studied. Unlike sexual orientation, gender categories are not automatically associated with normality or abnormality. Characteristics traditionally associated with the male gender are often valued more than those associated with females, but even this is not absolute. Historically, language use associated with women has been viewed more harshly than that linked to men (Coates, 1986). With the acceptance of general principles of gender equality and the increased legitimization of women's voices, women have redefined female-associated characteristics as positive. Rather than women's language being portrayed as passive, weak, and ineffective, authors in popular and academic circles are re-defining women's communication as nurturing, polite, and socio-emotional in orientation (Holmes, 1995; Tannen, 1990). This redefinition allows women as a group to create a more positive social identity (Smith, 1985; Williams & Giles, 1978).

Gender is also sometimes described as a state—something we are, or become. In this formulation, gender is static, a trait of individuals, an essence (Beall, 1993). When gender is thought of as a static trait, it is studied as bipolar categories to be described and maximally differentiated. Another conceptualization is that gender is something we do (West & Zimmerman, 1987). The focus here is not on acquiring or becoming; it is about acting in gendered ways. In this formulation, gender is not static. Depending on people's circumstances, they might behave more or less in ways that reflect society's ideas about being female or male. When gender is conceptualized in this way, researchers ask *how* gender is performed in context.

The Social Construction of Gender

In line with a self-categorization theory approach, it is difficult to avoid identifying oneself and being identified as a particular gender. Gender is one of the earliest learned social categories (Golombok & Fivush, 1994) and permeates almost every aspect of human existence. It is unlikely that gender identities could exist solely from the passive consumption of media images, societal roles, and parental expectations (Maccoby, 1998). Arguably, unlike some sexual orientation identities, gender identities are actively, not passively, constructed. They are created by perceiving oneself as a member of a particular gender, by actively seeking out information about a gender category, and by understanding one's gender in contrast to the "other." Ultimately, gender identity is constructed through social interaction.

One example of the fluid, socially constructed nature of gender is provided in Risman's (1987) study of men who mother. Risman noted that men who became the main caretaker of children by accident reported more "feminine" features than those who were not main caretakers. By having to play the role of the caretaker, men began to see themselves as more nurturing. A similar example is shown in the area of gendered communication. Leaper and Gleason (1996) asked parent-child dyads to perform one of two activities: playing grocer and building a car. They noted that when parents and children played grocer—an activity more associated with girls' play—their language was more like that used by girls and women. When parents and children built the car, their language reflected more features typically found with boys and men. In other words, their activity choice influenced their language, not their biological sex (or gender role).

One result of gender being created through social interaction is that individuals come to see themselves as members of a particular group (the ingroup) and not as members of the outgroup. This is how social identities are created (see Smith, 1985; Williams & Giles, 1978). When children participate in social interaction, their gendered membership becomes salient and important to them. This leads to gender segregation, or the importance of not only doing one's gender, but also not doing the other. Thus, for girls, it is important to not be like boys as well as to be like girls.

Gender Segregation

Gender segregation might be important for maintaining and intensifying gendered identities and gender-specific ways of behaving (Maccoby, 1998). We traditionally think of gender segregation as a childhood phenomenon. Indeed, standard developmental textbooks will tell us that gender segregation is evident by the third year of life and intensifies into middle childhood. During and after adolescence, the assumption is that gender segregation ceases to be a prime feature of social interaction. Yet the evidence shows that gender segregation remains the norm for adolescent social interaction and for adults in the workplace (Maccoby, 1998). Because most adults live and work with people of different genders, it is easy to be fooled into thinking that we have gone beyond segregation. Many workplaces are strongly segregated, either physically or by job description. Moreover, because female-male friendships are perceived to be sexualized, women and men find it difficult to establish close, nonsexual friendships except when one party is openly gay or lesbian, or when the relationship occurs as part of contact between two couples.

When gender is salient and groups are segregated, intergroup communication is sometimes characterized by overt or covert hostility. Games on the playground turn into "the boys" versus "the girls" and might involve behaviors such as raiding and chasing (Thorne,

1986). Boggs and Giles (1999) describe workplace conflict between female and male employees. They note, in particular, nonaccommodation—a resistance to converge toward the language used by employees of the other gender. Boggs and Giles document the many ways in which men, through their language use in the workplace, distance themselves from female co-workers and make it clear that the women are in the "other" group.

These examples raise an apparent contradiction. On the one hand, gendered identities can be enhanced by gender segregation. In some instances, gender differences in language between same-gender groups are greater than those found in mixed-gender groups (Bilous & Krauss, 1988; Fitzpatrick, Mulac, & Dindia, 1995). On the other hand, gendered behaviors can become more extreme in intergroup contexts (Boggs & Giles, 1999). Communication accommodation theory (CAT: Giles, Coupland, & Coupland, 1991) provides a conceptual framework in which to resolve this discrepancy.

The Role of Communication Accommodation in Gender Identity Differentiation

According to CAT, people converge in their communication toward others as a way of showing ingroup solidarity or to gain approval and show affiliation. Thus, when members interact within same-sex groups, convergence should lead to a set of features identifiable as gender-preferential. When segregated female and male groups are compared, convergence within a group should help to maximize group differences. In a problematic, intergroup situation, divergence between the two groups should also lead to increased intergroup differences. In both instances, group differences increase, but for different reasons (i.e., intragroup convergence vs. intergroup divergence).

This can be contrasted with the interpersonal situation of mixed-dyad conversation, where the desire to affiliate is greater than the need to define separate group identities. In these situations, where there is little inclination to perceive the situation as "them" and "us," women and men tend to converge in their communication, and gender differences are attenuated. Using a round-robin design, Fitzpatrick et al. (1995) demonstrated convergence in face-to-face conversations between adult couples. Similar effects have been shown in electronic communication (Thomson, Murachver, & Green, 2001) and in children's face-to-face communication (Robertson & Murachver, 2003). One important point from these studies is that a person's gender was never a strong predictor of their language use. Instead, the language used by their conversational partner exerted a greater effect.

Accommodation can occur not only in response to the actual behavior of the speaker, but also to perceived or expected behaviors of the speaker. As an example, we expect men to swear and use coarser language than women. As a consequence, when women speak with men, they sometimes increase their use of coarse terms, not because the men are doing so, but because the women expect the men to do so. This explains the overaccommodation Bayard (1995) reported in a sample of New Zealand university students. In same-sex conversations, men and women swore at similar rates. However, in mixed-sex conversations, the women out-swore the men. Accommodation to gender stereotypes is also shown by Thomson et al. (2001), who demonstrated accommodation to both the language of e-mail "netpals" and also to the gender label used to identify them. These examples show how even in an interpersonal context, gender identity can operate to influence communication.

One question to consider is whether accommodation occurs not just to a gender category, but to perceived masculinity or femininity. Would compliments or references to emotion—features associated as female-preferential—be given to a woman who was perceived to be highly masculine? It is possible that features associated with a gender rather than the gender label itself can invoke the gender category and related behaviors (see Smith, 1985 for related discussion).

In earlier sections of this chapter, we discussed the consequences of violating gender norms in the context of homosexuality. There is also some evidence that listeners treat women and men who violate gender norms of communication behavior differently from those who adhere to gender norms. Carli (1990) found that female speakers who used an assertive style to deliver a message had less influence on men's opinions than did those who used a more tentative style. Carli (1999) describes a study in which confederates manipulated their use of direct disagreements and agreements in conversations. Participants were particularly hostile to female confederates who violated their expectations and used direct disagreements. However, other studies have failed to find any interaction between speaker gender and speech style on listeners' ratings (Haleta, 1996; Thomson et al., 2001). One explanation for the variation in findings is that violations of gender norms are tolerated when the situational context is congruent with the atypical gendered language. For example, in the Haleta study, students rated female and male professors who used powerful or powerless language. When female professors used powerful language, the student raters did not penalize them. Powerful language is congruent with the social role of professor. Instead, they penalized both female and male professors who used powerless language.

Much is still unknown about parameters influencing accommodation to gendered language. Across similar social contexts, people vary in the extent of their convergence. Why do some people readily adapt to the speech of another gender, whereas others barely budge an utterance? One known influence is the extent to which a person holds very traditional ideas about gender. Both Fitzpatrick et al. (1995) and Robertson and Murachver (2003) found greater accommodation by males who held less traditional views about gender. An untested prediction is that people who more strongly identify with their gender will converge their language less in intergroup contexts than will those who show weaker gender identification.

Conclusion

Our combined application of SIT, self-categorization theory, CAT, and related constructs, explains some of the social complexities of identities based on sexual orientation and gender. This analysis has benefited the body of research in the area of communication studies by providing explanations for intergroup communication and discrimination, rather than solely describing the effects of such communicative behavior. Specifically, we have explained why some heterosexuals might discriminate against gay people. Furthermore, we have suggested reasons why various facets of gay culture target older gay men, bisexuals, and "bears" as opposed to members of other cognitively available groups, as well as suggesting reasons for differences in language use, given gender identity in various contexts. Our social identity perspective has informed gay and gender studies due to its consideration of both dominant and subordinate groups—an essential feature, given the notion that males and females, or gay people and heterosexuals, play either of these roles depending on the identity salient in a given encounter. This analysis has informed future work with SIT and the related theoretical perspectives, due to the examination here of group identities that have boundaries requiring communicative negotiation.

Such future research might examine verbal and nonverbal features of communication between group members, including conversational content, communicated affect, and feelings about the self during interaction. For example, future research can explore cognitive communication schemas (Harwood, McKee, & Lin, 2000) of conversations between men and women, or between older and younger gay men or lesbians, to examine the drive for positive distinctiveness, as well as determine the conversational salience of negative stereotypes of women, men, or older gay men.

In light of our previous discussion of heterosexuals' often "naming" gay people in insulting ways, future research might explore when and how sexual minorities use such derogatory labels to define and acknowledge *themselves* (e.g., gay men calling one another "nelly queens," lesbians calling one another "diesel dykes," etc.). Little is known about how and why sexual minorities engage in such intragroup behavior. Additionally, whereas we have addressed communicative issues of lesbians, gay men, and bisexuals, we have not examined transgendered individuals, due, in part, to a lack of current research. Future work might continue to expand the boundaries explored here by applying the above theoretical approaches to the intersection of transgender, gay, lesbian, bisexual, and gender identities.

To summarize, gender identities are actively constructed through social interaction. They are created by perceiving oneself as a member of a particular gender, by actively seeking out information about a gender category, and by understanding one's gender in contrast to the "other." Regardless of whether or not sexual orientation has its roots in biology, the same can be argued for the formation of *identities* based on sexual orientation. The boundaries of identities based upon both sexual orientation and gender—while likely both influenced by biological distinctions—nonetheless depend on subjective interpretation.

Although sexual orientation and gender are distinct dimensions, popular conceptualizations often confound the two. As suggested above, men, in particular, are less tolerant of gender role variations, and they are most critical of variations in their own gender. They are also generally less tolerant of homosexuality, especially in other men. One way of understanding this is to view the male gender role as defined by "what not to do"—in other words, not to be female. Thus, any behavior associated with women becomes taboo, including sex with men. A contributing factor to this masculine bias, including the greater tolerance shown to women who behave in a more masculine manner, is that maleness (and therefore masculinity) is more valued and associated with gender status. Men and women who adopt the behaviors associated with maleness gain status, whereas women and men who adopt behaviors associated with femaleness lose status. It is our view that social interaction plays a key role in all of these individual and group-based social identification and communication processes, and is influenced by the drive for self-esteem, differentiation, positive distinctiveness, and divergence from outgroup members.

References

Abrams, J. R., & Giles, H. (2004). An intergroup to communicating stigma: Gays and lesbians. In S. H. Ng, C. N. Candlin, & C. Y. Chiu (Eds.), *Language matters: Communication, identity, and culture* (pp. 27–61). Hong Kong: City of University of Hong Kong Press.

Adams, H. E., Wright, L. W. Jr., & Lohr, B. A. (1996). Is homophobia associated with homosexual arousal? *Journal of Abnormal Psychology, 105,* 440–445.

Bailey, J. M., Kim, P., Hills, A., & Linsenmeier, J. A. (1997). Butch, femme, or straight-acting?: Partner preferences of gay men and lesbians. *Journal of Personality and Social Psychology, 73,* 960–973.

Bayard, D. (1995). *Kiwitalk: Sociolinguistics and New Zealand society.* Palmerston North, New Zealand: Dunmore.

Beall, A. E. (1993). A social constructionist view of gender. In A. E. Beall & R. J. Sternberg (Eds.), *The psychology of gender* (pp. 127–147). New York: Guilford.

Bilous, F. R., & Krauss, R. M. (1988). Dominance and accommodation in the conversational behaviours of same- and mixed-gender dyads. *Language and Communication, 8,* 183–194.

Boggs, C., & Giles, H. (1999). "The canary in the coalmine": The nonaccommodation cycle in the gendered workplace. *International Journal of Applied Linguistics, 9,* 223–245.

Boon, S. D., & Miller, R. J. (1999). Exploring the links between interpersonal trust and the reasons underlying gay and bisexual males' disclosure of their sexual orientation to their mothers. *Journal of Homosexuality, 37,* 45–68.

Broido, E. M. (2000). Constructing identity: The nature and meaning of lesbian, gay, and bisexual identities. In R. M. Perez, K. A. DeBord, & K. J. Bieschke (Eds.), *Handbook of counseling and psychotherapy with lesbian, gay, and bisexual clients* (pp.

13–33). Washington, DC: American Psychological Association.

Brown, R. J., & Turner, J. C. (1981). Interpersonal and intergroup behavior. In J. Turner& H. Giles (Eds.), *Intergroup behavior* (pp. 33–65). Chicago: University of Chicago Press.

Carli, L. (1990). Gender, language, and influence. *Journal of Personality and Social Psychology, 59,* 941–951.

Carli, L. (1999). Gender, interpersonal power, and social influence. *Journal of Social Issues, 55,* 81–99.

Chapman, B. E., & Brannock, J. C. (1987). Proposed model of lesbian identity development: An empirical examination. *Journal of Homosexuality, 14,* 69–80.

Coates, J. (1986). *Women, men, and language: A sociolinguistic account of sex differences in language.* London: Longman.

Cox, S., & Gallois, C. (1996). Gay and lesbian identity development: A social identity perspective. *Journal of Homosexuality, 30,* 1–30.

Cuenot, R. G., & Fugita, S. S. (1982). Perceived homosexuality: Measuring heterosexual attitudinal and nonverbal reactions. *Personality and Social Psychology Bulletin, 8,* 100–106.

Dobinson, C. (1999). Confessions of an identity junkie. *Journal of Gay, Lesbian, and Bisexual Identity, 4,* 265–269.

Donovan, J. M. (1992). Homosexual, gay, and lesbian: defining the words and sampling the populations. *Journal of Homosexuality, 24,* 27–47.

Faderman, L. (1991). *Odd girls and twilight lovers.* New York: Columbia University Press.

Fitzpatrick, M. A., Mulac, A., & Dindia, K. (1995). Gender-preferential language use in spouse and stranger interaction. *Journal of Language and Social Psychology, 14,* 18–39.

Gaertner, S. L., Dovidio, J. F., Rust, M. C., Neir, J. A., Banker, B. S., Ward, C. M., Mottola, G. R., & Houlette, M. (1999). Reducing intergroup bias: Elements of intergroup cooperation. *Journal of Personality and Social Psychology, 76,* 388–402.

Gamson, J. (1997). Messages of exclusion: Gender, movements, and symbolic boundaries. *Gender and Society, 11,* 178–199.

Giles, H., Coupland, J., & Coupland, N. (1991). Accommodation theory: Communication, context, and consequences. In H. Giles, J. Coupland, & N. Coupland (Eds.), *Contexts of accommodation: Developments in applied sociolinguistics* (pp. 1–68). New York: Cambridge University Press.

Golombok, S., & Fivush, R. (1994). *Gender development.* Cambridge, UK: Cambridge University Press.

Gray, C., Russell, P., & Blockley, S. (1991). The effects upon helping behavior of wearing pro-gay identification. *British Journal of Social Psychology, 30,* 171–178.

Hajek, C., & Giles, H. (2002). The old man out: An intergroup analysis of intergenerational communication among gay men. *Journal of Communication, 52,* 698–714.

Haleta, L. L. (1996). Student perceptions of teachers' use of language: The effects of powerful and powerless language on impression formation and uncertainty. *Communication Education, 45,* 16–28.

Harwood, J., Giles, H., & Bourhis, R. Y. (1994). The genesis of vitality theory: Historical patterns and discoursal dimensions. *International Journal of the Sociology of Language, 108*, 167–206.

Harwood, J., McKee, J., & Lin, M-C. (2000). Younger and older adults' schematic representations of intergenerational communication. *Communication Monographs, 67*, 20–41.

Herek, G. M. (1988). Heterosexuals' attitudes toward lesbians and gay men: Correlates and gender differences. *The Journal of Sex Research, 25*, 451–477.

Herek, G . M., & Glunt, E. K. (1993). Interpersonal contact and heterosexuals' attitudes toward gay men: Results from a national survey. *Journal of Sex Research, 30*, 239–244.

Holmes, J. (1995). *Women, men, and politeness*. Essex: Longman Group Limited.

Horowitz, J. L., & Newcomb, M. D. (2001). A multidimensional approach to homosexual identity. *Journal of Homosexuality, 42*, 1–19.

Humphries, M. (1985). Gay machismo. In A. Metcalf & M. Humphries (Eds.), *The sexuality of men* (pp. 70–85). London: Pluto.

Kite, M. E., & Whitley, B. E. Jr. (1996). Sex differences in attitudes toward homosexual persons, behaviors, and civil rights: A meta-analysis. *Personality and Social Psychology Bulletin, 22*, 336–353.

Kurdek, L. A. (1988). Correlates of negative attitudes toward homosexuals in heterosexual college students. *Sex Roles, 18*, 727–738.

Leaper, C., & Gleason, J. B. (1996). The relationship of play activity and gender to parent and child sex-typed communication. *International Journal of Behavioral Development, 19*, 689–703.

Maccoby, E. E. (1998). *The two sexes: Growing up apart, coming together*. Cambridge, MA: Harvard University Press.

MacDonald, A. P. Jr. (1981). Bisexuality: Some comments on research and theory. *Journal of Homosexuality, 6*, 21–35.

Madon, S. (1997). What do people believe about gay males? A study of stereotyped content and strength. *Sex Roles, 37*, 663–685.

Miller, R. J., & Boon, S. D. (2000). Trust and disclosure of sexual orientation in gay males' mother-son relationships. *Journal of Homosexuality, 38*, 41–63.

Moorhead, C. (1999). Queering identities: The roles of integrity and belonging in becoming ourselves. *Journal of Gay, Lesbian, and Bisexual Identity, 4*, 327–343.

Oswald, R. F. (2000). Family and friendship relationships after young women come out as bisexuals or lesbian. *Journal of Homosexuality, 38*, 65–83.

Paul, J. P. (1984). The bisexual identity: An idea without social recognition. *Journal of Homosexuality, 9*, 45–63.

Paul, J. P. (1985). Bisexuality: Reassessing our paradigms of sexuality. In F. Klein & T. Wolf (Eds.), *Two lives to lead: Bisexuality in men and women* (pp. 21–34). New York: Blackwell.

Pennebaker, J. W., Barger, S. D., & Tiebout, J. (1989). Disclosure of traumas and health among holocaust survivors. *Psychosomatic Medicine, 51*, 577–589.

Risman, B. J. (1987). Intimate relationships from a microstructural perspective: Men who mother. *Gender and Society, 1*, 6–32.

Robertson, K., & Murachver, T. (2003). Children's speech accommodation to gendered language styles. *Journal of Language and Social Psychology, 22,* 321–333.

Rofes, E. (1998). *Dry bones breathe: Gay men creating post-AIDS identities and cultures.* Birmingham, NY: Haworth.

Ruble, D. N., & Martin, C. L. (1997). Gender development. In W. Damon & N. Eisenberg (Eds.), *Handbook of child psychology. Vol. 3: Social, emotional, and personality development* (pp. 933–1016). New York: Wiley.

Rust, P. C. (1993a). "Coming out" in the age of social constructionism: Sexual identity formation among lesbian and bisexual women. *Gender and Society, 7,* 50–77.

Rust, P. C. (1993b). Neutralizing the political threat of the marginal woman: lesbians' beliefs about bisexual women. *The Journal of Sex Research, 30,* 214–228.

Schwanberg, S. L. (1993). Attitudes toward gay men and lesbian women: Instrumentation issues. *Journal of Homosexuality, 26,* 99–136.

Smith, P. M. (1985). *Language, the sexes and society.* Oxford: Basil Blackwell.

Tajfel, H., & Turner, J. (1986). The social identity theory of intergroup behavior. In S. Worchel & W. G. Austin (Eds.), *Psychology of intergroup relations* (2nd ed., pp. 7–24). Chicago: Nelson.

Tannen, D. (1990). *You just don't understand: Women and men in conversation.* New York: William Morrow, Ballantine.

Taywaditep, K. J. (2001). Marginalization among the marginalized: Gay men's anti-effeminacy attitudes. *Journal of Homosexuality, 42,* 1–28.

Thomson, R., Murachver, T., & Green, J. (2001). Where is the gender in gendered language? *Psychological Science, 12,* 171–175.

Thorne, B. (1986). Girls and boys together, but mostly apart: Gender arrangements in elementary schools. In W. W. Hartup & Z. Rubin (Eds.), *Relationships and development* (pp. 167–184). Hillsdale, NJ: Erlbaum.

Thurlow, C. (2001). Naming the "outsider within": Homophobic pejoratives and the verbal abuse of lesbian, gay and bisexual high-school pupils. *Journal of Adolescence, 24,* 25–38.

Turner, J. C. (1982). Towards a cognitive redefinition of the social group. In H. Tajfel (Ed.), *Social identity and intergroup relations* (pp. 15–40). Cambridge: Cambridge University Press.

Turner, J. C. (1985). Social categorization and the self-concept: A social cognitive theory of group behavior. In E. J. Lawler (Ed.), *Advances in group processes: Theory and research* (vol. 2: pp. 77–121). Greenwich, CT: JAI Press.

Turner, J. C., Hogg, M. A., Oakes, P. J., Reicher, S. D., & Wetherell, M. S. (1987). *Rediscovering the social group: A self-categorization theory.* Oxford: Blackwell.

Valentine, D. (2003). "I went to bed with my own kind once": The erasure of desire in the name of identity. *Language and Communication, 23,* 123–138.

Valentine, J. (1998). Naming the other: Power, politeness and the inflation of euphemisms. *Sociological Research Online, 3,* 1–23.

West, C., & Zimmerman, D. (1987). Doing gender. *Gender & Society 1,* 125–151.

Whitley, B. E. Jr., & Egisdottir, S. (2000). The gender belief system, authoritarianism, social dominance orientation, and heterosexuals' attitudes toward lesbians and gay men. *Sex Roles, 42,* 947–967.

Williams, J., & Giles, H. (1978). The changing status of women in society: An intergroup perspective. In H. Tajfel (Ed.), *Differentiation between social groups: Studies in the social psychology of intergroup relations* (pp. 431–446). London: Academic Press.

Wolfgang, A., & Wolfgang, J. (1971). Exploration of attitudes via interpersonal distance toward the obese, drug users, homosexuals, police, and other marginal figures. *Journal of Clinical Psychology, 27,* 510–512.

Wong, F. Y., McCreary, D. R., Carpenter, K. M., Engle, A., & Korchynsky, R. (1999). Gender-related factors influencing perceptions of homosexuality. *Journal of Homosexuality, 37,* 19–31.

Wood, J. T. (1998). *But I thought you meant: Misunderstandings in human communication.* Mountain View, CA: Mayfield.

4
Multilingual Communication and Social Identification

Itesh Sachdev
Richard Y. Bourhis

> "Persons belonging to national or ethnic, religious and linguistic minori-
> ties...have the right to enjoy their own culture, to profess and practice their
> own religion, and to use their own language in private and in public, freely
> and without interference or any form of discrimination ..." (Article 2:1,
> United Nations Declaration on the Rights of Persons Belonging to National
> or Ethnic, Religious and Linguistic Minorities, 1992)

Being bilingual or multilingual is the norm for most people in the
world (Baker & Jones, 1998; Edwards, 1994, Grosjean, 1982; Hamers &
Blanc, 2000). Communication where two or more languages (and dialects) are used generally involves speakers of different ethnolinguistic
backgrounds sharing the same local, regional, or national jurisdiction
(Johnson, 2000). Which language is used, when, why, and by whom is
an important question given the crucial role that language plays not
only in fostering effective intergroup communication but also in as-
serting pride and loyalty for one's ethnolinguistic heritage (Fishman,
1977). The myriad of interethnic contexts, coupled with the equally
diverse array of ethnolinguistic behaviors and attitudes, represent a
considerable challenge to modeling the relationship between bilin-
gual/multilingual communication and social identifications (Sachdev
& Bourhis, 2001). In this chapter, references to bilingual communication will be subsumed under the more general term of multilingual
communication unless specifically indicated. In view of the complexity of multilingual communication, this chapter focuses on social psychological aspects of the phenomena (see also, Bourhis, 1979, 2001a;
Clément & Bourhis, 1996; Giles & Coupland, 1991; Liebkind, 1999;

Sachdev & Giles, 2004). The first part of this chapter addresses the importance of language as a pillar of ethnolinguistic identity and its importance for the achievement of a positive social identity. The second part examines micro-individual aspects of multilingual communication. The third explores macro-societal and public policy aspects of multilingual communication. It should be noted that although the division into micro and macro aspects is useful for our analytical purposes, the distinction is somewhat artificial, as these levels are interactive and interdependent (Bourhis, 1979; Sachdev & Bourhis, 2001). What the three parts of the chapter share is the usefulness of adopting a social identity approach to the study of multilingual communication (Tajfel & Turner, 1986).

Language, Ingroup Identification, and Positive Social Identity

Languages, accents, dialects, and lexical and syntactic diversity not only provide important cues for the categorization of speakers on the social map (Giles & Powesland, 1975; Scherer & Giles, 1979) but can also emerge as the most salient dimensions of group identity (Giles, Bourhis, & Taylor, 1977; Giles & Johnson, 1981; Sachdev & Bourhis, 1990). Social psychological research has shown that language competence and language use influences the formation of group identity (Clément & Bourhis, 1996). For instance, results of multidimensional scaling studies conducted in Quebec and Wales showed that ethnolinguistic group members felt they were more similar with categorized individuals who spoke their native tongue than with those who shared their cultural background or geographic origin, attesting to the role of language as the most salient dimension of ethnic identity in these cultural settings (Giles, Taylor, & Bourhis, 1977; Taylor, Bassili, & Aboud, 1973).

Although the literature on the centrality of language to group identity is substantial, some empirical evidence showing that language might not be the only, or even the most significant, variable related to group identity has also been obtained (Edwards, 1985). For instance, Sawaie (1986) documented how ethnic identification among Arabs in the United States remained high in spite of linguistic assimilation to English as the language of economic integration in the US. Similarly, Pak, Dion, and Dion (1985) found that Chinese Canadian students' self-rated confidence in English did not detract from their cultural identities. In reviewing such findings, Edwards (1985) suggested that language as a marker of group identity might be no different from other symbols of ethnic identification such as ethnic dress, ornamentation, dance, and song (for critiques of Edwards's position, see Coupland, 1986; Skutnabb-Kangas, 2000).

Multilinguals often identify not only with one of their languages but equally with all the languages they speak. This is more likely with individuals who are balanced bilinguals than among those whose degree of fluency in their first and second language is unequal (Hamers & Blanc, 2000). For instance, in a large-scale study of ethnolinguistic groups in California and Florida, Rumbaut (1994) found that adolescents who were more proficient in English as their second language (L2) than their mother tongue (L1), were more likely to define themselves as American than those who were more proficient in their L1 heritage language than their L2. Those who attained equal proficiency in their L1 and L2 (balanced bilinguals) were more likely to identify as "hyphenated" Americans (e.g., Mexican Americans).

Given the prevalence of multiple group identities, Hogg and McGarty (1990) sought to explain under what circumstances specific social categories and ingroup identities were activated during social interaction. They noted that:

> it became increasingly clear that to talk of social identification, ... "switching" of social identities, salience of social identities, ... simply begged the question by what process people come to conceptualize themselves in terms of social categories. Self-categorization theory was developed to address this question. (p. 11)

Starting with the premise that groups primarily exist cognitively, the fundamental argument of self-categorization theory (SCT) is that people form and internalize the different social categories to which they belong. These internalized categories (social identifications) guide intragroup and intergroup behavior (Turner, 1985). Self-categorization leads to stereotypical self-perception, depersonalization, and ingroup normative behavior (Turner, Hogg, Oakes, Reicher, & Wetherell, 1987). SCT provides the "possibility of addressing a classic social psychological problem of the relationship of the individual to the group and the emergence of collective phenomena from individual cognitions" (Brown, 2000, p. 746).

SCT proposes that social categorization operates at three broad levels of abstraction, which can each be activated by the self, depending on the setting and the category membership of those with whom we interact (Oakes, Haslam, & Turner, 1994). The group level category is the basic level of categorical activation, as it is related to the category memberships of those with whom we interact on a daily basis (e.g., gender, age, ethnicity, language group, social class; see relevant chapters in this volume). The individual level category is activated during interpersonal encounters with well-known others, such as family members and friends, about whom much idiographic information is known and is relevant for ensuring the quality of the encounter. Supraordinal category membership such as "we humans" is activated in cases where superordinate goals (ensuring world peace) or superordinate threats (avoiding ecological collapse) make base rate group-level categories less functional for addressing present needs and challenges. The social situation and the category memberships of those we interact with at a specific moment provide the cues that activate the level of category abstraction most heuristic for dealing with the encounter (individual, group, or supraordinal).

SCT provides a framework that clarifies the conditions under which language is activated as a marker of group identity. In situations where it is the group-level category that is activated, it is the contrasting category features of individuals relative to other individuals that determine the specific group-level category (e.g., linguistic vs. social class) that becomes the most salient for defining the self within the communication situation. Linguistic self-categorizations become salient when they provide the best "fit' for the available social context by maximizing the contrast between intracategory similarities and intercategory differences between group members (meta-contrast). For instance, in their analysis of language planning in Quebec, Sachdev and Bourhis (1990) argued that though religious values were central to French Quebecers' self-definitions in times past, language emerged as the best fit for self-categorization in contemporary Quebec where French/English linguistic background maximized the contrast in differences between, and similarities within, ethnolinguistic groups. Relatedly, Abrams and Hogg (1987) obtained evidence from Scotland suggesting that intranational accent evaluations (Dundee vs. Glasgow) were not relevant to their participants from Dundee when the level of comparison was *inter*national (Scottish vs. English), yet were extremely salient when the level of self-categorization was regional (east vs. west Scotland). These examples illustrate how SCT is not only useful in understanding when language can become the most important dimension of group identity, but might also help explain when language does *not* emerge as the main criterial attribute of ingroup identification.

While SCT provides a framework for understanding which category membership emerges as the most important dimension of group identity, ethnolinguistic identity theory (ELIT) was developed to account for the social psychological processes that account for how people achieve and maintain a positive social identity (Giles, Bourhis, et al., 1977; Giles & Johnson, 1981, 1987). ELIT is based on a fundamental premise of social identity theory (SIT): Individuals prefer to belong to groups that provide them with a positive social identity and will engage in personal and collective strategies for achieving and maintaining a "positive distinctiveness" vis-à-vis salient or rival outgroups (Tajfel & Turner, 1986). In the discrimination literature, minimal group studies have shown that the more individuals identify with their arbitrary category membership, the more they subsequently engage in discriminatory behavior, which, in turn, contributes to a more positive social identity (Perreault & Bourhis, 1998, 1999). In the language attitude literature, studies have consistently shown that speakers who identify with their ingroup tend to evaluate speakers of their ingroup more favorably than outgroup speakers (Ryan & Giles, 1982). This "ingroup favoritism effect" was obtained on ratings of both status and solidarity traits and enhanced the positive social identity of speakers whether they were differentiated by ethnicity, social class, or regional or national origin (Giles & Ryan, 1982).

Ethnolinguistic group members are more likely to enjoy a positive social identity when they belong to a language group that compares favorably with salient outgroups on important dimensions of social comparison, such as demographic strength, institutional support or control, and social prestige. But individuals can suffer from a negative social identity when they belong to an ethnolinguistic group that compares negatively in terms of status, a weak and declining demographic position or their subordinate position in institutions such as education, business, finance, and government. Based on SIT, ELIT proposes specific *identity management strategies* to counter the effects of a negative social identity (see Harwood, Giles, & Palomares, this volume). Members of low-status language groups might use individual mobility strategies to "pass" into the dominant outgroup by learning and speaking its prestige language and assimilating linguistically and culturally (Edwards & Chisholm, 1987). For instance, Albo (1979) showed how indigenous Andean group members increasingly employed Spanish vocabulary for reasons of prestige and modernity, leading to a diglossic situation in which their own aboriginal languages were restricted to low-status private domains, while the dominant language of the European colonizer was used for high-status public functions of the state. Also in South America, Kanazawa and Loveday (1988) found that third-generation immigrants of Japanese ancestry in Brazil, who had linguistically assimilated to the degree that they were monolingual in Portuguese, identified uniquely as Brazilian and not at all as Japanese. The widespread adoption of this assimilation strategy implies dis-identification with the former group and identification with the dominant majority. In the long run, this strategy could lead linguistic minorities to cease to exist as distinctive linguistic collectivities (Denison, 1977).

Of course, upward mobility through assimilation might not always be possible, especially when "objective" group barriers exist or when intergroup boundaries are perceived to be impermeable. SIT proposes that, under these conditions of dominant group exclusion, disparaged minorities who feel the situation to be illegitimate or unstable, might use "social creativity" strategies aimed at redefining evaluations associated with ingroup devaluation or construct new dimensions of comparisons on which the minority group will compare favorably with outgroups. Examples of creativity strategies adopted by ethnolinguistic minorities are many and include social movements associated with positively redefining previously negatively valued languages, such as Punjabi in Pakistan, African American vernacular English in the United States, and Welsh in the United Kingdom (Bourhis, Giles, & Tajfel, 1973; Giles, Taylor, et al., 1977; Lanehart, 1999; Williams, 1999).

Another identity management strategy proposed within SIT is that disparaged language minorities might challenge the status-quo directly through "social competition": acting collectively in seeking equal representation and power sharing with the dominant outgroup across domains of institutional support and control (Tajfel & Turner, 1986). Numerous examples of "language revival" movements around the world illustrate direct competition along linguistic dimensions in order for minority language communities to not only revive their language but to also be more fairly represented in formal functions of society, such as government services, education, the mass media, and the work world (Fishman, 1999; Skutnabb-Kangas, 2000). Recent instances of language minorities who have mobilized collectively by instituting "reversing language shift" policies (Fishman, 1991, 2001) include the Navajo in the United States (Lee & McLaughlin, 2001), the French in Quebec (Bourhis, 1984a, 2001b; Hamers & Hummel, 1994), the Basque and the Catalan in Spain (Azurmendi, Bachoc, & Zabaleta, 2001; McRoberts, 2001; Strubell, 2001), the Maoris in New Zealand and the Quechua in South America (Benton & Benton, 2001; Hornberger & King, 2001; Spolsky, 2003).

Efforts by linguistic minorities to revive or maintain their heritage language within the majority setting are often undermined and even repressed by majorities through assimilationist language policies such as those adopted in France (Bourhis, 1982; Lodge, 1993; Tabouret-Keller, 1999). In the United States, right-wing lobbies such as the "English-only movement" succeeded in having 18 state legislatures declare English as their only official language, thus limiting or banning schools and government agencies from using Spanish (Barker et al., 2001; Barker & Giles, 2002; Bourhis & Marshall, 1999; Ricento, 1998; Schmidt, 1998). Internationally, the economic and military dominance of the US and the concurrent rise of English as a world language have also resulted in increased levels of perceived threat for both linguistic minorities and for national languages of many countries across the world (Crystal, 1997; Flaitz, 1988; House, 2003).

Micro-Individual Aspects of
Multilingual Communication

When multilinguals initiate conversations in one language, their interlocutors can reply either in the same language, or in a different language, or in a combination of languages (Bourhis, 1979; Sachdev & Giles, 2004). When conversations involve code-switching, different languages might be used within the same sentence, or between sentences, or between speaker turns (Bourhis, 1984b; Gardner-Chloros, 1991; Milroy & Muysken, 1995; Myers-Scotton, 1997; Ng & He, 2004; Sachdev & Bourhis, 2001). Of course, conversations also include variation on other linguistic (e.g., accent, lexis, etc.), discoursal, and nonverbal dimensions, even when only one language is used in the dialogue (Coupland & Jaworski, 1997; Genesee & Bourhis, 1988).

Linguistic competence, desires to increase communication accuracy, and the normative demands of situations have been identified as important factors governing code-switching in multilingual situations (Beebe & Giles, 1984; Giles & Coupland, 1991; Sachdev & Bourhis, 2001). A key contribution in our understanding of the complexity and dynamic nature of multilingual communication has been the development of what is now known as communication accommodation theory (CAT: Bourhis, 1979; Coupland & Giles, 1988; Gallois, Giles, Jones, Cargile, & Ota, 1995; Giles, Taylor, & Bourhis, 1973; Niedzielski & Giles, 1996; Sachdev & Giles, 2004).

CAT was developed partly as a reaction to the normative bias in traditional sociolinguistics that explained code-switching in terms of language norms determining who speaks what to whom and when (Myers-Scotton, 1997; see Sachdev & Bourhis, 2001 for recent discussion). Without ignoring normative factors, CAT sought to account for language use in terms of interlocutors' motives, attitudes, perceptions, and group loyalties in a broad range of experimental and applied settings (Giles, Coupland, & Coupland, 1991; Giles, Mulac, Bradac, & Johnson, 1987). CAT expanded into an "interdisciplinary model of relational and identity processes in communicative interaction" (Coupland & Jaworski, 1997, pp. 241–242).

The dynamic variation of communicative behavior toward and away from others is referred to as accommodation. CAT was designed to account for three basic language strategies: convergence, divergence, and maintenance. Briefly, convergence was defined as a strategy whereby individuals adapt their communicative behaviors in terms of a wide range of linguistic (e.g., languages, accents, speech rates), paralinguistic (e.g., pauses, utterance length), and nonverbal features (e.g., smiling, gazing) in such a way as to become more similar to their interlocutor's behavior (Giles & Coupland, 1991). Conversely, divergence was defined as a strategy where individuals change their communicative behaviors to become more dissimilar to their interlocutor's behavior (Bourhis & Giles, 1977; Bourhis, Giles, Leyens, & Tajfel, 1979). Finally, the strategy of maintenance is an act of not converging (or actively diverging) from another but, instead, sustaining (somewhat purposively) one's own native language usage (Bourhis, 1979, 1984b). It is noteworthy that these phenomena have been found to occur simultaneously on a variety of levels and that speakers are not always aware that they are modifying their communicative behaviors (Giles et al., 1987). Levels of awareness about divergence and maintenance appear to be higher than for convergence (e.g., Bourhis, Giles, & Lambert, 1975; Street, 1982).

There are a multitude of reasons why multilinguals use different languages, including not finding the right word at that moment, desire for communicative efficiency, adhering to language norms, allowing others to have practice at one's language, the desire to convey one's loyalty to the local language community, or to project a multicultural cosmopolitan identity. CAT accounts for multilingual communication in terms of social psychological processes operating at both the interindividual level (e.g., similarity-attraction; Byrne, 1969) and at the intergroup level where social identity processes are of primary importance (SIT and ELIT: Giles, 1978; Giles, Bourhis, et al., 1977; Giles & Johnson, 1987; Tajfel & Turner, 1986).

At the interindividual level, motivations for social approval are thought to underlie communication convergence (Giles et al., 1987). Using research on similarity-attraction (Byrne, 1969) as a starting point, it was argued that when interlocutors became more similar in their speech styles they would like each other more. In support of this, a plethora of studies have suggested that language convergence generally facilitates interpersonal and intergroup interaction where linguistic dissimilarities might otherwise be a barrier to communication (Bourhis, 1979). Linguistic convergence has been thought likely to increase interlocutors' intelligibility (Triandis, 1960), predictability (Berger & Bradac, 1982), and interpersonal involvement (LaFrance, 1979). Additionally, convergence is perceived more favorably if it can be attributed to the converger's intentions rather than to external pressures (Simard, Taylor, & Giles, 1976). Bilinguals who make an effort to converge to the mother tongue of their interlocutor are likely to find their interlocutor reciprocate the effort through mutual language convergence (Giles et al., 1973). Convergence might also reflect motivations to maximize "rewards" and minimize "costs" (Homans, 1961). For instance, in interactions between bilingual Francophone and Anglophone Canadian civil servants, Francophones were more likely to converge to English than Anglophones were to converge to French (Bourhis, 1994). The enduring prestige of English as the language of work and upward mobility within the Canadian public service and in Canadian society contributed to the reward power of English use for both Anglophones and Francophones. Similarly, Berg (1986) observed that bilingual customers converged "downward" by using the local vernacular (Southern Min, Hakka) with street market attendants, yet converged "upward" by using Mandarin in their dealings with bank clerks, again maximizing their rewards in each context.

At the intergroup level, motivation for a positive social identity as proposed within social identity theory (SIT: Tajfel & Turner, 1986) was most clearly evident in studies demonstrating language divergence and language maintenance in many different parts of the world. Experimental studies have shown that positive ingroup identification was related to the positive evaluation of language maintenance and language divergence voiced by ingroup members in conversations with rival outgroup speakers (Bourhis et al., 1975; Genesee & Bourhis, 1988). A field study conducted in Hong Kong one year before its handover to the People's Republic of China, showed that respondents who identified with Hong Kong were more favorable about ingroup members who diverged (by using Cantonese) from Mandarin speakers than those who identified with mainland China (Tong, Hong, Lee, & Chiu, 1999).

As seen earlier, the primary motivational construct in ELIT was articulated as the search for "positive psycholinguistic distinctiveness" through the establishment of favorable social comparisons with outgroups on language and speech dimensions (Giles et al., 1987). ELIT proposes that language maintenance and divergence were ideal strategies of psycholinguistic distinctiveness, especially when language was an important dimension of ingroup identification. A language laboratory study conducted in Wales found that adults learning Welsh for cultural identity reasons diverged linguistically by emphasizing their Welsh accent in English when responding to an outgroup English speaker who had voiced a culturally threatening message using the standard English accent (Received Pronunciation) (Bourhis & Giles, 1977). Similarly, a language laboratory study in Belgium examined how trilingual Flemish undergraduates responded to a confederate with a French heritage who voiced a series of questions in English and then in French (Bourhis et al., 1979). When the French confederate used English to voice content-neutral questions, the Flemish students converged to English. However, when the confederate switched to French to voice a culturally threatening message, all the Flemish undergraduates demonstrated linguistic and content divergence by switching to Flemish, vehemently disagreeing with the disparaging statements about the Flemish language, and using insulting epithets to describe the French confederate.

Language strategies proposed within CAT can be investigated by using not only synchronic methodologies but also by using broader diachronic approaches. For instance, a series of field studies were conducted in bilingual Montreal from 1977 to 1997 to monitor multilingual communication between Francophone and Anglophone pedestrians following the adoption of a controversial language law designed to increase the status of French relative to English in Quebec (Bill 101, 1977: Bourhis 1984a, 2001a). Local Francophone and Anglophone pedestrians were randomly accosted in downtown Montreal by a female confederate who voiced a plea for directions in either fluent French or English. While controlling for the bilingual skills of respondents, results showed that Francophone pedestrians systematically converged to English (95 to 100%) when responding to the plea voiced in English by the confederate in the four studies conducted from 1977 to 1997. In contrast, as many as 30 to 40% of Anglophone pedestrians maintained English when responding to pleas for directions voiced in French in the studies conducted from 1977 to 1991 (Bourhis, 1984b; Moise & Bourhis, 1994). Results obtained in favor of English usage during this period reflected the power advantage of the elite Anglophone minority relative to the low-status Francophone majority in Montreal. It was only by the 1997 study that 95% of Anglophone pedestrians converged to French when providing directions to the Francophone confederate (Amiot & Bourhis, 1999). That both Anglophones and Francophones overwhelmingly converged to each other's linguistic needs by the 1997 study suggested that such multilingual communications were being emptied of their former tense intergroup symbolism, while being redefined as encounters that were more neutral, functional, and interpersonal in nature.

According to Hogg and Abrams (1988), language convergence/divergence may at times be considered as "conformity to language and speech style norms through self-categorization" (p. 202). Through self-stereotyping, group members might use language divergence as a way of conforming to the communication norms of their ingroup. For instance, Lawson-Sako and Sachdev (1996) found that Arab pedestrians in Tunisia diverged from an African confederate regardless of the language he used (Tunisian, Arabic, or French). Though the search for positive group distinctiveness could be proposed as an SIT explanation of these findings, the results could also be understood in terms of the self-stereotyping processes proposed within SCT. The request voiced by the Black African confederate might have "switched-on" the ethnic self-categorization of the pedestrians as "Arab" group members. The salience of this self-categorization might have been sufficient to trigger language divergence from the outgroup African regardless of the latter's language choices, a speech strategy concordant with the ingroup norm of how Arabs should communicate with Africans in Tunisia (see also Beebe, 1981; Clément & Noels, 1992). These results suggest that theoretical and empirical analyses of multilingual communication that incorporate SCT need to focus on speakers' *self*-stereotyping as well as outgroup stereotyping during intragroup and intergroup communication (Bourhis & Maass, in press).

Multilingual accommodation can be analyzed from three perspectives: a) objectively, from direct observation of language behavior; b) from the point of view of the intent of the speaker voicing the accommodation; and c) from the perspective of how the addressee perceives the behavior. Thakerar, Giles, and Cheshire (1982) referred to the latter two as psychological and subjective accommodation and argued that subjective accommodation does not always correspond with the objective language behavior nor with the intent behind it. For instance, Ross and Shortreed (1990) found that some Japanese were uncomfortable with Westerners who were proficient in Japanese. In response, Japanese residents sometimes adopt a "foreigner talk" register in Japanese or switch to English as a way of re-establishing the social distance preferred when interacting with Westerners living in

Japan. Similarly, Woolard (1989) reported that some Castilian speakers who converged to Catalan with Catalan speakers received replies voiced in Castilian, a reciprocal convergence interpreted as being intentionally divergent behavior designed to harden intergroup boundaries, rather than a strategy fostering interpersonal rapprochement. In line with the group differentiation motive proposed within SIT, such mutual convergence intended as psychological divergence will likely occur when interactants define the communication situation as an intergroup encounter (driven by social identity concerns) rather than being driven by personal identity. Communication defined as interpersonal might be seen as reflecting individual difference variables (e.g., temperament, personality), while intergroup communication is driven by salient social category memberships.

Macro-Societal and Public Policy
Aspects of Multilingual Communication

Within SIT, status variables were defined as intergroup comparisons on evaluative dimensions such as occupational status, education, and the prestige of ethnic and national groups within the social structure (Tajfel & Turner, 1986). *Group vitality* is a broader concept than group status and is used to compare the relative strength and weaknesses of linguistic minorities and dominant majorities on dimensions such as demography, institutional control, and social status (Bourhis, Giles, & Rosenthal, 1981). The group vitality of an ethnolinguistic group is that which makes the group likely to act as a distinctive and collective entity within the intergroup setting (Giles, Bourhis, et al., 1977). Demographic variables are those related to the sheer number of individuals composing the language group and their distribution throughout a particular urban, regional, or national territory. Informal institutional control refers to the extent to which a linguistic group has organized itself as a pressure group to represent and safeguard its own linguistic interests in various state and private activities. Formal institutional control refers to the degree to which members of a linguistic group have gained positions of control and power at decision-making levels in business, industry, cultural production, sports, mass media, politics, and within the state apparatus in education and the civil administration. Ethnolinguistic groups that have gained a measure of ascendancy on institutional control factors are also likely to enjoy much so-

cial status relative to weaker vitality language groups. Status variables are those related to the socio-historical prestige of the language
community and the status of its language regionally, nationally, and
internationally. Demographic, institutional and status factors combine
to affect the overall strength or vitality of language groups. A linguistic group might be relatively strong on the demographic front but suffer weak institutional support for its language and lack of prestige
both nationally and internationally. In contrast, a linguistic group
might be weak on the demographic front but enjoy strong institutional control and considerable language status internationally.

The stronger the vitality position of an ethnolinguistic group, the
more likely its members are to maintain the use of their own language
in a broad range of private and public settings (Bourhis, 2001a;
Sachdev & Bourhis, 1993). Conversely, ethnolinguistic groups that
have weak vitality might be forced to limit the use of their own language to private ingroup settings, while being pressured to converge
to the dominant language of the high-vitality group in public settings,
such as the work world and state services. In the long run, low-
vitality linguistic minorities are expected to experience language shift
pressures that might eventually lead to intergenerational language
loss and the possible disappearance of the group as a distinctive linguistic collectivity. However, as seen within the SIT framework, low-
vitality group members who strongly identify with their own language community can mobilize collectively and compete socially with
the high-vitality outgroup to gain support for their language in different sectors of the institutional control front. On the demographic
front, low-vitality groups can use increased birthrate and enforced
endogamy to boost the absolute and proportional number of ingroup
speakers within a given region. Such vitality-enhancing group strategies have the cumulative effect of increasing the number of ingroup
speakers in present and future generations, while expanding the settings in which linguistic minorities can use their own language. How
linguistic group members subjectively perceive their ingroup strength
on each dimension of group vitality and the degree to which members
of language groups are willing to mobilize individually or collectively
in order to increase the vitality of their ingroup has been the focus of
much research in the last decades (Bourhis & Sachdev, 1984; Harwood, Giles & Bourhis, 1994; Kindell & Lewis, 2000; Landry & Allard,

1994; Landry & Bourhis, 1997).

The interactive acculturation model (IAM) proposes that high-vitality groups have the institutional control and demographic base to impose state language policies that best serve the interests of their own linguistic community (Bourhis, 2001a; Bourhis, Moise, Perreault, & Senécal, 1997). Though low-vitality language groups can be given a say in the development of such policies in democratic states, their weaker vitality position undermines their capacity to influence the adoption of the language policies needed to sustain the use of minority languages in key domains such as education, government services, mass media, and the work world. The IAM is an intergroup model that proposes that high- and low-vitality language communities often compete to promote the vitality, development, and public use of their respective languages, and this competition is reflected in the language policies adopted in multilingual states (Bourhis, 1984a, 1994, 2001a; Kaplan & Baldauf, 1997). Language policies institutionalize language as the most salient dimension of national identity (Bouchard & Bourhis, 2002; Bourhis, 2001b; Sachdev & Bourhis, 1990). For example, the successful revival of Hebrew from being a "dead" language a century ago to the national language of Israel today can be attributed to the language-planning efforts conducted by the state to accommodate multilingualism since the creation of Israel in 1948 (Fishman, 1989; Spolsky & Shohamy, 1999, 2001).

Thus, at the collective level, the cumulative effects of language policies can result in *language maintenance* in the case of minorities who succeed in transmitting their minority language from one generation to the other without losing their demographic base in absolute and relative terms. *Language shift* implies a gain or a loss in the transmission of the minority language from one generation to the other, thus affecting the demographic and linguistic relationship between minority and majority group speakers in a given region or state. *Language loss* is the result of acculturation processes that undermine the capacity of a group to transmit its heritage language to its progeny, thus undermining its demographic vitality and potentially leading to *language death*.

The IAM proposed four clusters of state ideologies that shape language policies toward linguistic minorities (Bourhis, 2001a). These ideologies can be situated on a continuum that includes the pluralism, the civic, the assimilationist, and the ethnist ideology. Each of the four ideological clusters produces specific policies concerning the linguistic and cultural integration of language minorities within a given region or state. These clusters are not mutually exclusive, and the same democratic state can be situated at different points on the continuum depending on the specific configuration of their policies in different domains (e.g., education, public services, private or public sector work). This ideological continuum provides the public policy backdrop needed to contextualize the multilingual communication strategies of individual speakers in the intergroup setting. The cumulative and sustained implementation of these pro-diversity (pluralism) to intolerant (ethnist) language policies have a decisive impact on the identity of high- or low-vitality group speakers, their identity management strategies, and the multilingual communication strategies they adopt in cross-cultural encounters.

Along with the other three ideologies, the *pluralism ideology* shares the basic premise that in modern democratic states, language minorities should adopt the *public values* of the dominant majority (e.g., commitment to democratic ideals, adherence to civil and criminal codes, adherence to the constitution of the state and Human Rights Charter). Such values can also include the responsibility of all citizens to learn one or more languages adopted as official or co-official languages of the state (Bourhis, 2001a). However, the pluralism ideology upholds that the state has no right to regulate the *private values* of citizens whose individual liberties in personal domains must be respected. Private values include freedom of association in the linguistic, cultural, and political spheres, as well as freedom for linguistic minorities to learn and transmit languages of their choice for use at home, in interpersonal communication, in community and economic activities, and for cultural productions.

The pluralism ideology implies that the state is willing to support—financially and socially—the maintenance of the linguistic distinctiveness of its minorities. Such minorities are seen by the dominant group to enhance the cultural diversity and economic dynamism of mainstream society. The pluralism ideology proposes that because high- and low-vitality groups pay taxes, state funds should be distributed to support the cultural and linguistic activities of both groups (Fleras & Elliot, 1992). The ideology assumes that the endogenous culture and institutions of both groups will be more or less transformed by the sustained contact between these linguistic communities. However, it is recognized that by virtue of their weaker vitality position, linguistic minorities are more likely to be transformed by such contact (for instance, through assimilation) than the high-vitality majority (Bourhis, 2001a). An example of a language policy inspired by the pluralism policy is Canada's Official Languages Act, which recognizes the equality of French and English as official languages in Canada (Bourhis, 1994; Bourhis & Marshall, 1999; Schmidt, 1998). This policy was recognized as paving the way for the adoption of the 1988 Multiculturalism Act, the first official pluralism policy adopted for immigrant cultural communities in the world (Driedger, 1996; Fleras & Elliot, 1992).

Unlike the pluralism ideology, the *civic ideology* enshrines as a principle that the state does not fund or endorse the private values of groups, including linguistic heritage groups. Thus, this ideology is characterized by official state policies of nonintervention and non-support of minority languages and cultures. However, this ideology does respect the right of individuals to organize as community groups, using their own private financial means in order to maintain or promote their respective group identity based on cultural, linguistic, or religious affiliation. In multilingual states, the civic ideology amounts to state funding of the linguistic and cultural interests of the dominant language group, often portrayed as the "neutral" unifying embodiment of the nation and its common destiny. It is in the name of a "neutral state" that the civic ideology legitimizes the absence of official recognition and financial support of its linguistic and immigrant minorities (Bourhis, 2001a). The survival of linguistic minorities is thus left up to "free market forces," which, as the language-planning literature has demonstrated, usually favor the dominant language (Fishman, 1991). Linguistic minorities need institutional support for their language to stem the tide of assimilation and reverse language shift (Fishman, 2001). Under the pretext of "neutral nonintervention" on linguistic issues, dominant majorities can, in effect, accelerate the language shift and language loss of linguistic minorities in multilingual states.

The *assimilation ideology* expects language minorities to abandon their own linguistic and cultural distinctiveness and adopt the language and values of the dominant group. Some countries expect this linguistic and cultural assimilation to occur voluntarily and gradually over time, but other states impose assimilation through regulations that repress linguistic and cultural distinctiveness in public domains (e.g., the school system, the mass media). Usually, it is the economically and politically dominant group that is more successful in imposing its language and culture as the unifying "founding myth" of the nation state (Citron, 1991). For the "greater cause" of "national unity," assimilationist policies are designed to accelerate the language loss of minorities. Dominant group members who endorse assimilationist policies often portray language minorities as a threat to the authenticity, homogeneity, and indivisibility of the national state (Safran, 1999; Schmidt, 1998). State policies encouraging or enforcing linguistic assimilation have resulted in the assimilation of not only second- and third-generation immigrants established in Australia and the United States (Clyne, 2001; Ricento, 1998) but also of first-nation aboriginal minorities of Australia, Canada and the United States (Crawford, 1998; Fettes, 1998; Lo Bianco & Rhydwen, 2001; Sachdev, 1998; Taylor, Wright, Ruggiero, & Aitchison, 1993), and of national minorities such as the Basque, the Breton, and the Occitant in France (Bourhis, 1982; Lodge, 1993; Tabouret-Keller, 1999).

As in the case of the assimilationist ideology, the *ethnist ideology* encourages or forces linguistic minorities to give up their own language and culture for that of the dominant group. Unlike the assimilationist ideology, the ethnist ideology makes it difficult for linguistic minorities to be accepted legally or socially as authentic members of the majority, no matter how much such minorities assimilate linguistically and culturally to the dominant group. Unlike the other ideologies discussed so far, the ethnist ideology usually defines "who can be" and "who should be" citizens of the state in ethnically or religiously exclusive terms (e.g., Israel, Japan). This ideology is sometimes enshrined in the notion of "blood citizenship" whereby only members of selected racial groups can gain full legal access to citizenship. In such states, the nation is defined as being composed of a "kernel" ancestral ethnolinguistic group as determined by birth and kinship (e.g., Germany). Minorities and immigrants who do not share this kinship might never be accepted as legitimate citizens of the state, regardless of their assimilation levels.

In democracies, language policies usually reflect the most prevalent ideological orientations endorsed by the dominant majority. In a
given state, the majority of the population might endorse the assimilationist ideology, while the civic ideology receives moderate support
and the ethnist and pluralist ideologies are endorsed by only a minority (Bourhis, 2001a). Depending on economic, political, demographic,
and military events occurring at the national and international level,
politicians elected by the majority of citizens can shift language policies from one ideological orientation to the other. Political tensions
might emerge between factions of the dominant population holding
rival ideological views on language policies. The polarization of ideological positions regarding such issues might lead to the formation of
political parties whose main platform relates to state policies on language. Thus, backlash movements or political parties within the
dominant majority might succeed in shifting language policies from
the pluralism position to the assimilationist or ethnist ideology. However, mobilized linguistic minorities might succeed in forcing regional
or national governments to change existing assimilationist language
policies to more tolerant approaches, such as the pluralist or the civic
language policies. Once the language policies are adopted by the
state, regional and national governments can greatly influence public
attitudes concerning the legitimacy of such policies through control of
the educational system, public administration, and the mass media.
Thus, both top-down and bottom-up pressures can shift language
policies from one pole of the ideological continuum to the other over
time and across regions. Taken together, language policies can have a
substantial impact on multilingual communication, language maintenance, language shift, and on the acculturation orientations of both
linguistic minorities and members of the dominant language group
(Bourhis, 2001a).

Conclusion

In this chapter, multilingual communication was first addressed by
considering how language can emerge as a key marker of group
membership and a source of positive social identity using theoretical
frameworks such as ethnolinguistic identity theory and features of
both social identity and self-categorization theories. Micro-individual
aspects of multilingual communication were then considered by fo-

cusing on both interpersonal and intergroup communication using communication accommodation theory. Macro-societal considerations were addressed using the ethnolinguistic vitality framework and the interactive acculturation model as backdrops for analyzing how language policies can influence intergroup communication, language shift, and language loss of linguistic minorities and majorities sharing multilingual settings. Future theoretical and empirical efforts must integrate social psychological approaches with those of ethnography, sociolinguistics, discourse analysis, and language planning to more fully account for the complexity of multilingual communications in ever more diverse multilingual and multiethnic societies.

References

Abrams, D., & Hogg, M. (1987). Language attitudes, frames of reference and social identity: A Scottish dimension. *Journal of Language and Social Psychology, 6,* 201–213.

Albo, X. (1979). The future of oppressed languages in the Andes. In W. C. McCormack & S. A. Wurm (Eds.), *Language and society: Anthropological issues* (pp. 309–330). The Hague: Mouton.

Amiot, C., & Bourhis, R. Y. (1999). *Ethnicity and French-English communication in Montréal.* Poster presented at the 60th annual convention of the Canadian Psychological Association. Halifax, Nova Scotia, Canada.

Azurmendi, M. J., Bachoc, E., & Zabaleta, F. (2001). Reversing language shift: The case of Basque. In J. A. Fishman (Ed.), *Can threatened languages be saved?* (pp. 234–259). Clevedon, UK: Multilingual Matters.

Baker, C., & Jones, S. P. (1998). *Encyclopedia of bilingualism & bilingual education.* Clevedon, UK: Multilingual Matters.

Barker, V., & Giles, H. (2002). Who supports the English-only movement? Evidence for misconceptions about Latino group vitality. *Journal of Multilingual and Multicultural Development, 23,* 353–370.

Barker, V., Giles, H., Noels, K. A., Duck, J., Hecht, M. L., & Clément, R. (2001). The English-only movement: A communication analysis of changing perceptions of language vitality. *Journal of Communication, 51,* 3–37.

Beebe, L. (1981). Social and situational factors affecting the strategy of dialect code-switching. *International Journal of the Sociology of Language, 32,* 139–149.

Beebe, L., & Giles, H. (1984). Speech accommodation theories: A discussion in terms of second language acquisition. *International Journal of the Sociology of Language, 46,* 5–32.

Benton, R., & Benton, N. (2001). RLS in Aotearoa/New Zealand. In J. A. Fishman (Ed.). *Can threatened languages be saved?* (pp. 423–450). Clevedon, UK: Multilingual Matters.

Berg, van den M. E. (1986). Language planning and language use in Taiwan: Social identity, language accommodation and language choice behavior. *International Journal of the Sociology of Language, 59,* 97–115.

Berger, C. R., & Bradac, J. J. (1982). *Language and social knowledge.* London: Edward Arnold.

Bouchard, P., & Bourhis, R. Y. (Eds.) (2002). L'aménagement linguistique au Québec: 25 and d'application de la Charte de la langue française. (Language planning in Québec: 25 years of implementing the Charter of the French Language.) *Revue d'Aménagement Linguistique.* Québec: Publications du Québec.

Bourhis, R. Y. (1979). Language in ethnic interaction: A social psychological approach. In H. Giles & B. Saint-Jacques (Eds.), *Language and ethnic relations* (pp. 117–142). Oxford: Pergamon.

Bourhis, R. Y. (1982). Language policies and language attitudes: Le monde de la Francophonie. In E. B. Ryan & H. Giles (Eds.), *Attitudes toward language variation: Social and applied contexts* (pp. 34–62). London: Edward Arnold.

Bourhis, R. Y. (1984a). Language policies in multilingual settings. In R. Y. Bourhis (Ed.), *Conflict and language planning in Quebec* (pp. 1–28). Clevedon, UK: Multilingual Matters.

Bourhis, R. Y. (1984b). Cross-cultural communication in Montreal: Two field studies since Bill 101. *International Journal of the Sociology of Language, 46,* 33–47.

Bourhis, R. Y. (1994). Bilingualism and the language of work: The linguistic work environment survey. *International Journal of the Sociology of Language, 105–106,* 217–266.

Bourhis, R. Y. (2001a). Acculturation, language maintenance and language loss. In J. Klatter-Falmer & P. Van Avermaet (Eds.), *Theories on Language maintenance and loss of minority languages: Towards a more integrated explanatory framework* (pp. 5–37). New York: Waxmann Verlag.

Bourhis, R. Y. (2001b). Reversing language shift in Quebec. In J. A. Fishman (Ed.), *Can threatened languages be saved?* (pp. 101–141). Clevedon, UK. Multilingual Matters.

Bourhis, R. Y., & Giles, H. (1977). The language of intergroup distinctiveness. In H. Giles (Ed.), *Language, ethnicity and intergroup relations* (pp. 119–135). London: Academic Press.

Bourhis, R. Y., Giles, H., & Lambert, W. E. (1975). Social consequences of accommodating one's style of speech: A cross-national investigation. *International Journal of the Sociology of Language, 6,* 55–72.

Bourhis, R. Y., Giles, H., Leyens, J-P., & Tajfel, H. (1979). Psycholinguistic distinctiveness: Language divergence in Belgium. In H. Giles & R. N. St. Clair (Eds.), *Language and social psychology* (pp. 158–85). Oxford: Basil Blackwell.

Bourhis, R. Y., Giles, H., & Rosenthal, D. (1981). Notes on the construction of a "Subjective Vitality Questionnaire" for ethnolinguistic groups. *Journal of Multilingual and Multicultural Development, 2,* 144–155.

Bourhis, R. Y., Giles, H., & Tajfel, H. (1973). Language as a determinant of Welsh Identity. *European Journal of Social Psychology, 3,* 447–460.

Bourhis, R. Y., & Maass, A. (in press). Linguistic prejudice and stereotypes. In U. Ammon, N. Dittmar, K. J. Mattheir, & P. Trudgill (Eds.), *Sociolinguistics: An international handbook of the science of language and society* (2nd ed.). Berlin and New

York: Walter De Gruyter.

Bourhis, R. Y., & Marshall, D. E. (1999). The United States and Canada. In J. A. Fishman (Ed.), *Handbook of language and ethnic identity* (pp. 244–264). New York: Oxford University Press.

Bourhis, R. Y., Moise, L. C., Perreault, S., & Senécal, S. (1997). Towards an interactive acculturation model: A social psychological approach. *International Journal of Psychology, 32*, 369–386.

Bourhis, R. Y., & Sachdev, I. (1984). Vitality perceptions and language attitudes: some Canadian data. *Journal of Language and Social Psychology, 3*, 97–126.

Brown, R. (2000). Social identity theory: Past achievements, current problems and future challenges. *European Journal of Social Psychology, 30*, 745–778.

Byrne, D. (1969). Attitudes and attraction. *Advances in Experimental Social Psychology, 4*, 35–89.

Citron, S. (1991). *Le Mythe National: l'histoire de France en question*. Paris: Les Éditions Ouvrières.

Clément, R., & Bourhis, R. Y. (1996). Bilingualism and intergroup communication. *International Journal of Psycholinguistics, 12*, 171–191.

Clément, R., & Noels, K. A. (1992). Towards a situated approach to ethnolinguistic identity: The effects of status on individuals and groups. *Journal of Language and Social Psychology, 11*, 203–232.

Clyne, M. (2001). Can the shift from immigrant languages be reversed in Australia? In J. A. Fishman (Ed.), *Can threatened languages be saved?* (pp. 364–390). Clevedon, UK. Multilingual Matters.

Coupland, N. (1986). Review Article of J. Edwards' "Language, society and identity." *Journal of Language and Social Psychology, 5*, 63–70.

Coupland, N., & Giles, H. (Eds.). (1988). Communicative accommodation: Recent developments. *Language and Communication, 8*, 175–327.

Coupland, N., & Jaworski, A. (1997). Relevance, accommodation, and conversation: modeling the social dimension of communication. *Multilingua, 16*, 235–258.

Crawford, J. (1998). Endangered Native American languages: What is to be done, and why? In T. Ricento & B. Burnaby (Eds.), *Language and politics in the United States and Canada: Myths and realities* (pp. 151–165). Mahwah, NJ: Erlbaum.

Crystal, D. (1997). *English as a global language*. Cambridge: Cambridge University Press.

Denison, N. (1977). Language death or suicide? *International Journal of the Sociology of Language, 13*, 13–22.

Driedger, L. (1996). *Multi-ethnic Canada: Identities and inequalities*. Toronto: Oxford University Press.

Edwards, J. (1985). *Language, society and identity*, Oxford: Blackwell.

Edwards, J. (1994). *Multilingualism*. London: Routledge.

Edwards, J., & Chisholm, J. (1987). Language, multiculturalism and identity: A Canadian study. *Journal of Multilingual and Multicultural Development, 8*, 391–407.

Fettes, M. (1998). Life on the edge: Canada's Aboriginal languages under official bilingualism. In T. Ricento & B. Burnaby (Eds.), *Language and politics in the United States and Canada: Myths and realities* (pp. 117–149). Mahwah, NJ: Erlbaum.

Fishman, J. A. (1977). Language and ethnicity. In H. Giles (Ed.), *Language, ethnicity and intergroup relations* (pp. 15–57). London: Academic Press.

Fishman, J. A. (1989). *Language and ethnicity in minority sociolinguistic perspective.* Clevedon, UK: Multilingual Matters.

Fishman, J. A. (1991). *Reversing language shift: Theoretical and empirical foundations of assistance to threatened languages.* Clevedon, UK: Multilingual Matters.

Fishman, J. A. (Ed.) (1999). *Handbook of language and ethnic identity.* New York: Oxford University Press.

Fishman, J. A. (Ed.). (2001). Why is it so hard to save a threatened language? In J. A. Fishman (Ed), *Can threatened languages be saved?* (pp. 1–22). Clevedon, UK: Multilingual Matters.

Flaitz, J. (1988). *The ideology of English: French perceptions of English as a world language.* Berlin: Mouton de Gruyter.

Fleras, A., & Elliot, J. L. (1992). *The challenge of diversity: Multiculturalism in Canada.* Scarbourough: Nelson Canada.

Gallois, C., Giles, H., Jones, E., Cargile, A. C., & Ota, H. (1995). Accommodating intercultural encounters: Elaborations and extensions. In R. Wiseman (Ed.), *Theories of intercultural communication* (pp. 115–147). Thousand Oaks, CA: Sage.

Gardner-Chloros, P. (1991). *Language selection and switching in Strasbourg.* Oxford: Clarendon Press.

Genesee, F., & Bourhis, R. Y. (1988). Evaluative reactions to language choice strategies: The role of sociostructural factors. *Language and Communication, 8,* 229–250.

Giles, H. (1978). Linguistic differentiation between ethnic groups. In H. Tajfel (Ed.), *Differentiation between social groups* (pp. 361–393). London: Academic Press.

Giles, H., Bourhis, R. Y., & Taylor, D. M. (1977). Towards a theory of language in ethnic group relations. In H. Giles (Ed.), *Language, ethnicity and intergroup relations* (pp. 307–348). London: Academic Press.

Giles, H., & Coupland, N. (1991). *Language: Contexts and consequences.* Milton Keynes: Open University Press.

Giles, H., Coupland, J., & Coupland, N. (Eds.). (1991). *Contexts of accommodation: Developments in applied sociolinguistics.* Cambridge: Cambridge University Press.

Giles, H., & Johnson. P. (1981). The role of language in ethnic group relations. In J. C. Turner & H. Giles (Eds.), *Intergroup behavior* (pp. 199–243). Oxford: Blackwell.

Giles, H., & Johnson, P. (1987). Ethnolinguistic identity theory: A social psychological approach to language maintenance. *International Journal of the Sociology of Language, 68,* 69–99.

Giles, H., Mulac, A., Bradac, J. J., & Johnson, P. (1987). Speech accommodation theory: The first decade and beyond. In M. L. McLaughlin (Ed.), *Communication Yearbook 10* (pp. 13–48). Beverley Hills, CA: Sage.

Giles, H., & Powesland, P. (1975). *Speech style and social evaluation.* London: Academic Press.

Giles, H., & Ryan, E. B. (1982). Prolegomena for developing a social psychological theory of language attitudes. In E. B. Ryan & H. Giles (Eds.), *Attitudes toward language variation* (pp. 208–223). London: Academic Press.

Giles, H., Taylor, D. M., & Bourhis, R. Y. (1973). Toward a theory of interpersonal accommodation through speech: Some Canadian data. *Language in Society, 2,* 177–192.

Giles, H., Taylor, D. M., & Bourhis, R. Y. (1977). Dimensions of Welsh identity. *European Journal of Social Psychology, 7,* 165–174.

Grosjean, F. (1982). *Life with two languages: An introduction to bilingualism.* Cambridge, MA: Harvard University Press.

Hamers, J. F., & Blanc, M. H. A. (2000). *Bilinguality and bilingualism.* Cambridge: Cambridge University Press.

Hamers, J., & Hummel, K. (1994). The Francophones of Quebec: Language policies and language use. *International Journal of the Sociology of Language, 105–106,* 127–152

Harwood, J., Giles, H., & Bourhis, R. Y. (1994). The genesis of vitality theory: Historical patterns and discoursal dimensions. *International Journal of the Sociology of Language, 108,* 167–206.

Hogg, M., & Abrams, D. (1988). *Social identifications.* London: Methuen.

Hogg, M., & McGarty, C. (1990). Self-categorization and social identity. In D. Abrams & M. Hogg (Eds.), *Social identity theory: Constructive and critical advances* (pp. 10–27). Hemel Hempstead: Harvester Wheatsheaf.

Homans, G. C. (1961). *Social behavior.* New York: Harcourt, Brace and World.

Hornberger, N. H., & King, K. A. (2001). Reversing Quechua language shift in South America. In J. A. Fishman (Ed.), *Can threatened languages be saved?* (pp 166–194). Clevedon, UK: Multilingual Matters.

House, J. (2003). English as a lingua franca: a threat to multilingualism? *Journal of Sociolinguistics, 7,* 556–578.

Johnson, F. (2000). *Speaking culturally: Language diversity in the United States.* Thousand Oaks, CA: Sage.

Kanazawa, H., & Loveday, L. (1988). The Japanese immigrant community in Brazil: Language contact and shift. *Journal of Multilingual and Multicultural Development, 9,* 423–435.

Kaplan, R. B., & Baldauf, R. B. (1997). *Language planning: From practice to theory.* Clevedon, UK: Multilingual Matters.

Kindell, G., & Lewis, M. P. (Eds.). (2000). *Assessing ethnolinguistic vitality: Theory and practice.* Dallas, TX: SIL International.

LaFrance, M. (1979). Nonverbal synchrony and rapport: Analysis by the cross-lag panel technique. *Social Psychology Quarterly, 42,* 66–70.

Landry, R., & Allard, R. (1994). Diglossia, ethnolinguistic vitality and language behavior. *International Journal of the Sociology of Language, 108,* 15–42.

Landry, R., & Bourhis, R. Y. (1997). Linguistic landscape and ethnolinguistic vitality: An empirical study. *Journal of Language and Social Psychology, 16,* 23–49.

Lanehart, S. L. (1999). African American Vernacular English. In J. A. Fishman (Ed.), *Handbook of language and ethnic identity* (pp. 211–225). New York: Oxford University Press.

Lawson-Sako, S., & Sachdev, I. (1996). Ethnolinguistic communication in Tunisian streets. In Y. Suleiman (Ed.), *Language and ethnic identity in the Middle East and*

North Africa (pp. 61–79). Richmond: Curzon Press.

Lee, T., & McLaughlin, D. (2001). Reversing Navajo language shift, revisited. In J. A. Fishman (Ed.). *Can threatened languages be saved?* (pp. 23–43). Clevedon, UK: Multilingual Matters.

Liebkind, K. (1999). Social psychology. In J. A. Fishman (Ed.), *Handbook of language and ethnic identity* (pp. 140–151). Oxford: Oxford University Press.

Lo Bianco J., & Rhydwen, M. (2001). Is the extinction of Australia's indigenous languages inevitable? In J. A. Fishman (Ed.), *Can threatened languages be saved?* (pp. 391–422). Clevedon, UK: Multilingual Matters.

Lodge, R. A. (1993). *French: From dialect to standard*. London: Routledge.

McRoberts, R. (2001). *Catalonia: Nation building without a state*. Oxford: Oxford University Press.

Milroy, L., & Muysken, P. (1995). Introduction: Code-switching and bilingualism research. In L. Milroy & P. Muysken (Eds.), *One speaker, two languages: Cross-disciplinary perspectives on code-switching* (pp. 1–14). Cambridge: Cambridge University Press.

Moise, L. C., & Bourhis, R. Y. (1994). Langage et ethnicité: Communication interculturelle à Montréal, 1977–1991. *Canadian Ethnic Studies, 26*, 86–107.

Myers-Scotton, C. (1997). Code-switching. In F. Coulmas (Ed.), *The handbook of sociolinguistics* (pp. 217–237). Oxford: Blackwell.

Ng, S. H., & He, A. (2004). Code-switching in tri-generational family conversations among Chinese immigrants in New Zealand. *Journal of Language and Social Psychology, 23*, 28–48.

Niedzielski, N., & Giles, H. (1996). Linguistic accommodation. In H. Goebl, P. Nelde, H. Zdenek, S. Zdenek, & W. Wölck (Eds.), *Contact linguistics. An international handbook of contemporary research* (pp. 332–342). Berlin, New York: Walter de Gruyter.

Oakes, P. J., Haslam, S. A., & Turner, J. C. (1994). *Stereotyping and social reality*. Oxford: Blackwell.

Pak, A. W-P., Dion, K. L., & Dion, K. K. (1985). Correlates of self-confidence with English among Chinese students in Toronto. *Canadian Journal of Behavioral Science, 17*, 369–378.

Perreault, S., & Bourhis, R. Y. (1998). Social identification, interdependence and discrimination. *Group Processes and Intergroup Relations, 1*, 49–66.

Perreault, S., & Bourhis, R. Y. (1999). Ethnocentrism, social identification and discrimination. *Personality and Social Psychology Bulletin, 25*, 92–103.

Ricento, T. (1998). National language policy in the United States. In T. Ricento & B. Burnaby (Eds.), *Language and politics in the United States and Canada: Myths and realities* (pp. 85–112). Mahwah, NJ: Erlbaum.

Ross, S., & Shortreed, I. M. (1990). Japanese foreigner talk: Convergence or divergence? *Journal of Asian Pacific Communication, 1*, 135–145.

Rumbaut, R. G. (1994). The crucible within: Ethnic identity, self-esteem, and segmented assimilation among children of immigrants. *International Migration Review, 28*, 748–794.

Ryan, E. B., & Giles, H. (Eds.). (1982). *Attitudes toward language variation.* London: Academic Press.

Sachdev, I. (1998). Language use and attitudes amongst the Fisher River Cree in Manitoba. *Canadian Journal of Native Education, 22,* 108–119.

Sachdev, I., & Bourhis R. Y. (1990). Language and social identification. In D. Abrams & M. Hogg (Eds.), *Social identity theory: Constructive and critical advances* (pp. 33–51). Hemel Hempstead, UK: Harvester Wheatsheaf.

Sachdev, I., & Bourhis, R. Y. (1993). Ethnolinguistic vitality: Some motivational and cognitive considerations. In M. Hogg & D. Abrams (Eds.), *Group motivation: Social psychological perspectives* (pp. 33–51). New York and London: Harvester-Wheatsheaf.

Sachdev, I., & Bourhis, R. Y. (2001). Multilingual communication. In W. P. Robinson & H. Giles (Eds.), *The new handbook of language and social psychology* (pp. 407–428). Chichester, UK: Wiley.

Sachdev, I., & Giles, H. (2004). Bilingual accommodation. In T. K. Bhatia & W. Ritchie (Eds.), *Handbook of Bilingualism* (pp. 353–378). Oxford: Blackwell.

Safran, W. (1999). Nationalism. In J. A. Fishman (Ed.). *Handbook of language and ethnic identity* (pp. 77–93). New York: Oxford University Press.

Sawaie, M. (1986). The present and future of a minority language: The case of Arabic in the United States. *Journal of Multilingual and Multicultural Development, 7,* 379–392.

Scherer, K. R., & Giles, H. (Eds.). (1979). *Social markers in speech.* Cambridge: Cambridge University Press.

Schmidt, R. (1998). The politics of language in Canada and the United States: Explaining the differences. In T. Ricento & B. Burnaby, (Eds.), *Language and politics in the United States and Canada: Myths and realities* (pp. 37–70). Mahwah, NJ: Erlbaum.

Simard, L., Taylor, D. M., & Giles, H. (1976). Attribution processes and interpersonal accommodation in a bilingual setting. *Language and Speech, 19,* 374–387.

Skutnabb-Kangas, T. (2000). *Linguistic genocide in education or worldwide diversity and human rights?* London: Erlbaum.

Spolsky, B. (2003). Reassessing Maori regeneration. *Language in Society, 32,* 553–578.

Spolsky, B., & Shohamy, E. (1999). *The languages of Israel: Policy, ideology and practice.* Clevedon, UK: Multilingual Matters.

Spolsky, B., & Shohamy, E. (2001). Hebrew after a century of RLS efforts. In J. A. Fishman (Ed.), *Can threatened languages be saved?* (pp. 350–363). Clevedon, UK: Multilingual Matters.

Street, R. L. Jr. (1982). Evaluation of noncontent speech accommodation. *Language and Communication, 2,* 13–31.

Strubell, M. (2001). Catalan a decade later. In J. A. Fishman (Ed.), *Can threatened languages be saved?* (pp. 260–283). Clevedon, UK: Multilingual Matters.

Tabouret-Keller, A. (1999). Western Europe. In J. A. Fishman (Ed.), *Handbook of language and ethnic identity* (pp. 334–349). New York: Oxford University Press.

Tajfel, H., & Turner, J. C. (1986). The social identity theory of intergroup behavior. In S. Worchel & W. Austin (Eds.), *Psychology of intergroup relations* (2nd ed., pp. 7–24). Chicago: Nelson-Hall.

Taylor, D. M., Bassili, J., & Aboud, F. (1973). Dimensions of ethnic identity in Canada, *Journal of Social Psychology, 89*, 185–192.

Taylor, D. M., Wright, S. C., Ruggiero, K. M., & Aitchison, M. C. (1993). Language perceptions among the Inuit of Arctic Quebec: The future role of the heritage language. *Journal of Language and Social Psychology, 12*, 195–206.

Thakerar, J. N., Giles, H., & Cheshire, J. (1982). Psychological and linguistic parameters of speech accommodation theory. In C. Fraser & K. R. Scherer (Eds.), *Advances in the social psychology of language* (pp. 205–255). Cambridge: Cambridge University Press.

Tong, Y-Y., Hong, Y-Y., Lee, S-L., & Chiu, C-Y. (1999). Language use as a carrier of social identity. *International Journal of Intercultural Relations, 23*, 281–296.

Triandis, H. C. (1960). Cognitive similarity and communication in a dyad. *Human Relations, 13*, 175–183.

Turner, J. C. (1985). Social categorization and the self-concept: A social cognitive theory of group behavior. In E. J. Lawler (Ed.), *Advances in Group Processes* (pp. 77–122), Greenwich, CT: JAI Press.

Turner, J. C., Hogg, M., Oakes, P., Reicher, S., & Wetherell, M. (1987). *Rediscovering the social group: A self-categorization theory*. Oxford: Blackwell.

Williams, C. (1999). The Celtic world. In J. A. Fishman (Ed.), *Handbook of language and ethnic identity* (pp. 267–285). New York: Oxford University Press.

Woolard, K. A. (1989). *Double talk: Bilingualism and the politics of ethnicity in Catalonia*. Stanford, CA: Stanford University Press.

5

Intergroup Perspectives on Aging and Intergenerational Communication

Angie Williams
Peter Garrett

We begin this chapter with a discussion of the nature of age as a social category, and consider intergenerational communication as an intergroup process. We then review research into intergenerational communication, beginning with work on perceptions of (largely college students') communication with nonfamilial elders. Thereafter, we discuss more recent work that has broadened the intergenerational focus to include evaluations of and from a range of age groups, identifying some indications of developmental trends across the lifespan. Next, we shift the focus to the younger end of the lifespan: young teenagers (13 to 16 years old) and young adults between 18 and 25, and we consider whether communication between these two groups, close though they are in years, can also be understood in intergroup terms. We also consider data on "good communication," a notion currently much talked about in educational systems (e.g., Catan, Dennison, & Coleman, 1996) in relation to these different age groups. Finally, we turn our attention to communication *within* the family, focusing on grandparents in particular. There, we examine the usefulness of intergroup theory in a context where more individuation is arguably more likely, and we consider how intergroup strategies can provide useful resources for grandparents to pursue positive identities.

Intergenerational Communication:
A Special Case of Intergroup Communication

Can age groups be considered as "groups" in the social identity sense of the term? Strictly speaking, chronological age is a continuous variable. Aging is experienced as each passing year seamlessly merges into the next. However, aging can also be viewed as a linear but punctuated stream of experience. In social psychological terms, people typically perceive age as fairly discontinuous, grouping age into categorical bands. For example, research demonstrates the pervasiveness of broad age categorization labels (*young*, *middle-aged*, and *old*) (Giles, 1999).

We have fairly strong expectations about members of age bands, and we tend to homogenize and generalize about those within the bands. Adolescents are expected to experience a degree of "storm and stress," middle-aged people to experience midlife crises, older people to moan. Hence, it is fairly easy to categorize others into groups, to identify typical group attributes, and to generalize these attributes to the group. In communication and aging research, Hummert, Garstka, Ryan, and Bonnesen (2004) have shown that both older and younger adults have some well-defined stereotypes of older and younger people that influence communication. They have identified four predominantly negative (e.g., despondent, recluse) and three positive stereotypes (e.g., perfect grandparent) of older people held by young, middle-aged and older persons. Moreover, experimental studies indicate that unfavorable evaluations of older targets follow activation of negative stereotypes and, conversely, positive stereotype activation stimulates positive evaluations (Hummert et al., 2004).

These studies also revealed positive and negative stereotypes for young people (e.g., redneck, member of underclass vs. perfect friend, mature young professional). The teenage years and, as Arnett (2000) argues, emerging adulthood (18 to 25) are developmentally distinct but are crucial periods for developing social and personal identity (with "emerging adults" characterized by comparative independence from normative expectations, for example). In this respect, there is also research that reveals stereotypes that secondary (or high) school students have of their "same generation" groups and the part these play in exploring and constructing social identities (see, for example, Brown, Mory, & Kinney, 1994; Garrett, Coupland, & Williams, 2003). To sum up, it seems that when it comes to perceiving others, many intergroup processes map onto age categories.

Social identity issues also affect the way people perceive themselves in age-categorical terms. One derives a sense of identity as a social being from the groups and categories of which one is a member (Tajfel, 1978). In striving to achieve and maintain positive social identities, we might align ourselves with positively valued and high-status groups, or discursively construct our own groups as positive and valued when compared with other groups (e.g., the study of Generation X by Williams, Coupland, Folwell, & Sparks, 2000).

From the social identity perspective, age categorizations have distinct affective implications (Taylor, 1992). Hence, considerable energy might be invested in managing one's own age categorization to avoid an unsatisfyingly valenced social identity (Williams & Garrett, 2002a). Boundaries between some social groups and categories can have relatively high rigidity (e.g., race), and it is less likely that individuals will cross such boundaries in any sustained way. However, it has been suggested that definitions for what counts as a specific age group might be more contextually and communicatively negotiable than many other social group memberships (Coupland, 1999). Hence, social identity can be more crucial and "worked on" in the realm of age, as opposed to, for instance, differences where the physical characteristics underlying categorization allow less ambiguity.

Nevertheless, although we might view boundaries between age-groups as comparatively soft and negotiable (cf. Banton, 1983), there are certain criteria for traversing these boundaries. Williams and Harwood (2004) illustrate this by pointing to the unlikelihood of an unmarried male student with a full head of (not grey) hair being classified as "middle-aged." On the other hand, the relative flexibility and negotiability of age identities can allow opportunities for projecting quite different identities according to context. Coupland, Coupland, and Grainger (1991), for example, have shown how people can shift between being "old and dependent" for certain discursive purposes and being "young and vibrant" in other contexts. Hence, there might be attempts to recapture earlier stages of the lifespan through changing one's appearance (e.g., through clothing, cosmetics, even surgery) or one's peer affiliations (e.g., establishing new friendships with younger people).

In addition, age-category labels are a site for defining and negotiating age identities. Giles et al. (2000) found that young students from Canada, New Zealand, the United States, and Australia (average 20 years old) judged young adulthood to begin at 17 years and end at 28, and middle age to range from 29 to 48 years, with old age beginning at about 51 (see also Harwood & Giles, 1993). In the United Kingdom, Williams and Garrett (2002a) asked respondents aged 20 to 59 years to provide the upper and lower age boundaries they associated with the age labels *adolescence, young adulthood, middle age* and *old age*. Adolescence was associated with ages 12 to 17 and young adulthood with 18 to 26. Of particular interest here is the finding that there was no consensus on middle age and old age. The 20- to 29-year-olds suggested that middle age ranges from 37 and 54. The 40- to 59-year-olds differed significantly from the younger cohorts, moving the lower boundary up to 40 or 41 and the upper boundary to 57. It seemed that as they approached middle age, they were inclined to raise its lower limit to remain excluded longer and, thereby, to hold on to a more satisfying age identity. Similar findings applied to old age, with none of the respondents placing themselves in that category, and the lower boundary of old age varying according to respondent age. For the 20- to 29-year-olds, old age began at 62, whereas for the 50- to 59-year-olds, it began at 66. These findings align well with social identity theory, which postulates that people are disinclined to self-categorize in terms of negatively perceived groups (Garrett, Giles, & Coupland, 1989; Tajfel, & Turner, 1986; Williams & Giles, 1998).

So far, we have argued that intergenerational communication shares the primary characteristics of intergroup communication. It can be seen as a "special case" of intergroup communication, however, in that social identification is more communicatively negotiable. A great deal of research into intergenerational communication has employed communication accommodation theory (CAT) as its main analytical approach. We now explain this approach before commencing our review of research in this field.

Intergenerational Communication Research

CAT, in part, draws on social identity and intergroup theory to explain the processes by which individuals attune their communication to one another, as individuals and social-group members (Giles, Coupland, & Coupland, 1991). Accommodation is one process through which we attempt to move communicatively closer to a partner by, for example, attending to their conversational needs or adjusting the topic, pace, and timing of conversation. In contrast, nonaccommodation can signal distance from a partner; we might not attend carefully to what they say because we might be distracted, or we might push our own agenda, for instance. We generally prefer conversations in which our partner is accommodative to those in which they are nonaccommodative (Williams, 1992). CAT also posits that we attempt to attune to where we *believe* our partner is psychologically and communicatively. If erroneous, our belief can lead us to overshoot or undershoot the target. Overaccommodation occurs if we overadjust our communication—for example, talking to a very capable elderly or young person as if they were a baby. Underaccommodation occurs when we do not adjust our communication sufficiently for the target—for example, when a computer expert uses technical language with laypersons who are not technically trained.

A questionnaire study by Williams (1992) found that young people (18 to 20) rated interactions with adults (65 to 75) as less satisfying than interactions with same-aged peers. Four factors emerged that differentiated satisfying intergenerational encounters from less satisfying ones. *Old underaccommodative negativity* was noted where older persons talked excessively and exclusively about their own problems. *Mutuality* was seen when the age gap was diminished. *Elder individuation* occurred when the older person was treated as an individual rather than an old person. Finally, *young individuation* was a descriptor for when the young person felt individuated (and not treated stereotypically). These dimensions were related to reported emotions in predictable directions. For example, *old underaccommodative negativity* was associated with increased anger and frustration and decreased relaxation.

Drawing on Hewstone and Brown's (1986) intergroup contact theory, intergroup intergenerational contact was defined as occurring when respondents perceived age as salient and each person as typical of their respective age groups. In line with intergroup theory, Williams (1992) found that conversations high in group salience were less satisfying, less mutual, less differentiated, and less accommodative than those low in group salience. These results suggest that intergroup salience can be important in evaluations of intergenerational communication (see also Insko & Schopler, 1987). Of course, the data leave open the possibility that negative encounters are retrospectively evaluated (and attributed) in intergroup terms. The causal order here is yet to be established.

A further study investigating perceptions of intergenerational communication from a CAT perspective (Williams & Giles, 1996) asked college students to recall and recount recent satisfying and dissatisfying conversations with nonfamilial elders (65 to 75 years old). Content analysis showed that satisfying conversations were those in which older people were reportedly accommodative to the young person's needs (e.g., giving compliments and telling interesting stories). Satisfying conversations were also those in which a mutual understanding was achieved, and both the old and the young person expressed positive emotions. Interestingly, age differences in these conversations were frequently discounted by the young. The older people in satisfying encounters were either perceived to violate ageist expectations, or else age was thought to have no bearing on the conversation. Reports of dissatisfying conversations included frequent characterizations of older people as being underaccommodative (e.g., inattentive, closed-minded, out of touch), as complaining in an angry accusing fashion (e.g., in conflict situations), or as complaining despondently about their ill health and problematic life circumstances (Coupland, Coupland, Giles, & Wiemann, 1988). Moreover, some young participants felt that older people stereotyped them as irresponsible or naïve. Young people tended to describe themselves as "reluctantly accommodating" to dissatisfying older partners, restraining themselves by biting their tongue, and feeling an obligation to show respect for age, and they resented this.

Similar findings have emerged in other Western (non-European) contexts (reviewed by Giles, McCann, Ota, & Noels, 2002), where nonfamily elders have been perceived as more nonaccommodative and less accommodative than same-aged peers (but see McCann, Ota, Giles, & Caraker, 2003 for a recent exception). Younger people feel more respect and obligation to nonfamily elders than to peers, but a stronger desire to avoid conversations with them too.

Older people are not universally viewed negatively, however. Particularly salient in the satisfying conversations in Williams and Giles (1996) were those in which younger respondents described their older conversational partners as "like a typical grandparent." This aligns very well with research that shows adults having multiple positive and negative stereotypes of older people (Hummert et al.,

2004). Extending such findings, Harwood and Williams (1998) investigated young people's expectations for conversations with two different hypothetical elder (71 years old) substereotypes—the Despondent and the Perfect Grandparent. Participants presented with the Despondent subtype described themselves as more anxious and described the older adult as less accommodative and more likely to complain, as compared to those participants who were presented with the Perfect Grandparent subtype. But despite such effects for the substereotypes, more positive general attitudes toward contact with older adults were related to more positive expectations, independent of the specific nature of the older adult target. Interestingly, younger adults reported little variation in judgments of their own behavior across the target types; variation in perceptions of the older adults' behaviors were better predictors of perceived communication satisfaction.

In addition, a vignette study comparing an elder versus a peer who was portrayed as nonaccommodative indicated that elders are more likely to be forgiven for their nonaccommodation than peers, because elder nonaccommodation is stereotype-consistent and easier to explain away (Williams, 1996). When elders are noticeably *not* nonaccommodative, it is likely that positive stereotypes are activated and younger people might then tend to view elders in overly positive and accommodative ways. Thus, negative and positive stereotypes of elders are kept in play as "ready-made" attributions for dissatisfying or satisfying conversations (Williams, 1996). Elders seeking individuation might find themselves unable to step outside this "no-win" situation. This is a special case of ingroup-outgroup attributions—usually bad outgroup behavior is attributed negatively as a fixed and stable characteristic of the group and good outgroup behavior is explained away as due to situational and unstable factors (the "ultimate attribution error": Hewstone, 1990).

Overall, it seems that older adults are a marked communication outgroup for young people. Young adults' communication with older adults can be satisfying (within certain limits) or dissatisfying. Their conversational expectations, however, do not necessarily predict overall satisfaction. As we saw above in Williams and Giles (1996), younger people can tolerate elders' complaints, providing elders meet their communicative needs. In addition, for some conversational expectations, general stereotypes of older people might be stronger predictors than substereotypes. This suggests that, in some circumstances, specific individuating information about elders might be overlooked in favor of general positive or negative attitudes toward age (Caporael, 1981).

At this point, we should take stock of a few points in the research reviewed so far. First, the main focus has been on evaluations of communication with elders. Our own view is that an intergenerational perspective needs to include evaluations of a *range* of age groups; that is, a lifespan approach. Second, respondents have largely been young college students. Arguably, then, we need investigations of evaluations made *by* groups across the lifespan, not least elders themselves. Third, while research designs have included evaluations of communication with peers as a point of comparison, this communication, too, is bound to show features that are satisfying and dissatisfying. Hence, there remains the question of whether people evaluate communication with age peers any differently than the way they evaluate that with age outgroup members. Until this question is addressed empirically, we cannot be sure that intergenerational communication is very different to *intra*generational communication.

Recent work by Williams and Garrett (2002b) takes up these issues. Their respondents (community adults aged 20 to 59) were asked to judge their communication with elders (65 to 85 years), young teenagers (13 to 16 years), and peers. Including more age groups led to two additional evaluative dimensions emerging that are particularly relevant for perceptions of communication with young teenagers: *noncommunication* (e.g., gave short answers, dried up in conversation) and *self-promotion* (e.g., "tried to impress," "were cheeky"). Young teenagers were in fact the most negatively characterized of the three target groups. In addition, findings suggested changes in evaluations across the lifespan. Most notably, 30- to 39-year-olds, who have received scant attention in the current intergenerational and lifespan communication literature, stood out from the other respondent groups. In their evaluations of communication with the elderly, they marked a break with the reactive stance of younger adults and the beginning of a linear trend indicating that communication with elders was evaluated more positively as respondents got older. Additional indications of differences in communication evaluations according to where the judges and the judged are in the lifespan were found in

Williams, Garrett, and Tennant (2004) in their study of perceptions of "good communication" (see below). These findings provide important qualifications to earlier studies in which respondents were mainly young college students evaluating communication with elders. They also confirm the value of a lifespan approach in future research.

One of the many questions raised by Williams and Garrett's (2002b) study is: do older participants affiliate with older targets? As reported earlier, the study finds evidence that people who believe they are on the cusp of middle age and old age might be motivated to negotiate the chronological boundaries of these categories in order to be included in the younger age bracket. In this particular sample, there were no age-peer respondents from the over-65 target group (and affiliation with a category labeled "older adults aged 65-85" seems contentious, if not unlikely, for the oldest respondents in this study, aged 59). But, from other studies, there is nevertheless some evidence that elders view their peers as more nonaccommodative than they view younger people (e.g., Noels, Giles, Cai, & Turay, 1999). Thus, for some elders in some circumstances, *intra*generational communication can be dissatisfying. Whether all older people consider others of their supposedly same age bracket as being "age peers" is not entirely clear from these studies (Paoletti, 1998).

The results for accommodation in these studies support the ingroup preference notion that people favor their age peers. Both younger and older people feel that their own age peers are more supportive, attentive, complimenting, and so forth. However, the finding that older respondents perceived their own age group to be nonaccommodating could be interpreted in several ways. Either older people perceive elders to have communication problems and report them as nonaccommodation, or they are hanging on to and endorsing a commonly held negative stereotype of elders in order to distance themselves from a perceptual outgroup—perhaps a form of *social mobility*, that is, achieving a more satisfying identity through membership of a group one finds more desirable (Tajfel & Turner, 1986; see Harwood, Giles, & Palomares, this volume).

Williams and Guendouzi's (2000) interviews with elders (aged 78 to 90) in a sheltered retirement community shed additional light on this point. The residents, all in good health, discussed difficulties with peer communication and relationships. In contrast with communication with younger people (which respondents claimed was highly satisfactory), peers were characterized as nonaccommodative. However, the interviewees were careful to construct positive identities for *themselves* as physically active, cognitively alert, and able. Apart from demonstrating the very poignant difficulties for able elders living in sheltered residential communities, this study illustrates that these elders wished to distance themselves from a negatively stereotyped group—institutionalized elders.

Of course, the quality of intergenerational contact is not merely important in itself; it also might have consequences in terms of more general attitudes toward aging and older adults. The "contact hypothesis" suggests that contact with outgroup members has the potential to change attitudes (Allport, 1954). Support for this hypothesis has emerged in the intergenerational sphere. For instance, among student participants, those reporting more frequent contact with elders tend not to perceive elders as nonaccommodative, but tend to view elders as accommodative. They also tend to indicate respect for elders but are less likely to feel obligated or endorse the idea that large age-differences matter in intergenerational interaction (Williams et al., 1997). Some investigations have revealed similar effects (Soliz & Harwood, 2003), although others reveal nonsignificant correlations between frequency of contact and perceptions of intergenerational communication (Williams, Garrett, & Tennant, 2004).

One problem in examining contact theory issues in intergenerational relations is that intergenerational contact in some societies appears to be relatively infrequent. Sociologists have commented that modern post-industrial societies are increasingly age-segregated (Chudacoff, 1989). Contact between people of vastly different ages might be in decline partly as a result of increased geographic mobility and dispersion of families, and also more generally because of age-segregated living arrangements (e.g., university accommodation, retirement communities, child-free apartments). Williams (1992) found college students reporting spending only 5% of their time communicating with people over 65. Some work, however, suggests that community adults have more diverse intergenerational contact than has been previously found for young college students (Williams & Garrett, 2002a, 2002b). Earlier, we provided evidence that the nature and functions of intergenerational communication seem to change dramatically across the lifespan as peer reference groups, social networks, roles, and responsibilities change and develop. These results can be interpreted in the context of frequency of contact data showing that intergenerational contact becomes more varied across the lifespan and that young adults have the most contact with peers (Williams & Garrett, 2002b). Young adults in their twenties might be more inclined to orient to their own age group for support, advice, etc. As people have families, build careers and interact in multigenerational settings, younger people might rely more on older adults as mentors. Evaluations of elders in Williams and Garrett (2002b) reflect this changing picture across the lifespan. However, as we have argued earlier in this chapter, intergenerational research has tended to concentrate on one or two points in the lifespan, specifically college students and elders. But for a more comprehensive understanding of communication between generations, we need to widen our focus to incorporate more periods of the lifespan. Hence, in the spirit of such broader inquiry, we now consider communication in adolescence.

Teenagers and Emerging Adults

Adults tend to view adolescents as being fairly unskilled communicators (Thurlow, 2003). For example, Drury and Dennison (1999) found welfare benefits officers making negative generalizations about their communication encounters with adolescents compared to those with adults. Similar negative views emerge from data collected from police officers (Drury & Dennison, 2000) and teachers (Williams & Cockram, 2002). It is fair to say that communication with teenagers has not been systematically researched by communication scholars, however. In addition, in relation to Arnett's (2000) ideas regarding "emerging adulthood," we might expect to find important differences in comparative communication experiences and judgments of 18- to 25-year-olds when considering 13- to 16-year-olds. Williams, Garrett and Tennant (2004) found that 18- to 25-year-olds did indeed differentiate between their peers and adolescents. They judged peers as more accommodative, less nonaccommodative, and less noncommunicative than adolescents. They felt less discomfort, tension, and negativity, and more satisfaction when interacting with peers, and reported less need for communication adjustments. They did not differentiate between peers and adolescents in the degree of the other person's self-promotional communication or in their own feelings of support for the other, but overall, it is clear that emerging adults differentiate the age groups and that they upgrade the ingroup (peers) when compared to the outgroup (younger adolescents).

The suggestion that emerging adults view interactions with adolescents in intergroup terms is supported by their agreement that age differences were salient in these interactions. Finally, good communication (defined as satisfaction with the conversation) with peers was predicted by a linear combination of the other person's accommodation and self-promotion and their own feelings of supportiveness and low tension. These factors also predicted satisfaction in communication with adolescents with the addition of low levels of negativity and low salience of age differences. Thus, for this group of emerging adults, satisfaction is negatively associated with cognitive awareness and behavioral indices of the age differences.

The research reviewed so far concerns interactions with peers and other age groups who are not familial (chiefly between young people and nonfamily elders). It is probably easier to apply generalized stereotypes to strangers and acquaintances who are not well known and not individuated than it is to known or close family members. Family elders might be viewed in different ways, perhaps because they are more intimately known. In addition, the family appears to be one of the few contexts where intergenerational contact is relatively frequent (Harwood, 2000a). It is to this area that we now turn.

Intergenerational Communication in the Family

According to social theorists concerned with family relations (e.g., Bengtson, Marti, & Roberts, 1991), families are defined by a number of independent, complex, and stable features of solidarity (defined as close feelings and cohesion). The family is itself an ingroup with associated familial identity, albeit overlaid and interwoven with other group allegiances that emerge across the lifespan (Harwood, 2004). Solidarity is important to the emergence and coherence of any social group or category, including families. Familial solidarity has a number of components—associational, affectional, consensual, functional, and normative (Bengtson et al., 1991).

Associational solidarity refers to the frequency and pattern of interactions. Older people attempt to portray their familial interactions as frequent (subjectively defined) and harmonious, but on occasions will discuss tensions in interactions (Williams & Guendouzi, 2001). Affectional solidarity refers to the type and degree of positive sentiment for family members and the degree of reciprocity. Consensual solidarity is the degree of agreement on values, attitudes, and beliefs among family members—the subject of much management by elders. Functional solidarity is the degree to which family members exchange services. Normative solidarity is the perception and enactment of norms of the family (like rituals at Christmas) and intergenerational family structure refers to the number, type, and geographic proximity of family members.

Theory and research on intergenerational solidarity (Bengtson, Olander, & Haddad, 1976) and lifespan attachment (Cicirelli, 1991) suggest that relationships with elder family members might be viewed more positively than those with elder strangers (Williams & Nussbaum, 2001). But solidarity must be achieved by continual maintenance and management. Often, for instance, both adult children and elderly parents exercise a form of accommodative censorship, with each party understanding what topics not to discuss in front of the other. This helps to ensure a protective veneer of consensus (Noller & Bagi, 1985).

Williams and Guendouzi's (2001) interviews with elderly residents of a retirement community examine how older interviewees discursively portray interactions with family members. While family difficulties were not uncommon, interviewees were keen to present their own family as relatively harmonious, and themselves as relatively privileged in relation to their peers. Interviewees typically presented themselves as operating a "norm of noninterference" in their relationships with family members, especially where there was underlying conflict or disapproval. One particularly revealing aspect of these interviews was the suggestion that these older people not interfere in conflict and disapproval situations. In other words, they struggled to accommodate conversationally to their family members, but there was evidence that disapproval "leaked" verbally and nonverbally. This leakage might be one means of transmitting values to younger family members and might serve as one way that families try to control potentially risky behaviors without direct confrontation.

Harwood (2000b), using a questionnaire measure of accommodative behaviors, found that both grandparents' and grandchildren's levels of satisfaction in the relationship were influenced by the *other's* perceived involvement and accommodation in interactions (see also Harwood & Williams, 1998). Some of the accommodation behaviors previously identified as crucial in intergenerational relations (e.g., older underaccommodation) were not found to be significant predictors of satisfaction or closeness. In a recent replication conducted in Taiwan (Lin & Harwood, 2003), however, perceptions of *one's own* accommodation were the most influential in predicting satisfaction and closeness. In explanation, the authors point to the importance of collectivist beliefs in Asian cultures, with the family as the primary collective, resulting in a belief in personal responsibility for maintaining harmony and stability in the family.

Families have several layers of multigenerational interaction. Simple dyadic relationships are rare in such settings as, for example, middle-aged people might be managing their own relationships with their children and their own aging parents while simultaneously managing the relationship between the aging grandparents and their grandchildren (e.g., by encouraging contact, translating, negotiating misunderstandings). Similarly, older people frequently manage their relationships with grandchildren in the context of multiple relationships with other grandchildren as well as their own adult children (e.g., seeking to avoid perceptions of favoritism while treating each person as an individual). Each relationship influences the other to a greater or lesser degree in a multiplex network, and communication reflects this. One frequent medium of dyadic communication is the telephone. Harwood (2000a) found that telephone communication between grandparents and grandchildren was a more significant (positive) predictor of satisfaction than communication in other media (including face-to-face communication).

From our earlier discussion of intergroup communication (i.e., age is salient and the older person is seen as typical), it is clear that intergroup interaction can occur in the context of family relationships. The question "is intergroup theory valid for family interaction?" becomes less interesting than other questions. For example, when and under what circumstances do family members engage an intergroup stance, what local and more global purposes does it serve, and what consequences does it have? In this regard, it might be best to view group salience in terms of an intergroup-interindividual dialectic (Tajfel & Turner, 1986). Thus, relationships with an elderly family member, for example, can be characterized as swinging between two opposing dialectical poles, and family members can be conceived as struggling with this dialectic at certain crucial moments in time (e.g., extreme ill health and incapacity of an elder). In some contexts, the elderly family member is highly individuated and age does not matter, while in other circumstances the older individual is seen as a rather typical elder. Coupland and Coupland (2000) provide an excellent example of this in the discourse between a daughter and her mother's doctor during a medical examination of the mother.

While family members might be concerned to pursue the best interests of their loved ones (e.g., an aging parent or grandparent) they might also have some fairly stable and stereotypical expectations about old age. For example, they might expect parents or grandparents to behave in age-appropriate ways and be shocked and ashamed if they do not. Or they might expect a certain level of functioning associated with a particular age and are critical if elders do not conform to these expectations.

A recent study in the United Kingdom (Williams, 2003a) asked 65 university students (in their twenties) to write short accounts of occasions when age became salient in their relationships with grandparents. For some respondents, whose relationships with grandparents were not particularly intimate or frequent, age was always salient. More importantly, some respondents reported that age always was an issue because of their need to make adjustments and allowances for grandparents in various ways. In contrast, age was never an issue for respondents whose relationships were more intimate or whose grandparents were younger.

Age seemed particularly salient when grandparents were suffering health or mobility problems or talked about the past. Age was also salient when differences in attitudes, expectations, and values were obvious, when respondents had to modify their communication (e.g., avoid "talking back"), and when physical appearance differences were noticeable (e.g., grandmothers with purple curly perms). Lifestyle differences also featured (e.g., grandparents' gardening compared to their own clubbing, as well as grandparents' difficulties with new technology). However, age differences tended to diminish when respondents felt they were having "adult-adult" conversations with their grandparents, and when their focus was on shared social activities such as shopping, socializing, or family occasions (e.g., anniversary celebrations).

Respondents felt treated as typically young when grandparents spoiled them with gifts or treats, when they felt parented, when grandparents took the role of "wise advice giver," and when grandparents showed disapproval. They felt they acted typically young when they showed respect or adjusted their speech and other behavior (sometimes censoring information to avoid disapproval) or when they felt obligated.

As discussed by Williams and Harwood (2004), Gaertner's common ingroup identity model (Gaertner et al., 2000) might provide an account of why intergenerational family contact can have more positive outcomes than nonfamilial contact. Establishing a common ingroup identity is relatively easy within the family context (Banker & Gaertner, 1998). Focusing on the shared family issues (hence, an ingroup identity) will undoubtedly provide some sense of solidarity and might de-emphasize the extent to which age operates as a distancing mechanism. For example, in the study described above, family celebrations can have this effect.

One problem with such models is that they suggest positive consequences of de-emphasizing important group identities. Social identity (e.g., Brown, Vivian, & Hewstone, 1999) and social cognitive perspectives (Rothbart & John, 1985) maintain that generalization from a specific intergroup contact situation to more general intergroup attitudes is only likely if group memberships are salient in the contact situation. Support for this perspective has been provided by Harwood, Hewstone, Paolini, and Voci (in prèss) who found a positive relationship between the general quality of grandparent-grandchild contact and attitudes toward older adults *only* among grandchildren who find their grandparents' age to be salient within the interaction. Paradoxically, and as noted earlier, contact in which group memberships are salient is not always the most positive. Harwood et al. also found that age-salient interactions tend, in general, to be less positive, despite their potential for a positive impact on attitudes (Williams & Giles, 1996). The family context seems to require more careful theorizing, but there does appear to be tension between the need for quality familial and other intergenerational interactions and the need to maintain age salience to facilitate the extension of positive consequences to more general attitudes toward aging.

As suggested by Williams and Harwood (2004), an area where familial intergenerational communication research links with the intergroup literature is in terms of strategies outlined by social identity theory for dealing with low-status (Tajfel & Turner, 1986). Recent studies have pointed to the grandparent role as one that might offer more positive connotations associated with age than are generally apparent (Harwood, 2004; Harwood & Lin, 2000). In addition, behaviors within the grandparent role might provide rewards to older adults experiencing identity threat (Harwood, 2004). These might, in some situations, resemble strategies of *social mobility*—grandchildren might offer an opportunity to engage in activities or behaviors characteristic of younger age groups, through involvement either in childhood or parenting activities. A grandparent doing parenting might be seen as having "transferred" to the middle-aged. Grandparenting can also offer *social creativity* options to grandparents. For example, being a "good grandparent" might be a way to pursue a positive identity while the status quo is left unchallenged (note Hummert, Garstka, Shaner, and Strahm's [1994] *perfect grandparent* positive stereotypes of older adults). The family can similarly provide opportunities for older adults to claim status and even influence decisions—roles that are often denied outside the family. Lastly, grandparents can sometimes involve themselves in actions best characterized as *social competition*. Recent US Supreme Court decisions (e.g., Troxell v. Granville, 2000) on custody rights of grandparents, for example, have affirmed that grandparents can successfully challenge the status quo. One important direction for the future, however, is to consider how far being a grandparent can reasonably be considered as a social identity (i.e., are grandparents joining together, addressing issues of mutual collective concern, or sharing in other ways that indicate a sense of group identity with other grandparents?). In addition, if we discover a meaningful sense of *social identity* among grandparents, then in what ways might social identity interact with the more general identification as an older adult, given that many grandparents are older adults (Harwood, 2004)?

Adolescence also can be seen in intergroup terms within the family. As mentioned above, during adolescence and emerging adulthood young people are typically developing social identities outside the family of origin (Drury, 2003; Fortman, 2003). These identities might emerge in conjunction with a series of struggles with parents (Petronio, 1994). At these times, the intergroup nature of their interactions can be most salient for both adolescents and parents (Williams, 2003b). Beginning with the early writings of Hall (1904), Mead (1928), and Erikson (1968), the perception of adolescence as a period of storm and stress has entered the public psyche and been accepted as normal. As part of our cultural understandings, such notions influence our expectations and interpretations of teenage behavior. Studies by Buchanan and colleagues (1990, 1998) indicate that parents and other adults endorse "storm and stress" models of adolescent development. They have also shown that parents might even increase their efforts to control teenagers in anticipation of rebellion, recklessness, and conflict (Buchanan & Holmbeck, 1998). A recent study in the United Kingdom (Anderson, Tunaley, & Walker, 2000) elicited the following comment from a parent regarding her relationship with her teenage son: "So far it's very good…. I'm still holding my breath a bit because you are waiting for it (trouble) to happen. You can't get through life and there not be any major problems, especially when you get to the sixteen to eighteen bit" (p. 21). Such expectations have wide-ranging consequences and are worthy of further study for the insights promised by an intergroup perspective on this relationship.

Conclusion

This chapter demonstrates that intergenerational communication can be regarded as intergroup communication in terms of labels, boundaries, attributions, stereotypes, typicality, and age salience. Even though intergenerational communication within the family is viewed more positively than that with strangers, it can nonetheless be intergroup in nature. We need to do more work on the conditions and consequences of this. With the dominant focus hitherto on evaluations of the elderly, the lack of knowledge of other age groups has become more conspicuous as we have developed our research program to cover other parts of the lifespan. We have also demonstrated the importance and value of investigating age groups across the lifespan with respect to our recent research on young teenagers and emerging adults, as well as the distinctive profile of people in their thirties. An evaluative atlas to map out more elaborate and differentiated profiles of various other lifespan age groups is an imperative for future research.

References

Allport, G. W. (1954). *The nature of prejudice.* Reading, MA: Addison-Wesley.

Anderson, M., Tunaley, J., & Walker, J. (2000). *Relatively speaking: Communication in families.* London: BT Future Talk.

Arnett, J. J. (2000). Emerging adulthood: A theory of development from the late teens through the twenties. *American Psychologist, 55,* 469–480.

Banker, B. S., & Gaertner, S. L. (1998). Achieving stepfamily harmony: An intergroup-relations approach. *Journal of Family Psychology, 12,* 310–325.

Banton, M. (1983). *Racial and ethnic competition.* Cambridge: Cambridge University Press.

Bengtson, V. L., Marti, G., & Roberts, H. E. L. (1991). Age-group relationships: Generational equity and inequity. In K. Pillemer & K. McCartney (Eds.), *Parent-child relations throughout life* (pp. 253–278). Hillsdale, NJ: Erlbaum.

Bengtson, V. L., Olander, E. B., & Haddad, A. A. (1976). The generation gap and aging family members: towards a conceptual model. In J. E. Gubrium (Ed.), *Time, roles and the self in old age* (pp. 237–263). New York: Human Sciences Press.

Brown, B., Mory, M., & Kinney, D. (1994). Casting adolescent crowds in a relational perspective: Caricature, channel, and context. In R. Montemayor, G. Adams, & T. Gullotta (Eds.), *Personal relationships during adolescence* (pp. 123–160). Thousand Oaks, CA: Sage.

Brown, R., Vivian, J., & Hewstone, M. (1999). Changing attitudes through intergroup contact: The effects of group membership salience. *European Journal of Social Psychology, 29,* 741–764.

Buchanan, C. M., Eccles, J. S., Flanagan, C., Midgley, C., Feldlaufer, H., & Harold, R. D. (1990). Parents' and teachers' beliefs about adolescents: Effects of sex and experience. *Journal of Youth and Adolescence, 19,* 363–394.

Buchanan, C. M., & Holmbeck, G. N. (1998). Measuring beliefs about adolescent personality and behavior. *Journal of Youth and Adolescence, 27,* 609–629.

Caporael, L. R. (1981). The paralanguage of caregiving: Baby talk to the institutionalized elderly. *Journal of Personality and Social Psychology, 40,* 876–884.

Catan, L., Dennison, C., & Coleman, J. (1996). *Getting through: Effective communication in the teenage years.* London: The BT Forum.

Chudacoff, H. P. (1989). *How old are you? Age consciousness in American culture.* Princeton, NJ: Princeton University Press.

Cicirelli, V. (1991). Attachment theory in old age: Protection of the attached figure. In K. Pillemer & K. McCartney (Eds.), *Parent-child relationships throughout life* (pp. 2–42). Hillsdale, NJ: Erlbaum.

Coupland, J., Coupland, N., & Grainger, K. (1991). Intergenerational discourse: Contextual versions of aging and elderliness. *Aging and Society, 11,* 189–208.

Coupland, J., Coupland, N., Giles, H., & Wiemann, J. M. (1988). My life in your hands: Processes of self-disclosure in intergenerational talk. In N. Coupland (Ed.), *Styles of discourse* (pp. 201–253). London: Croom Helm.

Coupland, N. (1999). "Other" representation. In J. Verschueren, J-O. Ostman, J. Blommaert, & C. Bulcaen (Eds.), *Handbook of Pragmatics* (pp. 1–24). Amsterdam: Benjamins.

Coupland, N., & Coupland, J. (2000). Relational frames and pronominal address/reference: The discourse of geriatric medical triads. In S. Sarangi & M. Coultard (Eds.), *Discourse and social life* (pp. 207–229). London: Longman.

Drury, J. (2003). Adolescent communication with adults in authority. *Journal of Language and Social Psychology, 22,* 66–73.

Drury, J., & Dennison, C. (1999) Individual responsibility versus social category problems: Benefit officers' perceptions of communication with young people. *Journal of Youth Studies, 2,* 171–192.

Drury, J., & Dennison, C. (2000) Representations of teenagers among police officers: Some implications for their communication with young people. *Youth and Policy, 66,* 62–87.

Erikson, E. H. (1968). *Identity: Youth and crisis.* New York: Norton.

Fortman, J. (2003). Adolescent language and communication from an intergroup perspective. *Journal of Language and Social Psychology, 22,* 104–111.

Gaertner, S. L., Dovidio, J. F., Nier, J. A., Banker, B. S., Ward, C. M., Houlette, M., & Loux, S. (2000). The common ingroup identity model for reducing intergroup bias: Progress and challenges. In D. Capozza & R. Brown (Eds.), *Social identity processes: Trends in theory and research* (pp. 133–148). London: Sage.

Garrett, P., Coupland, N., & Williams, A. (2003). *Investigating language attitudes: Social meanings of dialect, ethnicity and performance.* Cardiff: University of Wales Press.

Garrett, P., Giles, H., & Coupland, N. (1989). The contexts of language learning: Extending the intergroup model of second language acquisition. In S. Ting-Toomey & F. Korzenny (Eds.), *Language, communication and culture: Current directions* (pp. 201–221). Newbury Park, CA: Sage.

Giles, H. (1999). Managing dilemmas in the "silent revolution": A call to arms! *Journal of Communication, 49,* 170–182.

Giles, H., Coupland, J., & Coupland, N. (Eds.). (1991). *Contexts of accommodation: Developments in applied sociolinguistics.* Cambridge: Cambridge University Press.

Giles, H., McCann, R., Ota, H., & Noels, K. (2002). Challenging intergenerational stereotypes across Eastern and Western cultures. In M. S. Kaplan, N. Z. Henkin, & A. T. Kusano (Eds.), *Intergenerational program strategies from a global perspective* (pp. 13–28). Honolulu: University Press of America.

Giles, H., Noels, K., Ota, H., Ng, S. H., Gallois, C., Ryan, E. B., Williams, A., Lim, T-S., Somera, L., Tao, H., & Sachdev, I. (2000). Age vitality across eleven nations. *Journal of Multilingual & Multicultural Development, 21,* 308–323.

Hall, G. S. (1904). *Adolescence: Its psychology and its relation to physiology, anthropology, sociology, sex, crime, religion and education.* (Vols. 1 & 11). Englewood Cliffs, NJ:

Prentice-Hall.

Harwood, J. (2000a). Communication media use in the grandparent-grandchild relationship. *Journal of Communication, 50,* 56–78.

Harwood, J. (2000b). Communicative predictors of solidarity in the grandparent-grandchild relationship. *Journal of Social and Personal Relationships, 17,* 743–766.

Harwood, J. (2004). Relational role and social identity as expressed in grandparents' personal websites. *Communication Studies, 55,* 268–286.

Harwood, J., & Giles, H. (1993). Creating intergenerational distance: Language, communication and middle-age. *Language Sciences, 15,* 1–24.

Harwood, J., Hewstone, M., Paolini, S., & Voci, A. (in press). Grandparent-grandchild contact and attitudes towards older adults: Moderator and mediator effects. *Personality and Social Psychology Bulletin.*

Harwood, J., & Lin M-C. (2000). Affiliation, pride, exchange, and distance: Grandparents' accounts of relationships with their college-aged grandchildren. *Journal of Communication, 50,* 31–47.

Harwood, J., & Williams, A. (1998). Expectations for communication with positive and negative subtypes of older adults. *International Journal of Aging and Human Development, 47,* 11–33.

Hewstone, M. (1990). The "ultimate attribution error"? A review of the literature on intergroup causal attribution. *European Journal of Social Psychology, 20,* 311–335.

Hewstone, M., & Brown, R. J. (1986). "Contact is not enough": An intergroup perspective on the contact hypothesis. In M. Hewstone and R. Brown (Eds.), *Contact and conflict in intergroup relations* (pp. 1–44). Oxford: Blackwell.

Hummert, M. L., Garstka, T. A., Ryan, E. B., & Bonnesen, J. L. (2004). The role of age stereotypes in interpersonal communication. In J. F. Nussbaum & J. Coupland (Eds.), *Handbook of communication and aging research* (2nd ed., pp. 91–114). Mahwah, NJ: Erlbaum.

Hummert, M. L., Garstka, T. A., Shaner, J. L., & Strahm, S. (1994). Stereotypes of the elderly held by young, middle-aged and elderly adults. *Journal of Gerontology: Psychological Sciences, 49,* 240–249.

Insko, C. A., & Schopler, J. (1987). Categorization, competition, and collectivity. In C. Hendrick (Ed.), *Group processes. Review of personality and social psychology* (Vol. 8, pp. 213–251). Beverly Hills, CA: Sage.

Lin, M-C., & Harwood, J. (2003). Predictors of grandparent-grandchild relational solidarity in Taiwan. *Journal of Social and Personal Relationships, 20,* 537–563.

McCann, R. M., Ota, H., Giles, H., & Caraker, R. (2003). Perceptions of intra- and intergenerational communication among adults in Thailand, Japan, and the USA. *Communication Reports, 16,* 1–23.

Mead, M. (1928). *Coming of age in Samoa.* New York: Morrow.

Noels, K., Giles, H., Cai, D., & Turay, L. (1999). Intergenerational communication and health in the United States and the People's Republic of China. *South Pacific Journal of Psychology, 10,* 120–134.

Noller, P., & Bagi, S. (1985). Parent adolescent communication. *Journal of Adolescence, 8,* 125–144.

Paoletti, I. (1998). *Being an older woman: A case study in the social production of identity.*

Mahwah, NJ: Erlbaum.

Petronio, S. (1994). Privacy binds in family interactions: The case of parental privacy invasion. In W. R. Cupach & B. H. Spitzberg (Eds.), *The dark side of interpersonal communication* (pp. 241–258). Hillsdale, NJ: Erlbaum.

Rothbart, M., & John, O. P. (1985). Social categorization and behavior episodes: A cognitive analysis of the effects of intergroup contact. *Journal of Social Issues, 41,* 81–104.

Soliz, J., & Harwood, J. (2003). Communication in a close family relationship and the reduction of prejudice. *Journal of Applied Communication Research, 31,* 320–345.

Tajfel, H. (Ed.). (1978). *Differentiation between social groups.* London: Academic Press.

Tajfel, H., & Turner, J. C. (1986). The social identity theory of intergroup behavior. In S. Worchel & W. G. Austin (Eds.), *The social psychology of intergroup relations* (2nd ed., pp. 7–24). Chicago: Nelson-Hall.

Taylor, B. C. (1992). Elderly identity in conversation: Producing frailty. *Communication Research, 19,* 493–515.

Thurlow, C. (2003). Teenagers in communication, teenagers on communication. *Journal of Language and Social Psychology, 22,* 50–57.

Troxell vs. Granville, 99–138 S. Ct. (2000).

Williams, A. (1992). *Intergenerational communication satisfaction: An intergroup analysis.* Unpublished M.A. Thesis: University of California, Santa Barbara.

Williams, A. (1996). Young people's evaluations of intergenerational versus peer underaccommodation: Sometimes older is better? *Journal of Language and Social Psychology, 15,* 291–311.

Williams, A. (2003a). *Emerging adults' perceptions of age salience and typicality in their relationships with their grandparents.* Unpublished manuscript. Cardiff University, Wales.

Williams, A. (2003b). Adolescents' relationships with parents. *Journal of Language and Social Psychology, 22,* 58–65.

Williams, A., & Cockram, M. (2002, July). *Authority versus affiliation: Dialectics of teachers' communication with adolescent pupils.* Paper presented at the 8th International conference on Language and Social Psychology, Hong Kong.

Williams, A., Coupland, J., Folwell, A., & Sparks, L. (2000). Talking about Generation X: Defining them as they define themselves. *Journal of Language and Social Psychology, 16,* 251–227.

Williams, A., & Garrett, P. (2002a). *Moving the goalposts: Adults' estimates of chronological age corresponding with age labels.* Unpublished manuscript: Cardiff University.

Williams, A., & Garrett, P. (2002b). Communication evaluations across the lifespan: From adolescent storm and stress to elder aches and pains. *Journal of Language and Social Psychology, 21,* 101–126.

Williams, A., Garrett, P., & Tennant, R. (2004). Young adults' perceptions of communication with peers and adolescents. In S. H. Ng, C. N. Candlin, & C. Y. Chiu (Eds.), *Language matters: Communication, identity, and culture* (pp. 111–136). Hong Kong: City University of Hong Kong Press.

Williams, A., & Giles, H. (1996). Intergenerational conversations: Young adults' retrospective accounts. *Human Communication Research, 23,* 220–250.

Williams, A., & Giles, H. (1998). Communication of ageism. In M. Hecht (Ed.), *Communication and prejudice* (pp. 136–160). Thousand Oaks, CA: Sage.

Williams, A., & Guendouzi, J. (2000). Adjusting to "the home" dialectical dilemmas and personal relationships in a retirement community. *Journal of Communication, 50,* 65–82.

Williams, A., & Guendouzi, J. (2001, May). *Constructing family relationships: Intimacy, harmony and social value in accounts of retirement community residents.* Paper presented to the International Communication Convention, Washington DC.

Williams, A., & Harwood, J. (2004). Intergenerational communication: Intergroup, accommodation and family perspectives. In J. F. Nussbaum & J. Coupland (Eds.), *Handbook of communication and aging research* (2nd ed., pp. 115–138). Mahwah, NJ: Erlbaum.

Williams, A., & Nussbaum, J. F. (2001). *Intergenerational communication across the lifespan.* Mahwah, NJ: Erlbaum.

Williams, A., Ota, H., Giles, H., Pierson, H. D., Gallois, C., Ng, S. H., Lim, T-S., Ryan, E. B., Somera, L., Maher, J., & Harwood, J. (1997). Young people's beliefs about intergenerational communication: An initial cross-cultural comparison. *Communication Research, 24,* 370–393.

6

"I Just Want You to Know That 'Them' is Me": Intergroup Perspectives on Communication and Disability

Ellen B. Ryan
Selina Bajorek
Amanda Beaman
Ann P. Anas

It has been noted before that a telephone call can change your life forever. In my case, it was a visit to the eye doctor. I was told that I had had a retinal hemorrhage. While he admitted that this was probably the beginning of a very serious condition, he urged me not to tell anyone, especially the people at work. I was sent to a retinal specialist who looked at my eyes briefly and in a nonchalant manner noted that there was absolutely nothing that he could do for me and briskly guided me out to the hallway. Thus, the stage seemed to be set for a fight. And for a couple of years it was difficult to do anything but count the casualties. My boss informed me that if she was losing her vision, "she would kill herself." And my family doctor urged me to apply for my pension. Thus, the first battle involved the struggle to stay at work as long as possible. Eventually, however, I realized that I had lost my job but more importantly I seemed to have lost a sense of myself. Financial losses quickly followed, and I realized that losing my vision was not the tough part. It was what people did to you that was the most difficult. Thus, the battle was being waged on two fronts—with others and within myself.

Happily, the skirmishes eventually settled. I have become wiser about where I should struggle, how to find allies, and when to avoid the battle all together. My friends and family experience a similar grief to my own. They are not the enemy, and they need my patience and understanding, as I need theirs.

My volunteer work has brought me into contact with others who are also struggling alone and invisible to others, but their inner strength refuses to diminish. Allies such as these are a source of spiritual strength and endurance. The people who avoid me, who try to help by telling every salesperson that I am visually impaired, and who yell in my ear to make sure that I can hear them—these actions no longer evoke my anger. The anger has been replaced with an inner smile of new secret knowledge. I have won the battle within myself, and occasionally I give others something to think about. (S.B.)

Acquiring a physical disability in adulthood necessitates a process of adjustment to the new social milieu, as recounted above by the second author. Negative attitudes and constraining expectations about behavior can result from a discrediting attribute, the stigma associated with disability (Goffman, 1963). Once disabled, one's conversations with able-bodied people might now be interpreted as intergroup encounters in which the person with the disability is marginalized. Intergroup communication can simultaneously affect the physically challenged person's evolving social identity and their communication patterns with others. Adjustment to the changed social milieu can lead to a limited social identity, but more positive outcomes are possible through the use of empowering communication strategies.

In this chapter, we introduce the communication predicament of disability model to provide a framework for understanding the intergroup communication challenges and threatened social identity resulting from stigma. After providing evidence for this negative feedback process, we characterize the manner in which people with disabilities can interrupt the cycle through the use of "selective assertiveness" in conversation, as well as group-empowered communication to challenge the status quo. Our discussion is constructed from the standpoint of persons with disabilities and has been informed as much as possible by *their* perspective. Examples from empirical research on communication predicaments and assertiveness in aging are provided to support interpretations and speculations about disability. Finally, we suggest productive areas for future research emerging from this intergroup conceptualization of communication and disability.

Communication Predicament of Disability Model: A Negative Feedback Cycle

Major recent reviews have outlined a variety of relevant theoretical approaches for conceptualizing communication and disability (see Braithwaite & Thompson, 2000). Interability communication theory, the one most relevant to this volume, will be discussed later in the chapter (Fox & Giles, 1997; Fox, Giles, Orbe, & Bourhis, 2000). We introduce here an alternate model that is also derived primarily from social identity and communication accommodation (Giles, Coupland, & Coupland, 1991) theories.

The communication predicament of disability model (see Figure 1) builds on the empirical success of the communication predicament of aging model (Hummert, Garstka, Ryan, & Bonnesen, 2004; Ryan, Giles, Bartolucci, & Henwood, 1986). This new negative feedback model emphasizes the disempowerment involved in much intergroup communication experienced by individuals with a disability and draws attention to selective assertiveness as a key to re-establishing more respectful interpersonal communication. The model postulates that stereotypes of disability such as dependence, lack of control, and incompetence bias the ways in which able-bodied people treat persons with disabilities. The resulting communication modifications constrain opportunities for satisfying communication and reinforce disability-based stereotypes. The momentum of the predicament process increasingly presses upon the person with a disability to react passively or resist aggressively. Frequent interactions of this type can lead the person to withdraw socially, feel less in control, conform more to disability stereotypes, and eventually adopt a reduced sense of self as disabled. However, the model portrays the opportunity for people with a disability to interrupt the cycle through selective assertiveness, either through individual conversational strategies in dyadic situations or through group-based strategies. The following sections are organized around the model.

Stage One of Predicament: Stigmatization

Able-bodied individuals commonly stereotype persons with disabilities as dependent (Coleman & DePaulo, 1991; Fine & Asch, 1988), incompetent (Emry & Wiseman, 1987; Fox & Giles, 1996), unproductive (Chouinard, 2003; Susman, 1994), sick (Braithwaite, 1990; Emry & Wiseman, 1987), burdensome (Chouinard, 2003; Fox & Giles, 1996), unattractive (Frank, 1988; Susman, 1994), and hypersensitive and bitter (Coleman & DePaulo, 1991; Emry & Wiseman, 1987). There are many theories concerning the origin of the negative stereotypes associated with persons with disabilities (Goffman, 1963; Rubington &

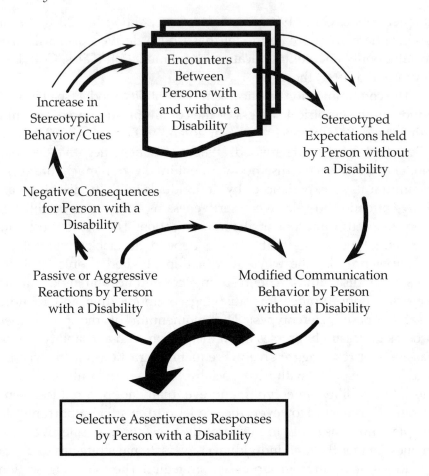

Figure 1: *The Communication Predicament of Disability: Interrupting the Cycle with Selective Assertiveness*

Weinberg, 1987; Yuker, 1988). For example, social exchange theorists argue that "unmarked" (able-bodied) individuals, in a social exchange with "marked" (person with disability) individuals, might wish to place the blame for the "mark" on the person with the disability so as to maximize the social exchange in their favor (Gramling & Forsyth, 1987). Assigning stereotypes to the marked group effectively attributes responsibility to disabled persons for their situation (e.g., they are incompetent). This "blame the victim" mentality has been documented with minority groups identified by race, gender, language, and age (see relevant chapters in this volume). From a broader perspective, negative stereotypes and attitudes are hypothesized to be sustained by values such as Western society's emphasis on the sociocultural ideals of independence, beauty, and marketability (Livneh, 1988; Susman, 1994). As noted by Higgins (1992, p. 8), "we create disability when we accept a portion of human variation as "natural" and mark off the rest of human variation as significantly different."

Categorization of people into social groups can lead to mindless behavior whereby people minimize differences within the group and exaggerate intergroup differences (Coleman & DePaulo, 1991; Langer & Chanowitz, 1988). Individuals within the outgroup are believed to possess homogeneous characteristics, although, despite very specific labels (e.g., older native Canadians with visual impairment), there is inevitably a great deal of heterogeneity among any group's members. The able-bodied often accept the illusion of homogeneity, communicating in fixed ways with "the disabled," rather than responding to the varied backgrounds and abilities of the individuals in this population (Fox & Giles, 1997; Rubington & Weinberg, 1987).

Goffman (1963) highlighted the different issues faced in everyday interactions by persons with visible vs. invisible disabilities. Namely, those with visible disabilities (discredited) must deal with the anxiety resulting from their disability being public knowledge, while those with invisible disabilities (discreditable) contend with concealing any information that might give away their disability and the predicament of finding the appropriate time to disclose their disability to others (Fine & Asch, 1988; Matthews & Harrington, 2000).

Stereotypes can cause nondisabled people to hold rigid expectations of persons with disabilities. For example, a person with an invisible disability might require more help than a person with a visible disability, but conflicting cues regarding dependence and independence can lead to inappropriate helping. Often, witnessing one instance of dependence causes the nondisabled to overgeneralize that an individual is dependent in every situation. For example, with many types of disability, such as multiple sclerosis and arthritis, individuals might or might not need to use an assistive device from one day to the next. For many individuals, changes occur in the level of dependence across time and situations, potentially changing the visibility of a disability (Fine & Asch, 1988; Morris, 1991). In addition, an observed instance of dependency might not be internal to the individual but a result of environmental constraints. For example, a person with visual impairment might only need to use a white cane when the light is poor. Able-bodied individuals can become upset when the behavior of a person with a disability does not fit with an all-or-none concept of impairment (e.g., a person with hearing loss overhearing a personal comment, a blind person seeing something with peripheral vision, or a person in a wheelchair standing up) (see Emry & Wiseman, 1987).

Stage Two of Predicament: Modified Communication

> Recently, in a coffee shop, I was approached by someone who said "Hello, Selina" and she stood at our table while I tried to identify her. While most people know that I cannot see their face, they continue to refuse to adapt to a pattern of identifying themselves. My companion, sensing a moment of awkwardness, shouted at me, "Stand up, Selina and see who it is!" (SB)

Social categorization and stereotyping lead to modified nonverbal and verbal communication behaviors by both the able-bodied and the person with the disability. Communication accommodation theory argues that people draw on their existing knowledge, including negative stereotypes, to accommodate communication behaviors toward members of a particular group (Coupland, Coupland & Giles, 1991; Giles et al., 1991). Accommodations are motivated by the individual's needs to express values, attitudes, and intentions, as well as social approval or disapproval, and group loyalty (Fox & Giles, 1996; Fox et al., 2000). Encounters with disabled persons might threaten their social identity as a fully functioning human being and as a charitable person (Fox & Giles, 1997). Thus, able-bodied people often use communication strategies that emphasize their distinctiveness from their disabled conversational partner and that present themselves as "good persons" (Fox & Giles, 1997; Rubington & Weinberg, 1987).

Research on intergenerational communication with older adults is relevant, since disability stereotypes are also commonly applied to old people. Younger adults and service providers often make speech overaccommodations that communicate a patronizing attitude toward older adults (Hummert et al., 2004; Hummert & Ryan, 2001; see also Williams & Garrett, this volume). Modifications such as simplified vocabulary, simple sentences, overly familiar talk, overly directive talk, disapproval, and baby talk (including exaggerated intonation) stem from the stereotypes of older adults as dependent and incompetent (Fox & Giles, 1996, 1997). These communication patterns are driven by two different motivations: task efficiency, which leads to impatience, and an automatic sense of nurturance, which leads to overhelping or inappropriate helping (Hummert & Ryan, 2001). Many of the same behaviors have been found to occur in conversations experienced by individuals with disabilities (Emry & Wiseman, 1987; Liesener & Mills, 1999).

Persons with disabilities have also described the tendency of the able-bodied either to center the interaction around the disability, giving it "master status," or to avoid the topic altogether (Coleman & DePaulo, 1991; Goffman, 1963). In their preoccupation with the disability, nondisabled persons might ask overly personal questions (e.g., intimate questions from strangers about grooming and sexuality) (Braithwaite, 1990). The power differential created when strangers are asked by a person with a disability for help can also give the helper a false sense of permission to ask personal questions.

Overhelping behavior is one of the most commonly cited communication modifications in interactions with persons with disabilities (Fox & Giles, 1997; Fox et al., 2000). Braithwaite and Eckstein (2003) showed that managing unwanted assistance from able-bodied others is a primary communication challenge for people with disabilities. They found that help was deemed unwanted by persons with disabilities when able-bodied helpers' communication reflected stereotypes such as incompetence and dependence. Help from a nondisabled person was unwanted when they were patronizing, they offered more help than needed, gave help when not asked, made a spectacle of helping, or put a person's safety in jeopardy by not following instructions.

Finally, avoidance behavior is thought to result from anxiety about interacting with a person with a disability (Fox & Giles, 1996; Hebl & Kleck, 2000). The initial emotional reactions of fear, surprise, or repulsion displayed in the nondisabled person's facial expressions are often not well hidden. Their failed attempts to try and replace them with more socially desirable expressions (e.g., ingratiation) are often detected by the person with the disability (Coleman & DePaulo, 1991). Braithwaite (1990) found that persons with disabilities sensed the able-bodied person's discomfort through verbal and nonverbal signs such as fidgeting, lack of eye contact, keeping a large physical distance, staring, statements of sympathy, avoidance, or pretending the disability does not exist. There are competing responses: you want to look and you cannot (Goffman, 1963; Yuker, 1988). When a person with disability is with another person, the able-bodied often ignore them, carrying on the conversation with the companion due to their discomfort and the inappropriate assumption of incompetence (Braithwaite & Thompson, 2000; Yuker, 1988).

Stage Three of Predicament: Passive or Aggressive Reactions of the Person with a Disability

Individuals with a disability have several options for responding to the modified communication of members of the able-bodied group. However, repeated experiences of stereotype-based communication can limit their apparent options to passive or aggressive reactions. Thus, individuals might take the path of least resistance to make the interaction run more smoothly (which reinforces the dependent stereotype), or react aggressively to defend themselves, which reinforces the "sensitive" and "bitter" stereotype. Finally, they might react outwardly with passive behavior with the intention of thwarting the goals of the able-bodied individual through passive aggressiveness (e.g., inefficiency, procrastination), thereby confirming the stereotype of incompetence (Emry & Wiseman, 1987; Fox et al., 2000; Paterson, 2000). For the purposes of this chapter, we have chosen to focus on the more automatic passive and aggressive reactions.

Passive communication is characterized by an inhibited, self-denying, and apologetic style, and by language that is indirect, overly polite, and filled with hidden meaning (Paterson, 2000; Rakos, 1991). Passive responses are accompanied by stooped, sagging posture, fidgeting, lack of eye contact, and tense facial gestures. When behaving in this manner, individuals often allow others to make choices for them, usually resulting in their goals being unmet. The negative feedback loop operates to encourage acknowledgment of a physical disability as a passive response to the uncertainty of the conversational partner, allowing the interaction to run more smoothly. However, this behavior often contributes to the relinquishment of control in a conversation (Coleman & DePaulo, 1991; Hebl & Kleck, 2000). Research with older adults has revealed that nursing home residents often passively accept patronizing communication due to fears of jeopardizing the care they receive from healthcare workers, perpetuating the perception that they are incompetent (Hummert et al., 2004). Persons with disabilities who are dependent on others for services also sometimes feel they must accept inappropriate behavior for the sake of continued services. Yet, individuals going along with the stereotypes risk being further stigmatized and might begin to believe that they are helpless (Fox et al., 2000; Scott, cited in Rubington & Weinberg, 1987).

Aggressive communication is typically identified as a controlling style involving accusatory and angry language, rigid gestures, and highly charged emotions. In terms of disability, the emotional language and bristly gestures inherent in these responses might halt inappropriate behaviors of others but, in turn, act as cues that call up negative stereotypes (e.g., sensitive, bitter) (Fox & Giles, 1997). Subsequently, as predicted by the negative feedback cycle, the nondisabled person might respond with equally stereotypical behavior, cutting the interaction short or responding in a rigid manner, spoiling the opportunity for a satisfying interaction (Coleman & DePaulo, 1991; Emry & Wiseman, 1987). While the initial aggressive reaction of the individual with the disability might be a result of their pent-up frustration with continually experiencing poor communication from others, it might only result in their needs being left unmet.

Stage Four of Predicament: Negative Consequences for Social Identity
While adaptations to one's physical environment are expected after acquiring a disability, the adjustments that must be made to a new social identity as disabled might only become apparent after living with the disability for some time (Braithwaite, 1990). Furthermore, it has been argued that it is not the physical, but the social and psychological changes described above that cause the most problems for people with acquired disabilities (Fine & Asch, 1988; Higgins, 1992; Oliver, 1996).

After exposure to stereotype-driven communication, individuals with a disability might internalize the expectations that the able-bodied assign and, in line with self-fulfilling prophecy theory, might begin acting or feeling how they think others perceive them, leading to lowered self-esteem (Coleman & DePaulo, 1991; Goffman, 1963).

The modified behaviors of the nondisabled can produce feelings of anger, humiliation, and depression in persons with disabilities. Recipients of inappropriate communication might become overly sensitive to the evaluations of others or contemptuous toward other persons with disabilities (Coleman & DePaulo, 1991; Langer & Chanowitz, 1988).

While individuals might not be consciously aware of them, implicit stereotypes held about one's own social group can have far-reaching effects on behavior. Research shows that activation of negative aging stereotypes without the participants' awareness causes older adults to behave "older" in terms of reduced memory performance, handwriting quality, and cardiovascular stress indicators. However, when positive stereotypes were primed, their memory, handwriting, walking gait, and health indicators improved (Levy, 2003). Furthermore, as compared to explicit discriminatory behaviors, it might be more difficult for stigmatized groups to defend against negative behaviors implicitly driven by stereotypes since these behaviors are often subtle or easily attributable to other causes (e.g., the other candidate was more qualified for the job) (Coleman & DePaulo, 1991; Levy, 2003). The link to communication is highlighted by the finding that marginalized individuals experience lower self-esteem and increased depression after receiving unwarranted help (Schneider, Major, Luhtanen, & Crocker, 1996).

Selective Assertiveness: Conversational Options

Given the negative consequences associated with stereotype-reinforcing reactions, persons with disabilities might cultivate other options that are more likely to elicit respectful behavior on the part of the able-bodied. As depicted in Figure 1, selective assertiveness can break the cycle of automatic intergroup conduct, creating person-to-person interactions. Of course, we offer this perspective while recognizing the great variation in relevance and implementation, given the complexity of people's lives.

Possible responses to inappropriate communication can be viewed along a continuum from passive to aggressive. Choosing an assertive response from the middle of that continuum is intended to avoid the dangers associated with the extremes and to take control over managing others' impressions of oneself (Rakos, 1991; Twenge, 2001; Wilson

& Gallois, 1993). Some authors have suggested that assertiveness is multidimensional and requires a conceptualization more like a triangle or pyramid to contrast the ideal style from passive, aggressive, offensive, and manipulative responses (e.g., Fox et al., 2000; Paterson, 2000). Assertive communication involves the tactful, straightforward expression of feelings and desires. Clear messages are associated with a confident, calm tone of voice and relaxed facial expressions and gestures. Assertive messages can be especially effective when expressing appreciation and acknowledging the conversational partner's needs (Hummert et al., 2004; Rakos, 1991).

We use the term "selective" to emphasize the goal-based, situational choices involved in when and how to be assertive. Selectively assertive people take responsibility for meeting their own goals. In contrast, passive people fail to take responsibility, while aggressive people are likely to hurt others (Fox et al., 2000; Taylor & Epstein, 1999). Our emphasis on selection derives from decades of research establishing the necessity of contextualizing assertive responses and of choosing one's battles (Rakos, 1991; Street, 2001; Wilson & Gallois, 1993).

Assertive behavior is associated with high-status, self-esteem, a positive self-concept, and empowerment (Hebl, Tickle, & Heatherton, 2000; Twenge, 2001; Wilson & Gallois, 1993). Those who engage in assertive behavior are less likely to be victimized, experience less depression, sustain increased effectiveness in interpersonal power relationships, and enjoy higher levels of social support (e.g., Hersen et al., 1995). The correlation between assertiveness and positive acceptance of disability underlies the incorporation of communication skills training into rehabilitation programs (Joiner, Lovett, & Goodwin, 1989).

Fox and Giles (1996, 1997; Fox et al., 2000) have formulated interability communication theory to account for the one-down position of people with disabilities in intergroup situations and for the limited effects of intergroup contact with disabled individuals on able-bodied people's attitudes and communication behaviors. They propose social identity motivations underlying response strategies. Passing as able-bodied motivates nonassertion, while establishing a totally separate group motivates aggression. In contrast, assertion flows from a desire for positive social identity within an intergroup exchange.

In a study of older adults with and without hearing loss, assertive responding was rated as more competent than either passive or aggressive responding and also more likely to result in satisfying interactions in the future (Ryan, Anas, & Friedman, 2004; see also Harwood, Ryan, Giles, & Tysoski, 1997). Other related studies have shown the promise of humor and appreciation as indirectly assertive responses that can be useful selectively when saving the face of the conversational partner is important (e.g., with a service provider: Hummert et al., 2004; Ryan, Kennaley, Pratt, & Shumovich, 2000).

Braithwaite (1990) derived six impression management strategies from interviews with persons with disability. These task-oriented communication strategies serve to manage the conversation so that individuals with a disability present themselves first as persons for the sake of building a relationship with nondisabled others, instead of accepting inappropriate attention to the disability. These strategies fit within our concept of selective assertiveness: 1) establish normalcy by showing the able-bodied person more likenesses than the salient difference or minimizing the disability; 2) use modeling behavior to show how one would like to be treated; 3) limit attention to an assistive device (e.g., use the device unobtrusively, or divert attention away from it); 4) limit responses to personal questions; 5) delay disclosure about the disability; 6) manage the able-bodied tendency to overhelp (e.g., ignore unwanted helping attempts, turn down the offer with humor, educate the helper with straightforward description of what is most useful, engage a formal helper) (see also Braithwaite & Eckstein, 2003; Taylor & Epstein, 1999). SB offers these illustrations: a) "I have trouble seeing" instead of "I am legally blind"; b) using a collapsible cane that can be put away once in familiar territory; c) "Please take my arm rather than pushing me."

Potential benefits of selective assertiveness include satisfying communication, positive social identity, a sense of control, managing help effectively, and generally meeting one's goals. When empowered with a sense of equality as a human being, the person with a disability can more effectively manage the communication predicaments that are part of everyday life.

Intergroup Communication
Strategies of the Disability Group

Once persons with disabilities decide to be members of a disability group, intergroup communication strategies can be used selectively to meet the social identity goals of social creativity (creating positive in-group norms) and social competition (vying for resources). These approaches focus on empowerment of the disadvantaged group as a whole rather than individual members (see Harwood, Giles, & Palomares, this volume).

Social Creativity

Social creativity involves seeking new positive dimensions for intergroup comparison to improve the self-concept of members of the disadvantaged group. The disability community has worked toward redefining models of disability. Meanings derived from the medical model or the model of "personal tragedy" focus on the internal, functional limitations of the person with the disability. For instance, care plans for disabled individuals have usually been defined in terms of a rehabilitation model. This model is inappropriate because of the assumption that it is necessary and possible for persons with disabilities to overcome their health problems (Emry & Wiseman, 1987; Zola, 1981). In addition, the competence level of the person has been traditionally defined by a healthcare professional and their family, thereby taking control away from the individual (Emry & Wiseman, 1987). Newer perspectives see the limitations as resulting from forces external to the individual (Marinelli & Dell Orto, 1999; Morris, 1991; Rauscher & McClintock, 1997). Furthermore, these alternate perspectives challenge the political and attitudinal forces that nurture a disabling environment (Oliver, 1996).

The independent living model was developed in the 1980s during the disabled persons' movement, which emphasized the competence of the person with the disability to develop their own goals and make their own care decisions (Institute on Disability Culture, 2003; Morris, 1995). Contrary to the focus of rehabilitation on maximizing physical function, care under this model recognizes that an individual might not overcome health problems. People with disabilities redefined the meanings of "independence" and "dependence" in alignment with the philosophy of independent living. The traditional Western meaning of independence as "self-reliant" and "self-supportive" prevented an individual who needed any assistance from being considered independent. The new independence is equated with the ability to access assistance when and how one needs it and not with the intellectual or physical ability to care for oneself. The Americans with Disabilities Act (US Department of Labor, 1990) also redefined the concept of competence in the workplace by stating that an employee with a disability is qualified if able to perform the job "with the necessary accommodations."

Labels can be powerful enough to sway the attitudes of individuals, which may cause them to modify their behavior (DePaulo & Coleman, 1986; Office for Disability Issues, 1998). By creating alternatives to negative language, persons with disabilities can separate from the stereotypes associated with a label. Advocates for persons with disabilities have attempted to educate the public regarding the effects that inappropriate language can have on persons with disabilities (Office for Disability Issues, 1998; Rauscher & McClintock, 1997). However, this process is ongoing, since previously innocuous language can inevitably become negative over time. Here again, individual-based strategies such as controlling information flow (Braithwaite, 1990) work toward the larger goal of social creativity in that they are redefining the dominant group's perception about them (e.g., persons with disabilities have many other characteristics that make them competent besides the disability).

During the 1950s, people with disabilities were referred to as "cripples" and defined as "useless" or "imperfect," which had clear consequences for them. Later, the label of "handicapped" was used but it came to mean "crippled." By creating a word that symbolizes environmental obstacles (inaccessible), the existence of the obstacles has been legitimized. People with disabilities have also deemed the phrase "the disabled" as unacceptable because the disability is equated with the person when the adjective is used as a noun (Office for Disability Issues, 1998; Susman, 1994). The use of "nondisabled" to refer to the dominant group has the unfamiliar effect of transferring negative connotation from persons with disabilities to those without. Some persons with disability suggest the term "temporarily able-bodied" to minimize the difference between themselves and members of the nondisabled group. Also, the phrase "differently abled" switches the focus from what individuals cannot do to what they can do. However, these alternate labels can be viewed as euphemisms that perpetuate societal ignorance about disabilities. Overall, the goal of changing the language is to ensure that individuals are addressed less in terms of their disability and more in terms of their personhood (Hebl & Kleck, 2000). Hence, we have chosen to use the term "person with disability" (Office for Disability Issues, 1998; US Department of Labor, 1990). The project of reassigning meaning to disability has even extended to the establishment of disability studies programs at some universities as an important contribution to the study of diversity and an enhanced understanding of human lives (Linton, 1998).

While many groups strive to have their impairment viewed in terms of environmental limitations, others covet a definition that excludes them from the disability group altogether (Institute on Disability Culture, 2003). Deaf activists have fought to be viewed not as a disability subgroup but as a culture, no different from any other culture that has its own language (Young, 1990). Similarly, persons with limb deficiencies challenge the existence of stigma, rather than simply reacting to it, by refusing to wear prosthetic devices (Frank, 1988). Thus, these groups attempt to create new norms that could remove the stigma altogether.

Social Competition

Engaging in social competition, various disability groups strive politically to gain status and societal resources for their members. Disability advocates in North America in the 1970s gathered together across disability subgroup boundaries to fight "ableism," a newly identified source of societal discrimination (Rauscher & McClintock, 1997). Advocates were successful in obtaining equal rights "without discrimination based on... mental or physical disability" in the Canadian Charter of Rights and Freedoms (1982, section 15(1)). The Americans with Disabilities Act of 1990 challenged society's notions of competence and productivity, among many other issues, by demanding equal consideration for employment opportunities (US Department of Labor, 1990). The act stated that the decreased status of the disabled resulted from barriers in the environment such as architectural, transportation, and communication barriers. Thus, people with disabilities were *legally* considered equal to those without and, therefore, granted resources that would allow them to take advantage of the same opportunities as the dominant group (Oliver, 1996).

Conclusion

This chapter speaks from the perspective of persons with disabilities, following the lead of Emry and Wiseman (1987) and Braithwaite (1990). We have argued that as one adjusts to an acquired disability, one can learn to interrupt the negative feedback cycle depicted by the communication predicament of disability model. By exercising control, choice, and assertiveness, one can move effectively beyond the limits imposed by stigmatization and environmental barriers (Fox & Giles, 1997; Fox et al., 2000; Marinelli & Dell Orto, 1999). One can acknowledge the social stigma of "disabled" without internalizing it. As a result, one can manage conversations with others proactively and thereby create a positive new social identity.

Nevertheless, we must not underestimate the importance of awakening the nondisabled world to their common practice of "mindless" communication. Langer and Moldoveanu (2000, p. 138) argue that mindful communication with others is really about mindful *listening*, whereby one actively listens, free of the "preexisting categories that constrain the attention of the listener to a pre-specified set of characteristics of the other." Given the ever-present stereotypes and the negative consequences of communication predicaments imposed upon persons with disability, sensitizing the nondisabled to inappropriate communication patterns should continue to be an important area of research, practice, and policy. In addition, learning that the boundary between able-bodied and disabled is illusory can help people prepare for their own possible acquisition of disability later in life (Beaulaurier & Taylor, 2001). The assertive communication techniques we have outlined could be effective beyond the issues of disability for any recipient of inappropriate attention or disempowering communication.

The most important direction for future research is to record the multiplicity of voices among people with disabilities. Social identity theory and the communication predicament of disability model provide valuable frameworks within which to interpret data concerning the intergroup predicaments faced by people with disabilities. Further extending the work of Braithwaite and colleagues, ethnographic and interview methodology could highlight the most important conversational dilemmas as well as the range of selective assertiveness and group-based strategies that might be available for managing those dilemmas. This research could elaborate distinctions in the intergroup experiences of those with visible and invisible disabilities.

Person perception studies are particularly useful for assessing the impact of group memberships and interpersonal and contextual manipulations on the interpretation of conversational strategies. This paradigm can systematically examine the range of assertive behaviors realistically available to people with different disabilities under particular circumstances (see Fox & Giles, 1996; Hummert et al., 2004). As identified earlier, the primary assertiveness issues for people with disabilities involve when and how to disclose information and how to manage helping behaviors (needed and unwanted). Future research needs to document which strategies work best for different personalities, different disabilities, and in different situations.

Dyadic experiments offer the opportunity to observe the conversational behavior of disabled and nondisabled conversational partners under controlled conditions to determine the impact of the situation, role, and interactive components of context (see Hebl & Kleck, 2000). Role-plays can be developed from these dyadic studies for use in training professional service providers (social workers, therapists, nursing staff, medical staff). As well, the dyadic conversational paradigm provides a technique for evaluating the effects of communication skills training.

Finally, links between social identity in disability and communication can profitably be addressed in terms of the following research questions: What sorts of communication experiences lead persons with an acquired disability to shift from social mobility (trying to pass as able-bodied) to identification as a disabled person? What communication experiences might lead a person with a disability to choose collective identity with people with different disabilities? How does degree of identification with disability relate to the use of assertive conversational strategies? How does the use of assertive conversational strategies in intergroup contexts relate to endorsement of social creativity and social competition group strategies?

Author Note

The authors express their appreciation for partial support for this research by a grant from the Social Sciences and Humanities Research Council of Canada. We thank Jake Harwood and Howard Giles for their thoughtful comments on earlier versions of this chapter. We also gratefully acknowledge the assistance of Judith Dueck and Kathleen Banchoff.

References

Beaulaurier, R. L., & Taylor, S. H. (2001). Dispelling fears about aging with a disability: Lessons from the disability rights community. *Journal of Gerontological Social Work, 35*, 81–98.

Braithwaite, D. O. (1990). From majority to minority: An analysis of cultural change from ablebodied to disabled. *International Journal of Intercultural Relations, 14*, 465–483.

Braithwaite, D. O., & Eckstein, N. (2003). Reconceptualizing supportive interactions: How persons with disabilities communicatively manage assistance. *Journal of Applied Communication Research, 31*, 1–26.

Braithwaite, D., & Thompson, T. (Eds.). (2000). *The handbook of communication and physical disability*. Mahwah, NJ: Erlbaum.

Canadian Charter of Rights and Freedoms (1982). Ottawa. Government of Canada.

Chouinard, V. (2003). *Embodying gender and disability II: Understanding disabled women's places in Canadian society and space*. Unpublished manuscript: McMaster University, Hamilton, ON, Canada.

Coleman, L., & DePaulo, B. (1991). Uncovering the human spirit: Moving beyond disability and "missed" communication. In N. Coupland, H. Giles, & J. Wiemann (Eds.), *Miscommunication and problematic talk* (pp. 61–85). Newbury Park, CA: Sage.

Coupland, N., Coupland, J., & Giles, H. (1991). *Language, society and the elderly: Discourse, identity and ageing*. Oxford: Blackwell.

DePaulo, B. M., & Coleman L. M. (1986). Talking to children, foreigners, and retarded adults. *Journal of Personality and Social Psychology, 51*, 945–959.

Emry, R., & Wiseman, R. L. (1987). An intercultural understanding of ablebodied and disabled persons' communication. *International Journal of Intercultural Relations, 11*, 7–27.

Fine, M., & Asch, A. (1988). Disability beyond stigma: Social interaction, discrimination, and activism. *Journal of Social Issues, 44*, 3–21.

Fox, S. A., & Giles, H. (1996). Interability communication: Evaluating patronizing encounters. *Journal of Language and Social Psychology, 15*, 265–290.

Fox, S. A., & Giles, H. (1997). Let the wheelchair through: An intergroup approach to interability communication. In W. P. Robinson (Ed.), *Social groups and identity: The developing legacy of Henri Tajfel* (pp. 215–248). Oxford: Heineman.

Fox, S. A., Giles, H., Orbe, M. P., & Bourhis, R. Y. (2000). Interability communication: Theoretical perspectives. In D. Braithwaite & T. Thompson (Eds.), *The handbook of communication and physical disability* (pp. 193–222). Mahwah, NJ: Erlbaum.

Frank, G. (1988). Beyond stigma: Visibility and self-empowerment of persons with congenital limb deficiencies. *Journal of Social Issues, 44* (1), 95–115.

Giles, H., Coupland, N., & Coupland, J. (1991). Accommodation theory: Communication, context, and consequence. In H. Giles, J. Coupland, & N. Coupland (Eds.), *Contexts of accommodation: Developments in applied sociolinguistics* (pp. 1–68). Cambridge: Cambridge University Press.

Goffman, E. (1963). *Stigma: Notes on the management of spoiled identity.* Englewood Cliffs, NJ: Prentice Hall.

Gramling, R., & Forsyth, C. J. (1987). Exploiting stigma. *Sociological Forum, 2,* 401–415.

Harwood, J., Ryan, E. B., Giles, H., & Tysoski, S. (1997). Evaluations of patronizing speech and three response styles in a non-service-providing context. *Journal of Applied Communication Research, 25,* 170–195.

Hebl, M. R., & Kleck, R. E. (2000). The social consequences of physical disability. In T. F. Heatherton, R. E. Kleck, M. R. Hebl, & J. G. Hull (Eds.), *The social psychology of stigma* (pp. 419–439). New York: Guilford.

Hebl, M. R., Tickle, J., & Heatherton, T. F. (2000). Awkward moments in interactions between nonstigmatized and stigmatized individuals. In T. F. Heatherton, R. E. Kleck, M. R. Hebl, & J. G. Hull (Eds.), *The social psychology of stigma* (pp. 275–306). New York: Guilford.

Hersen, M., Kabacoff, R. I., Van Hasselt, V. B., Null, J. A., Ryan, C. F., Melton, M. A., & Segal, D. L. (1995). Assertiveness, depression, and social support in older visually impaired adults. *Journal of Visual Impairment and Blindness, 89,* 524–530.

Higgins, P. (1992). *Making disability: Exploring the social transformation of human variation.* Springfield: Charles C. Thomas Publishers.

Hummert, M. L., Garstka, T. A., Ryan, E. B., & Bonnesen, J. L. (2004). The role of age stereotypes in interpersonal communication. In J. F. Nussbaum & J. Coupland (Eds.), *The handbook of communication and aging,* (2nd ed., pp. 91–114). Mahwah, NJ: Erlbaum.

Hummert, M. L., & Ryan, E. B. (2001). Patronizing. In W. P. Robinson & H. Giles (Eds.), *The new handbook of language and social psychology* (2nd ed., pp. 253–269). Chichester, UK: Wiley.

Joiner, J. G., Lovett, P. S., & Goodwin, L. K. (1989). Positive assertion and acceptance among persons with disabilities. *Journal of Rehabilitation, 55,* 22–29.

Institute on Disability Culture (2003). *Disability Culture home page.* Retrieved February 14, 2003 from http://www.dimenet.com/disculture/

Langer, E. J., & Chanowitz, B. (1988). Mindfulness/mindlessness: A new perspective for the study of disability. In H. Yuker (Ed.), *Attitudes towards persons with disabilities* (pp. 68–81). New York: Springer.

Langer, E. J., & Moldoveanu, M. (2000). Mindfulness research and the future. *Journal of Social Issues, 56,* 129–139.

Levy, B. R. (2003). Mind matters: Cognitive and physical effects of aging self-stereotypes. *Journal of Gerontology: Psychological Sciences, 58B,* P203–211.

Liesener, J. J., & Mills, J. (1999). An experimental study of disability spread: Talking to an adult in a wheelchair like a child. *Journal of Applied Social Psychology, 29,* 2083–2092.

Linton, S. (1998). *Claiming disability: Knowledge and identity.* New York: New York University Press.

Livneh, H. (1988). A dimensional perspective on the origin of negative attitudes toward persons with disabilities. In H. Yuker (Ed.), *Attitudes towards persons with disabilities* (pp. 35–46). New York: Springer.

Marinelli, R. P., & Dell Orto, A. E. (Eds.). (1999). *The psychological and social impact of disability* (4th ed.). New York: Springer.

Matthews, C. K., & Harrington, N. G. (2000). Invisible disability. In D. Braithwaite & T. Thompson (Eds.), *The handbook of communication and physical disability* (pp. 405–421). Mahwah, NJ: Erlbaum.

Morris, J. (1991). *Pride against prejudice: Transforming attitudes to disability.* Philadelphia: New Society Publishers.

Morris, J. (1995). Creating a space for absent voices: Disabled women's experience of receiving assistance with daily living activities. *Feminist Review, 51,* 68–93.

Office for Disability Issues (1998). *A way with words: Guidelines and appropriate terminology for the portrayal of persons with disabilities.* Hull, Quebec: Human Resources Development Canada.

Oliver, M. (1996). *Understanding disability: From theory to practice.* New York: St Martin's Press.

Paterson, R. J. (2000). *The assertiveness workbook: How to express your ideas and stand up for yourself at work and in relationships.* Oakland, CA: New Harbinger.

Rakos, R. F. (Ed.) (1991). *Assertive behavior: Theory, research, and training.* London: Routledge.

Rauscher, L., & McClintock, M. (1997). Ableism curriculum design. In M. Adams, L. A. Bell, & P. Griffen (Eds.), *Teaching for diversity and social justice: A sourcebook* (pp. 198–227). New York: Routledge.

Rubington, E., & Weinberg, M. S. (Eds.). (1987). *Deviance: An interactionist perspective* (5th ed.). New York: Macmillan.

Ryan, E. B., Anas, A. P., & Friedman, D. (2004). *Evaluations of older adult assertiveness in problematic clinical encounters.* Manuscript submitted for publication.

Ryan, E. B., Giles, H., Bartolucci, G., & Henwood, K. (1986). Psycholinguistic and social psychological components of communication by and with the elderly. *Language and Communication, 6,* 1–24.

Ryan, E. B., Kennaley, D. E., Pratt, M. W., & Shumovich, M. A. (2000). Evaluations by staff, residents, and community seniors of patronizing speech in the nursing home: Impact of passive, assertive or humorous responses. *Psychology and Aging, 15,* 272–328.

Schneider, M. E., Major, B., Luhtanen, R., & Crocker, J. (1996). Social stigma and the potential costs of assumptive help. *Personality and Social Psychology Bulletin, 22,* 201–209.

Street, R. L. Jr. (2001). Active patients as powerful communicators. In W. P. Robinson & H. Giles (Eds.), *The new handbook of language and social psychology* (pp. 541–560). London: Wiley.

Susman, J. (1994). Disability, stigma and deviance. *Social Sciences and Medicine, 38,* 15–22.

Taylor, S., & Epstein, R. (1999). *Living well with a hidden disability: Transcending doubt and shame and reclaiming your life.* Oakland, CA: New Harbinger.

Twenge, J. M. (2001). Changes in women's assertiveness in response to status and roles: A cross-temporal meta-analysis, 1931–1993. *Journal of Personality and Social Psychology, 81,* 133–145.

U.S. Department of Labor (1990). *The Americans with Disabilities Act of 1990,* Retrieved March 30, 2004 from http://www.dol.gov/esa/regs/statutes/ ofccp/ada.htm

Wilson, K., & Gallois, C. (1993). *Assertion and its social context.* New York: Pergamon.

Young, I. M. (1990). *Justice and the politics of difference.* Princeton, NJ: Princeton University Press.

Yuker, H. (Ed.). (1988). *Attitudes towards persons with disabilities.* New York: Springer.

Zola, I. K. (1981). Communication barriers between "the able-bodied" and "the handicapped." *Archives of Physical Medicine and Rehabilitation, 62,* 355–359.

PART 2

Communicating Identity Across Communication Contexts

7

Social Identity, Influence, and Communication in Small Groups

Michael A. Hogg
R. Scott Tindale

The social identity perspective is a mid-range theory of group membership, self-conception, and group behavior that attributes a causal role to collective self-conception (i.e., social identity). Because social identity is grounded in group life contextualized by intergroup relations, the social identity perspective maintains that an explanation of what happens *within* groups is incomplete without consideration of the group's relations to other groups. It is not a perspective only on intergroup relations or large-scale social categories. It is a perspective that is equally applicable to what happens within small face-to-face task-oriented groups (e.g., Hogg, Abrams, Otten, & Hinkle, 2004).

In this chapter, we focus on aspects of the social identity perspective that have relevance to an understanding of influence and communication processes among people in small interactive groups (also see Hogg, 2004, in press a). The pivotal idea is that in certain circumstances, group norms, cognitively represented as prototypes, are a fundamental feature of social life. Norms not only guide social interaction and influence, but are themselves the consequence of influence processes. People in groups spend a great deal of time talking about who "we" are, and how we are different from "them." Indeed, talk within and between groups is about group norms or is contextualized by group norms—it identifies, establishes, maintains, or changes group norms, and influence rests on perceptions of group membership and the group normativeness or prototypicality of interlocutors. Group membership is a crucible for what we might term "norm talk."

We overview the social identity perspective and describe its analysis of group norms and social influence, and then focus on two aspects of group processes—group decision-making (social decision schemes, intellective vs. judgmental tasks, and shared vs. unshared information), and differential influence within groups (leadership, deviance, criticism, and schisms and minority influence).

The Social Identity Perspective

The social identity perspective is a general social psychological analysis of group behavior, group membership, and the collective self-concept (for overview see Hogg, 2003; Hogg & Abrams, 1988, 2003). Its two key components are an analysis of intergroup relations (social identity theory: Tajfel & Turner, 1986), and an analysis of social cognitive processes (self-categorization theory: Turner, Hogg, Oakes, Reicher, & Wetherell, 1987).

Selves, Identities, and Salience

A distinction is drawn between two ways in which people's self-concept and sense of identity can be structured: personal identity and social identity. Personal identity is a definition and evaluation of one-self in terms of idiosyncratic personal attributes (e.g., I have a trusting personality) or one's relationships with specific other people (e.g., I am David's brother). Social identity is a definition and evaluation of oneself in terms of the shared attributes that define membership of the specific groups one belongs to (e.g., we English are eccentric). Personal identity is tied to the personal self; social identity is tied to the collective self.

People have many social and personal identities that vary in how subjectively important they are and how frequently they are used—how chronically accessible they are in one's self-concept. Chronic accessibility in conjunction with immediate situational cues, and deliberate personal or group goals, work together to prime ways to categorize oneself and others in a particular situation. The primed social categorization is automatically used to make sense of that situation. If it fits the ways that people differ in the context (comparative fit) and makes sense of why people are behaving in the way they are (normative fit), then that particular social categorization becomes psychologically *salient*. When a social categorization, self-conception, or identity is psychologically salient, it becomes one's subjective reality in that context. It is how one represents oneself and others, and it governs the way one perceives, thinks, feels, and behaves.

Social Categorization, Prototypes, and Depersonalization

Social categorization lies at the core of social identity processes and group and intergroup phenomena. People cognitively represent groups in terms of *prototypes*—these are fuzzy sets (not checklists) of interrelated attributes (e.g., perceptions, beliefs, attitudes, values, feelings, behaviors) that simultaneously capture similarities within groups and differences between groups. The prototype describes and prescribes all the attributes of an ideal group member. Prototypes are social-cognitively constructed according to the principle of metacontrast (maximizing the ratio of perceived intergroup differences to intragroup differences). They maximize entitativity—the extent to which a category appears to be a distinct and bounded entity (e.g., Hamilton & Sherman, 1996). However, prototypes are also constructed to represent the ingroup more favorably than relevant outgroups. As such, prototypes rarely describe average or typical ingroup members—rather, they are polarized away from outgroup features and describe ideal, often hypothetical, ingroup members. Prototypes cannot form or be sustained purely by intragroup comparisons—they are dependent on intergroup comparisons. Thus, intragroup processes are inextricable from the wider intergroup context—this is one important way in which the social identity perspective is an intergroup analysis.

Prototypes are generally shared among group members. As such, they are the cognitive analogue of the social interactive construct of group norm, where the norm is not simply the average of members' behavior (e.g., Turner, 1991). Prototypes vary from situation to situation as a function of the social comparative frame—that is, the specific ingroup members and the specific outgroup that are the basis for comparison. This variability can be dramatic (for example, in relatively small and new groups), but it can also be more modest due to the inertial anchoring effect of enduring group representations (for example, in large ethnic groups). In salient groups, the prototype is the basis of perception, inference, and behavior. Within such groups, people are highly attuned to prototypicality. Reactions to and feelings about fellow members are underpinned by perceptions of how prototypical those others are—how closely they match the group proto-type. Hence, if the prototype changes, then feelings for and percep-tions of specific members will change as their degree of prototypical-ity varies.

When you categorize someone, rather than viewing that person as an idiosyncratic individual, you view them through the lens of the prototype—they become *depersonalized*. Prototype-based perception of outgroup members is more commonly called stereotyping—ingroupers have a shared view of "them" as being similar to one an-other and all having outgroup attributes. When you categorize your-self, exactly the same depersonalization process applies to self—the individual self is replaced by the group self (e.g., Postmes, Spears, & Lea, 1998; Reicher, Spears, & Postmes, 1995). You view yourself in terms of the attributes of the ingroup (self-stereotyping), and, since prototypes also describe and prescribe group-appropriate ways to feel and behave, you feel and behave normatively. In this way, self-categorization produces, within a group, conformity and normative behavior (e.g., Abrams, Wetherell, Cochrane, Hogg, & Turner, 1990; Turner, 1991), and patterns of ingroup liking, trust and solidarity (e.g., Hogg, 1993, in press b).

Uncertainty Reduction and Self-Enhancement

Social identity and self-categorization processes are psychologically motivated by uncertainty reduction and self-enhancement (e.g., Hogg, 2000). People strive for a sense of relative certainty about their social world and about their place within it—they like to know who they are and how to behave, and who others are and how they might behave. Social categorization ties self-definition, behavior, and perception to prescriptive and descriptive prototypes. Prototypes define who we are and who others are, how we should behave and how others will behave, and how we should interact with members of our own group and of other groups. Thus, prototypes reduce social and self-conceptual uncertainty.

Communication plays a dual role in reducing self-conceptual un-certainty. It reduces uncertainty directly by disambiguating percep-tions (e.g., Berger & Bradac, 1982; Bradac, 2001; Gudykunst, 1995), and it reduces uncertainty indirectly by clarifying contextually rele-vant category prototypes and associated social identities that are the basis of social categorization of self and others.

People also strive to feel good about themselves and to have relatively positive self-esteem. Prototypes are evaluative—they evaluate groups and, thus, those who belong to those groups. Therefore, people strive to belong to groups that have favorable prototypes and, thus, relatively higher status. The precise way in which people and the groups they belong to compete for status and evaluatively positive social identity is influenced by beliefs about the nature of intergroup relations—for example the stability and legitimacy of status differences and the possibility of psychologically passing from one group to another (e.g., Ellemers, 1993; Tajfel & Turner, 1986).

Group Norms and Social Influence

As mentioned above, group prototypes are the way we cognitively represent group norms. From a social identity perspective, prototypes (and, thus, norms) are prescriptive as well as descriptive, and they do not necessarily express average ingroup properties or central tendencies of the group—they are more likely to be polarized away from a salient outgroup. The self-categorization and depersonalization processes describe how people's thoughts, feelings, and behavior become prototype-consistent within a salient group. Across a group in which all members have roughly the same prototype, as is typically the case, this process produces conformity and ingroup normative behavior.

The social influence process associated with norm formation, norm modification, and norm recognition, and with group normative behavior is *referent informational influence* (e.g., Abrams & Hogg, 1990; Turner & Oakes, 1989). In group contexts, people pay attention to information about the context-specific group norm. Typically, the most immediate and reliable source of this information is identity-consistent behavior of core group members. However, outgroups can also provide relevant information ("whatever they are, we are not"), and core ingroup members, such as leaders, can have extensive freedom to redefine group norms in ways that might not appear to be very identity consistent. Once the norm has been recognized or established, it is internalized by members as the context specific ingroup prototype and conformed to via the self-categorization process. Contextual norms serve at least two functions—to express ingroup similarities and ingroup identity and also to distance the ingroup from all that the outgroup stands for. Because of this, they tend to be polarized away from outgroup norms and, thus, to be more extreme than any central normative tendency of the ingroup.

Although communication must, quite obviously, be central to referent informational influence, this dimension has not been systematically explored by social identity researchers. People obtain norm-relevant information from others, either through face-to-face social interaction or indirectly via, for example, mass media. In either case, there is a communication dynamic involving the development, transmittal, and receipt of verbal and nonverbal information, and the assessment of the normative relevance of the source of information, the information itself, and the match between the two. In small interactive groups, this process could be characterized as "norm talk"—but this idea is applicable to any situation where someone is trying to influence people's perceptions of what is group normative or not (for example the rhetoric of political leaders, or the motivational talk of corporate managers).

Norm-oriented communication is not only predicated on salient social identity but also renders social identity salient. It can consolidate existing identities and their prototypes, or it can transform them. Because prototypes, norms, and social identities are fundamentally social, they are based on communication.

Social Identity, Small Groups, and Communication

Initially, the social identity approach was an analysis of large-scale intergroup relations. It did not prioritize the study of small groups or intragroup processes. However, it provided a conceptual springboard for the development of a social psychology of language. Language and speech style were seen as group-, and thus self-, defining attributes that were influenced by social identity processes (e.g., see Clément, 1996; Giles, 1996; Noels, Giles, & Le Poire, 2003). By the mid-1980s, social identity research had become increasingly cognitive (e.g., Turner et al., 1987). The consequence was, with some exceptions, a separation of mainstream social identity research from language and communication research.

Recent years have, however, witnessed new opportunities for integrative research on social identity, communication, and small interactive groups (Hogg, 1996, 2004; Ng, 2001). This is primarily because the cognitive underpinning of social identity processes is better understood, and social identity research has now become more open, diverse, and inclusive. Of particular relevance is a new social identity engagement with small group processes and phenomena (see Hogg & Tindale, 2001; Poole & Hollingshead, in press; Wheelan, in press).

In this chapter, we focus on a handful of small interactive group contexts, under the general headings of decision-making and differential influence, in which communication aspects of social identity influence processes have been explored or have the potential to be explored. In all cases, the communication aspect is in its infancy, and our emphasis is on "norm talk"—how language and communication influence, and are influenced by, the norms and prototypes that govern social identity-contingent depersonalized behavior.

Small Group Decision-Making

One of the most common reasons for small interactive face-to-face groups to assemble or to exist is to make decisions and, of course, decision-making involves communication and, almost always, talk. For a group to make a decision or choose a course of action, the members must reach consensus on what that course of action should be. In most cases, not all members will initially agree on the same alternative. Thus, social influence is a key aspect of group decision-making, and communication, in all its forms, is the medium through which social influence operates. Much of the recent theory and research in small group decision-making has shown that "social sharedness" plays a major role in how groups reach consensus. Norms, ideas, cognitive representations of the task, heuristic task strategies, and so forth, that are shared among group members exert an inordinate influence on both the group process and outcomes (Kameda, Tindale, & Davis, 2003; Tindale & Kameda, 2000; Tindale, Meisenhelder, Dykema-Engblade, & Hogg, 2001).

Intellective and Judgmental Tasks

Laughlin (1980) has argued that group tasks fall along a dimension of intellective to judgmental. Intellective tasks are those where the members share an axiomatic system of knowledge that allows them to reach consensus on a "demonstrably correct" solution (see also Laughlin & Ellis, 1986). The shared representation of the task and the background knowledge associated with it allow members who favor the correct alternative to convince other members of its "correctness." Thus, small but correct factions within the group can have influence over larger factions favoring incorrect solutions. Tindale, Smith, Thomas, Filkins, and Sheffey (1996) showed similar effects (i.e., small factions winning) even for incorrect answers when the shared task representation favored or was consistent with such answers. Thus, shared task knowledge plays a large role in group decision-making, particularly when the principal goal is to achieve consensus on a correct or optimal solution.

According to Laughlin (1980), other types of tasks are more judgmental in nature, and a demonstrably correct solution might not exist or be readily apparent. In such circumstances, shared perspectives among group members take on a larger role (Tindale & Kameda, 2000). For example, for judgmental tasks, usually the largest faction in the group (a majority or plurality) tends to prevail due to greater sharing at the preference level. For these types of tasks, shared identity becomes particularly important. First, in many cases, member preferences will be consistent with the normative position of the group so that the chosen response (based on a majority decision) will reflect the group norm. Second, groups will often polarize or shift toward the dominant position in the group so that member preferences better represent the prototypic position (Mackie, 1986). Thus, even if the member preference distribution does not exactly reflect the group norm, group discussion will tend to move the group in the normative direction. In such cases, being "correct" means being prototypical or "more like the group." Here, rather than the task defining what is correct, the socially dominant position defines correctness. Social identity-contingent norm talk can have a greater role in judgmental than intellective tasks.

Shared and Unshared Information

Prior to the 1980s, much of the work on group decision-making emphasized members' preferences (e.g., Davis, 1973; Kerr, 1981). More recent work has focused on the cognitive or information processing capabilities of groups (Hinsz, Tindale, & Vollrath, 1997; Tindale et al., 2001). The dominant paradigm for much of this research stems from research by Stasser and associates on information sharing and hidden information profiles (e.g., Stasser & Titus, 1985, 1987). By systematically distributing decision-relevant information among group members, these scholars were able to show that groups are not very proficient at ensuring that all relevant information gets discussed. Groups tend to discuss information that everyone already knows, both in terms of initial mentions and later repetitions (Larson, Foster-Fishman, & Keys, 1994). This favors normative as compared to informational social influence in that unique information available to only one group member rarely gets discussed. Thus, normative positions (usually held by the majority) tend to win out even when the group has information at its disposal that would favor alternative positions. There is also a fair amount of recent work showing that group members who communicate shared information are viewed more favorably than are members who bring up unshared information (Wittenbaum, Hubbell, & Zuckerman, 1999). Shared information is seen as more valid, consistent with the ideas of Hardin and Higgins (1996) that "saying is believing." Hearing information that one already knows increases its perceived validity and, thus, increases the likelihood of it being repeated in the future.

Recent research has shown that communication plays a central role in formulating and promulgating shared ideas in groups. Kashima (2000) studied how stories told by one group member to the next over time change as a function of the number of tellings (cf. research on rumor: Rosnow, 1980). Kashima included both stereotypic and counter-stereotypic information in the stories and had group members retell the stories to other group members. Although both stereotypic and counter-stereotypic information was prevalent in early rounds, as the story developed over retellings, the counter stereotypic information faded and stereotypic information remained. Social identity and self-categorization processes lead to outgroup stereotyping, and communication among the ingroup members not only endorses these stereotypes, but actually works to hide information inconsistent with the stereotypes over time. More recent work (Kashima, 2003) has shown that certain types of communication networks reverse this trend in hiding inconsistent information, but more research is needed to both replicate these findings and to flush out the key characteristics of the networks that show this effect.

Given that groups do not communicate effectively (i.e., share information in optimal ways), a number of researchers have tried to find ways to increase group communication effectiveness (e.g., Stasser & Birchmeier, 2003). Although many of these approaches can work well for task-oriented groups with a limited sense of group identity, such interventions might prove more difficult for situations where group norms are strong and firmly tied to members' self-construals. Research has shown that non-normative behavior by a group member leads to derogation and negative evaluations of that member by others (Marques, Abrams, & Serôdio, 2001). In fact, non-normative information and behavior seems to be better tolerated within groups if it comes from an outgroup member (see also, Phillips, 2001).

Overall, research on shared and unshared information reveals a paradox. The existence of a shared reality based at least in part on shared social identity allows communication to flow smoothly and efficiently (shared definitions of terms, implicit knowledge inferred, and so forth). However, a diversity of opinions, viewpoints, and identities, which is associated with more bumpy communication, often produces better group decisions (e.g., Stasser, Stewart, & Wittenbaum, 1995)—for example, it helps prevent groupthink (e.g., Postmes, Spears, & Cihangir, 2001). The challenge for groups is to hit the contextually optimal balance between efficient communication through shared worldviews, and communication that is effective in delivering good decisions. This is a matter of group composition, which should be a major area of future research.

Differential Influence Within Groups

All groups are internally differentiated. Differentiation can be in terms of general or specific roles that can sometimes be associated with socio-demographic category membership (e.g., Levine & Moreland, 1994; Ridgeway, 2001), nested and cross-cutting categories (e.g., Crisp, Ensari, Hewstone, & Miller, 2003), or members' membership credentials or membership centrality or prototypicality (e.g., Hogg & Hornsey, in press; Wenzel, Mummendey, Weber, & Waldzus, 2003). Associated with structural differentiation is differential influence over the group and its members—some positions within the group are more influential than others in determining what is normative or prototypical of group membership, and what membership means. The vehicle for this influence is communication—usually via talk.

Leadership

One the most fundamental differentiations within groups is into leader(s) and followers, where leadership can be defined as the ability to transform individual action into group action by influencing others to embrace as their own, and exert effort on behalf of and in pursuit of, new values, attitudes, goals, and behaviors. For the social identity analysis of leadership (Hogg, 2001; Hogg & van Knippenberg, 2003; van Knippenberg & Hogg, 2003), the core idea is that as group membership becomes increasingly salient, members pay more attention to prototypicality and endorse prototypical leaders more strongly than nonprototypical leaders. Prototypicality is a significant basis for effective leadership in high salience groups. This idea is supported empirically by a number of studies that manipulate leader prototypicality and followers' social identity salience or strength of identification (e.g., Hogg, Hains, & Mason, 1998).

Prototypicality facilitates leadership via a number of processes. Group behavior conforms to the prototype, and thus, prototypical members are the focus of conformity within the group—follower behavior automatically conforms to their behavior. Prototypical members are the focus of consensual prototype-based depersonalized social attraction—they are "popular" and, thus, not only able to gain compliance with their wishes, but they appear to occupy a higher status position within the group than less prototypical members. Prototypical members are figural against the background of the group, and thus, their behavior is more likely to be dispositionally attributed so that they are seen to have a personality that suits them to effective leadership. Prototypical members often identify more highly with the group than do others, and as such, they tend automatically to behave in more group-oriented and group-serving ways. These behaviors, that benefit the group as a whole and generate trust in the leader not to do things that will harm the group, cause followers to allow the leader to be innovative and to trust the leader to take the group in beneficial directions. If, however, innovation causes followers to see the leader as less prototypical and less identified with the group, then the leadership magic of prototype-based trust disappears.

Communication is central to prototype-based leadership—indeed to leadership in general. If prototypicality is a powerful basis of effective leadership in salient groups, then leaders need to be able to manage their prototypicality—they need to communicate their own image of their prototypicality to their followers (e.g., Reid & Ng, 2000) through what we have called "norm talk." Leaders can manipulate their prototypicality in many ways. They can talk up their own prototypicality or talk down aspects of their own behavior that are nonprototypical. They can identify deviants or marginal members in such a way as to highlight their own prototypicality or to construct a particular prototype for the group that enhances their own prototypicality. They can secure their own leadership position by vilifying contenders for leadership and casting the latter as nonprototypical. They can identify as relevant comparison outgroups those outgroups that are most favorable to their own prototypicality—that is, they can manipulate the social comparative frame and, thus, the prototype and their own prototypicality. They can engage in a discourse that raises or lowers salience. If one is highly prototypical, then raising salience will provide one with the leadership benefits of high prototypicality; if one is not very prototypical, then lowering salience will protect one from the leadership pitfalls of not being very prototypical.

Research by Reicher and Hopkins (1996, 2001) on the rhetoric used by political leaders shows that such leaders are particularly prone to accentuate the existing ingroup prototype, pillory ingroup deviants, and demonize an appropriate outgroup. Furthermore, the very act of employing these powerful rhetorical devices is often viewed as convincing evidence of effective leadership. Reicher and Hopkins proposed that leaders are in this sense "entrepreneurs of identity"—and we might add that they are experts in norm management through talk. Effective organizational leadership often rests on norm management through talk (e.g., Gardner, Paulsen, Gallois, Callan, & Monaghan, 2001).

Prototypicality management through talk is also central to the way that leaders of social movements can politicize members and mobilize them to engage in social action (Reid & Ng, 1999). The central problematic of mobilization is that although members might subscribe strongly to group normative attitudes (e.g., anti-whaling), there are many barriers to translating such attitudes into behavior (e.g., protest)—among other things social action carries personal risk (e.g., Klandermans, 1997; Reicher, 2001; Stürmer & Simon, in press). Prototypical leaders are effective mobilizers probably because they reduce self-conceptual and normative uncertainty, and because followers trust them and are therefore prepared to take risks on their behalf (e.g., Hogg, in press a; Tyler, 1997).

Other social identity research on leadership suggests that high and low prototypical leaders of high salience groups need to behave differently to manage their prototypicality. For example, Rabbie and Bekkers (1978) show that leaders whose position is insecure are more likely to seek conflict with other groups. More generally, leaders who feel they are not, or are no longer, prototypical might strategically engage in a range of group-oriented behaviors to strengthen their membership credentials (e.g., Platow & van Knippenberg, 2001).

The leadership behavior of low and high prototypical leaders can differ because they are differently positioned within the group, such that highly prototypical leaders do not need to establish their prototype-based leadership credentials as much as do less prototypical leaders. Highly prototypical leaders' membership credentials are not called into question, and so they do not need to behave in ways that either demonstrate prototypicality or confirm membership. They are trusted by the group to be doing the best for the group, because, after all, they are central members themselves and what benefits the group must benefit them. They can be innovative and creative, and ironically can actually behave in relatively nonprototypical ways (cf. Hollander's, 1958, notion of idiosyncrasy credits). As long as they are trusted and viewed as highly identified members, they are permitted a wide latitude of behavior. Of course, behaviors that are clearly not in the group's best interest will shatter trust and diminish perceived prototypicality and commitment. This is where norm talk comes into play—the rhetoric of justification of actions as being in the group's best interest and reflecting the essential identity of the group.

In contrast, low prototypical leaders' membership credentials are not established and might be called into question. They, therefore, need to be much more careful to behave overtly in ways that confirm their prototypicality, and establish that they are good, loyal, and valid group members. Low prototypical leaders need to behave highly prototypically—they need to conform, engage in prototypicality talk and behavior, show greater outgroup derogation and ingroup loyalty, and display greater ingroup procedural justice.

Deviance

The flip side of leadership is deviance (e.g., Abrams, Hogg, & Marques, in press). The social identity analysis of deviance (e.g., Hogg, Fielding, & Darley, in press; Marques, Abrams, Páez, & Hogg, 2001) rests on the premise that deviant members are people who are not very prototypical and, therefore, they are not liked as group members (social attraction) or trusted as much as more prototypical members. In this respect, deviants have less influence over the group than do other members, in particular more central members (e.g., leaders).

Marques and colleagues (e.g., Marques & Páez, 1994) describe how, in high-salience groups, low prototypical ingroup members are marginalized and evaluatively downgraded. In particular, they showed that a person located on an intergroup boundary was evaluated more negatively if he or she were an ingroup member (i.e., a "black sheep") than an outgroup member. This analysis has been elaborated into the wider theory of subjective group dynamics (e.g., Abrams, Marques, Bown, & Henson, 2000; Marques, Abrams, Páez, et al., 2001) which argues that rejection of members who deviate from the group prototype occurs if and because such members threaten the integrity of group norms.

Hogg, Fielding, and Darley (in press; also see Fielding, Hogg, & Annandale, submitted) have suggested that how ingroup deviants are treated depends on two factors: (a) whether the deviant holds a prototypical position that borders the outgroup (a borderline, or negative, deviant) or is remote from the outgroup (an extremist, or positive deviant) and (b) whether the group's dominant motivation in the situation is for positive social identity or for uncertainty reduction and enhanced entitativity. As group membership becomes more salient, a borderline member is increasingly marginalized and evaluatively downgraded under conditions that threaten either the valence or entitativity of the group. Borderline or negative deviants compromise both the valence and entitativity of the group because they muddy group boundaries and lean toward the relatively less favorably evaluated outgroup prototype. Therefore, threats to group valence or entitativity lead to marginalization of borderline deviants. In contrast, although extremists (positive deviants) muddy the group's boundary, they lean away from the outgroup prototype. This means that although under entitativity threat they will be marginalized like border-lines, under valence threat they will be less marginalized and might even be celebrated as they contribute positively to group valence.

Marques's work, and associated research, does not incorporate an analysis of communication processes that might be the vehicle for marginalization or the justification of marginalization. However, Fielding's work does explicitly build in a communication component that has attracted some preliminary support (Fielding et al., submitted). Fielding and associates argue that the treatment of prototypically marginal members might rest on how these people explain their borderline/negative or extreme/positive position. Specifically, positive deviants who publicly attribute their positive deviance to the actions of the group (modesty), and thus allow the group to own their contribution to the group's positive valence, will be favorably treated and embraced by the group as "one of us." Those who publicly take personal responsibility and deny that the group had anything to do with their positive deviance (self-aggrandizement), do not allow the group to own their contribution to the group's positive valence and will be marginalized by the group. For negative deviants, the opposite is the case. If they take personal responsibility for their borderline position (self-blame) the group might have some sympathy and attempt to re-socialize them. If they do not take personal responsibility (but, rather, blame the group), they will certainly be marginalized.

The communication and language component of this analysis needs further elaboration and empirical investigation. We might be able to learn from one area of social identity research on deviance that does integrate language and communication data to some extent. This is work by Emler and Reicher (1995) on adolescent delinquency. For Emler and Reicher, delinquency is reputation management. It is a matter of constructing a distinctive deviant identity that casts one as a deviant in society's eyes, but attracts some respect from one's peer group—as such, delinquency helps resolve adolescent identity problems for scholastic underachievers, particularly boys. The thing about delinquency is that it has to be publicly communicated for it to attract attention and serve its social identity function—if no one knows that you are a delinquent, then that identity is not validated. This communication can take many forms, ranging from types of dress to boasting and telling tales of one's escapades.

Another aspect of deviance that is ripe for a systematic communication analysis is criticism. Research by Hornsey and his associates on the intergroup sensitivity effect reveals that people are more tolerant of criticism of group norms and practices if such criticism comes from an ingroup, rather than an outgroup, member (e.g., Hornsey & Imani, 2004; Hornsey, Oppes, & Svensson, 2002). Internal criticism can even be encouraged and can act as a basis for normative change. In contrast, outgroup criticism spawns defensiveness, and can enhance intergroup polarization and conflict.

Initially this appears to conflict with the research on deviance discussed earlier—non-normative (deviant) information and behavior is better tolerated within groups if it comes from an outgroup member (Marques, Abrams, & Serôdio, 2001; Phillips, 2001). Violation of norms and criticism of normative practices can, however, be quite different phenomena. The former conveys that one is not a group member or that one is marginal or does not wish to belong. The latter, if it comes from outside the group, conveys a deliberate attempt to discredit the group and all that it stands for. If it comes from inside the group, particularly from prototypical members (cf. leadership discussion above), it might be viewed more positively as a constructive attempt to improve the group.

Schism and Minority Influence

Deviants do not have to be lone or disparate individuals. Quite often a group can contain a deviant minority subgroup or some other collective that represents a schism in the overall group's normative structure. The idea of schism is usually associated with profound attitudinal and value differences within ideological groups such as religions, cults, political parties, artistic movements, scientific doctrines, schools of thought, and so forth (e.g., Liebman, Sutton, & Wuthnow, 1988).

In their analysis of schisms, Sani and Reicher (1998, 1999) describe the way that identity threat, self-conceptual uncertainty, and a sense of self-conceptual impermanence and instability can arise in groups whose prototypical or normative properties are suddenly changed. The change can be brought about by the actions of a subgroup or a leadership clique. Members feel that the group is no longer what it used to be—its normative attitudes, values, perceptions, and behaviors have uncompromisingly changed. The prototype has changed, and, thus, the group's identity has changed.

Those who are taken off guard by this change suddenly feel acutely uncertain about how, and whether, they fit into the new group. Under these circumstances members can try to re-establish the group's original identity through discussion, persuasion, and negotiation, or they can split into a separate subgroup that is in conflict with the rest of the group. A split, or schism, is most likely to occur if members feel the group is intolerant of dissent, unable to embrace diverse views, and inclined toward marginalization of dissenting individuals. A schism effectively transforms one group, a single category, into two separate groups that are engaged in often highly charged intergroup conflict. The split rests on a profound social identity threat that engages a powerful drive to reduce the acute self-conceptual uncertainty that has been aroused. Not surprisingly schisms can sometimes be very destructive of groups—for example, factional conflicts within political ideologies (e.g., Stalinists vs. Trotskyites within the Communist Party), and interpretational differences within religions (e.g., Sunnis vs. Shi'ites within Islam).

Where a schism exists, the subgroup that holds the minority position might paradoxically stand a chance of winning over the rest of the group and reinstating a degree of normative consensus. This can happen if the minority's position is novel, the minority can lay some claim to being a bona fide part of the larger ingroup, and the minority adopts a consistent yet flexible style of social influence and persuasion (e.g., Mugny, 1982; Nemeth, 1986). Indeed, although schisms are often highly destructive, the fact that they can spur critical thinking, creativity and innovation might, if properly managed, enhance the larger group (e.g., Nemeth & Owens, 1996; Nemeth & Staw, 1989).

Conclusion

Where people define themselves in terms of group membership (social identity), group norms become a key influence on perception, cognition, and behavior. What people say and do is largely oriented by relevant norms. In these contexts communication influences norms and is influenced by norms—people engage in "norm talk."

In this chapter, we overviewed the social identity perspective, showing that it is an intergroup perspective because it attributes a key role to the outgroup in both inter- and intragroup processes and that it is equally applicable to large-scale social categories as small interactive groups. Although norms are central to social identity processes, and the dynamics of norm formation, maintenance, and change rest on communication, the social identity approach has not gone as far as it could in incorporating a communication analysis.

We discuss a number of areas with significant potential for development of a social identity and interpersonal communication analysis of the role of norms. These include small group decision-making and differential influence within groups. Much of what goes on in small decision-making groups is communication to recognize, establish, maintain, or change the group's normative position—and this is particularly the case when the task is judgmental rather than intellective. Although opinion diversity (unshared information) can actually improve decision-making, groups tend to be overwhelmed by consensus (shared information). Leaders, as highly prototypical group members, play a pivotal role in group influence—a role that rests on the fact that they are normative and are, thus, paradoxically, trusted to be doing the right thing for the group even when they violate, criticize, or redefine the group norm. Marginal members, or deviants, have a much harder time directly influencing group norms. However, they play a role in defining what is not normative and, under some circumstances, they can influence the group through minority influence or by being part of an ideological schism within the group.

A research agenda for the future might rest on collaboration between social psychologists, communication scholars, and, perhaps, political and organizational scientists. The task would be to focus on exactly what is communicated (verbally, nonverbally, through talk and text), and how it is influenced by and, in turn, influences group norms and prototypes and associated group memberships and social identity. For example, just how much nonprototypical talk by a highly prototypical member will a group be influenced by before the speaker's membership credentials are called into question? Communication would be a dependent variable affected by social identity processes, but also an independent variable that influences social identity processes, prototypicality, and norm construction.

References
Abrams, D., & Hogg, M. A. (1990). Social identification, self-categorization and social influence. *European Review of Social Psychology, 1*, 195–228.

Abrams, D., Hogg, M. A., & Marques, J. (Eds.). (in press). *The social psychology of inclusion and exclusion*. Philadelphia, PA: Psychology Press.

Abrams, D., Marques, J. M., Bown, N. J., & Henson, M. (2000). Pro-norm and anti-norm deviance within in-groups and out-groups. *Journal of Personality and Social Psychology, 78*, 906–912.

Abrams, D., Wetherell, M. S., Cochrane, S., Hogg, M. A., & Turner, J. C. (1990). Knowing what to think by knowing who you are: Self-categorization and the nature of norm formation, conformity, and group polarization. *British Journal of Social Psychology, 29*, 97–119.

Berger, C. R., & Bradac, J. J. (1982). *Language and social knowledge*. London: Edward Arnold.

Bradac, J. J. (2001). Theory comparison: Uncertainty reduction, problematic integration, uncertainty management, and other curious constructs. *Journal of Communication, 51*, 456–476.

Clément, R. (1996). Social psychology and intergroup communication. *Journal of Language and Social Psychology, 15*, 222–229.

Crisp, R. J., Ensari, N., Hewstone, M., & Miller, N. (2003). A dual-route model of crossed categorization effects. In W. Stroebe & M. Hewstone (Eds.), *European Review of Social Psychology* (Vol. 13, pp. 35–74). New York: Psychology Press.

Davis, J. H. (1973). Group decisions and social interactions: A theory of social decision schemes. *Psychological Review, 80*, 97–125.

Ellemers, N. (1993). The influence of socio-structural variables on identity management strategies. *European Review of Social Psychology, 4*, 27–57.

Emler, N., & Reicher, S. D. (1995). *Adolescence and delinquency: The collective management of reputation*. Oxford: Blackwell.

Fielding, K. S., Hogg, M. A., & Annandale, N. (submitted). *The effects of personal and group attributions for success on evaluations of high achievers*.

Gardner, M. J., Paulsen, N., Gallois, C., Callan, V. J., & Monaghan, P. (2001). Communication in organizations: An intergroup perspective. In W. P. Robinson & H. Giles (Eds.), *The new handbook of language and social psychology* (pp. 561–584). Chichester, UK: Wiley.

Giles, H. (Ed.). (1996). Language, communication, and social psychology [Special issue]. *International Journal of Psychology, 12*(2).

Gudykunst, W. B. (1995). Anxiety/uncertainty management (AUM) theory: Current status. In R. L. Wiseman (Ed.), *Intercultural communication theory* (pp. 8–58). Thousand Oaks, CA: Sage.

Hamilton, D. L., & Sherman, S. J. (1996). Perceiving persons and groups. *Psychological Review, 103*, 336–355.

Hardin, C. D., & Higgins, E. T. (1996). Shared reality: How social verification makes the subjective objective. In R. M. Sorrentino & E. T. Higgins (Eds.) *Handbook of motivation and cognition* (Vol. 3, pp. 28–84). New York: Guilford.

Hinsz, V. B., Tindale, R. S., & Vollrath, D. A. (1997). The emerging conception of groups as information processors. *Psychological Bulletin, 121,* 43–64.

Hogg, M. A. (1993). Group cohesiveness: A critical review and some new directions. *European Review of Social Psychology, 4,* 85–111.

Hogg, M. A. (1996). Identity, cognition, and language in intergroup context. *Journal of Language and Social Psychology, 15,* 372–384.

Hogg, M. A. (2000). Subjective uncertainty reduction through self-categorization: A motivational theory of social identity processes. *European Review of Social Psychology, 11,* 223–255.

Hogg, M. A. (2001). A social identity theory of leadership. *Personality and Social Psychology Review, 5,* 184–200.

Hogg, M. A. (2003). Social identity. In M. R. Leary & J. P. Tangney (Eds.), *Handbook of self and identity* (pp. 462–479). New York: Guilford.

Hogg, M. A. (2004). Social identity, self-categorization, and communication in small groups. In S. H. Ng, C. N. Candlin, & C. Y. Chiu (Eds.), *Language matters: Communication, identity, and culture* (pp. 221–243). Hong Kong: City University of Hong Kong Press.

Hogg, M. A. (in press a). The social identity perspective. In S. A. Wheelan (Ed.), *Handbook of group research and practice.* Thousand Oaks, CA: Sage.

Hogg, M. A. (in press b). Social identity and the group context of trust: Managing risk and building trust through belonging. In M. Siegrist & H. Gutscher (Eds.), *Trust, technology, and society: Studies in cooperative risk management.* London: Earthscan.

Hogg, M. A., & Abrams, D. (1988). *Social identifications: A social psychology of intergroup relations and group processes.* London & New York: Routledge.

Hogg, M. A., & Abrams, D. (2003). Intergroup behavior and social identity. In M. A. Hogg & J. Cooper (Eds.), *The Sage handbook of social psychology* (pp. 407–431). London: Sage.

Hogg, M. A., Abrams, D., Otten, S., & Hinkle, S. (2004). The social identity perspective: Intergroup relations, self-conception, and small groups. *Small Group Research, 35,* 246–276.

Hogg, M. A., Fielding, K. S., & Darley, J. (in press). Deviance and marginalization. In D. Abrams, M. A. Hogg, & J. Marques (Eds.), *The social psychology of inclusion and exclusion.* New York: Psychology Press.

Hogg, M. A., Hains, S. C., & Mason, I. (1998). Identification and leadership in small groups: Salience, frame of reference, and leader stereotypicality effects on leader evaluations. *Journal of Personality and Social Psychology, 75,* 1248–1263.

Hogg, M. A., & Hornsey, M. J. (in press). Self-concept threat and differentiation within groups. In R. J. Crisp & M. Hewstone (Eds.), *Multiple social categorization: Processes, models, and applications.* New York: Psychology Press.

Hogg, M. A., & Tindale, R. S. (Eds.). (2001). *Blackwell handbook of social psychology: Group processes.* Oxford, UK: Blackwell.

Hogg, M. A., & van Knippenberg, D. (2003). Social identity and leadership processes in groups. In M. P. Zanna (Ed.), *Advances in experimental social psychology* (Vol. 35, pp. 1–52). San Diego, CA: Academic Press.

Hollander, E. P. (1958). Conformity, status, and idiosyncrasy credit. *Psychological Re-*

view, 65, 117–127.

Hornsey, M. J., & Imani, A. (2004). Criticizing groups from the inside and the outside: An identity perspective on the intergroup sensitivity effect. *Personality and Social Psychology Bulletin, 30,* 365–383.

Hornsey, M. J., Oppes, T., & Svensson, A. (2002). "It's OK if we say it, but you can't": Responses to intergroup and intragroup criticism. *European Journal of Social Psychology, 32,* 293–307.

Kameda, T., Tindale, R. S., & Davis, J. H. (2003). Cognitions, preferences, and social sharedness: Past, present and future directions in group decision-making. In S. L. Schneider & J. Shanteau (Eds.) *Emerging perspectives on judgment and decision research* (pp. 458–485). New York: Cambridge University Press.

Kashima, Y. (2000). Maintaining cultural stereotypes in the serial reproduction of narratives. *Personality and Social Psychology Bulletin, 26,* 594–604.

Kashima, Y. (2003). *Cultural dynamics of stereotypes: Grounding a social reality in symbolic communication.* Paper presented at the conference on Communication-Based Approaches to Stereotype Research, Heidelberg, Germany.

Kerr, N. (1981). Social transition schemes: Charting the group's road to agreement. *Journal of Personality and Social Psychology, 41,* 684–702.

Klandermans, B. (1997). *The social psychology of protest.* Oxford: Blackwell.

Larson, J. R. Jr., Foster-Fishman, P. G., & Keys, C. B. (1994). Discussion of shared and unshared information in decision-making groups. *Journal of Personality and Social Psychology, 67,* 446–461.

Laughlin, P. R. (1980). Social combination processes of cooperative problem-solving groups on verbal intellective tasks. In M. Fishbein (Ed.), *Progress in social psychology* (pp. 127–155). Hillsdale, NJ: Erlbaum.

Laughlin, P. R., & Ellis, A. L. (1986). Demonstrability and social combination processes on mathematical intellective tasks. *Journal of Experimental Social Psychology, 22,* 177–189.

Levine, J. M., & Moreland, R. L. (1994). Group socialization: Theory and research. *European Review of Social Psychology, 5,* 305–336.

Liebman, R. C., Sutton, J. R., & Wuthnow, R. (1988). Exploring the social sources of denominationalism: Schisms in American Protestant denominations, 1890–1980. *American Sociological Review, 53,* 343–352.

Mackie, D. M. (1986). Social identification effects in group polarization. *Journal of Personality and Social Psychology, 50,* 720–728.

Marques, J. M., Abrams, D., Páez, D., & Hogg, M. A. (2001). Social categorization, social identification, and rejection of deviant group members. In M. A. Hogg & R. S. Tindale (Eds.), *Blackwell handbook of social psychology: Group processes* (pp. 400–424). Oxford: Blackwell.

Marques, J. M., Abrams, D., & Serôdio, R. (2001). Being better by being right: Subjective group dynamics and derogation of in-group deviants when generic norms are undermined. *Journal of Personality and Social Psychology, 81,* 436–447.

Marques, J. M., & Páez, D. (1994). The "black sheep effect": Social categorization, rejection of ingroup deviates and perception of group variability. *European Review of Social Psychology, 5,* 37–68.

Mugny, G. (1982). *The power of minorities.* London: Academic Press.

Nemeth, C. (1986). Differential contributions of majority and minority influence. *Psychological Review, 93,* 23–32.

Nemeth, C., & Owens, P. (1996). Making work groups more effective: The value of minority dissent. In M. A. West (Ed.), *The handbook of workgroup psychology* (pp. 125–141). Chichester, UK: Wiley.

Nemeth, C., & Staw, B. M. (1989). The tradeoffs of social control and innovation in groups and organizations. In L. Berkowitz (Ed.), *Advances in experimental social psychology* (Vol. 22, pp. 175–210). San Diego, CA: Academic Press.

Ng, S. H. (2001). Influencing through the power of language. In J. P. Forgas & K. D. Williams (Eds.), *Social influence: Direct and indirect processes* (pp. 185–197). Philadelphia, PA: Psychology Press.

Noels, K. A., Giles, H., & Le Poire, B. (2003). Language and communication processes. In M. A. Hogg & J. Cooper (Eds.), *The Sage handbook of social psychology* (pp. 232–257). London: Sage.

Phillips, K. W. (2001). *The effects of categorically based expectations on minority influence: The importance of congruence.* Working paper, Northwestern University, Kellogg School of Management.

Platow, M. J., & van Knippenberg, D. (2001). A social identity analysis of leadership endorsement: The effects of leader ingroup prototypicality and distributive intergroup fairness. *Personality and Social Psychology Bulletin, 27,* 1508–1519.

Poole, M. S., & Hollingshead, A. B. (Eds.). (in press). *Theories of small groups: An interdisciplinary perspective.* Thousand Oaks, CA: Sage.

Postmes, T., Spears, R., & Cihangir, S. (2001). Quality of decision-making and group norms. *Journal of Personality and Social Psychology, 80,* 918–930.

Postmes, T., Spears, R., & Lea, M. (1998). Breaching or building social boundaries? SIDE-effects of computer-mediated communication. *Communication Research, 25,* 689–715.

Rabbie, J. M., & Bekkers, F. (1978). Threatened leadership and intergroup competition. *European Journal of Social Psychology, 8,* 9–20.

Reicher, S. D. (2001). The psychology of crowd dynamics. In M. A. Hogg & R. S. Tindale (Eds.), *Blackwell handbook of social psychology: Group processes* (pp. 182–207). Oxford: Blackwell.

Reicher, S. D., & Hopkins, N. (1996). Self-category constructions in political rhetoric: An analysis of Thatcher's and Kinnock's speeches concerning the British miners' strike (1984–1985). *European Journal of Social Psychology, 26,* 353–371.

Reicher, S. D., & Hopkins, N. (2001). *Self and nation.* London: Sage.

Reicher, S. D., Spears, R., & Postmes, T. (1995). A social identity model of deindividuation phenomena. *European Review of Social Psychology, 6,* 161–198.

Reid, S. A., & Ng, S. H. (1999). Language, power and intergroup relations. *Journal of Social Issues, 55,* 119–139.

Reid, S. A., & Ng, S. H. (2000). Conversation as a resource for influence: Evidence for prototypical arguments and social identification processes. *European Journal of Social Psychology, 30,* 83–100.

Ridgeway, C. L. (2001). Social status and group structure. In M. A. Hogg & R. S. Tindale (Eds.), *Blackwell handbook of social psychology: Group processes* (pp. 352–375). Oxford, UK: Blackwell.

Rosnow, R. L. (1980). Psychology of rumor reconsidered. *Psychological Bulletin, 87,* 578–591.

Sani, F., & Reicher, S. D. (1998). When consensus fails: An analysis of the schism within the Italian Communist Party (1991). *European Journal of Social Psychology, 28,* 623–645.

Sani, F., & Reicher, S. D. (1999). Identity, argument and schisms: Two longitudinal studies of the split in the Church of England over the ordination of women to the priesthood. *Group Processes and Intergroup Relations, 2,* 279–300.

Stasser, G., & Birchmeier, Z. (2003). Group creativity and collective choice. In P. Paulus & B. Nijstadt (Eds.), *Group creativity: Innovation through collaboration* (pp. 85–109). Oxford: Oxford University Press.

Stasser, G., Stewart, D. D., & Wittenbaum, G. M. (1995). Expert roles and information exchange during discussion: The importance of knowing who knows what. *Journal of Experimental Social Psychology, 31,* 244–265.

Stasser, G., & Titus, W. (1985). Pooling of unshared information in group decision-making: Biased information sampling during discussion. *Journal of Personality and Social Psychology, 48,* 1467–1478.

Stasser, G., & Titus, W. (1987). Effects of information load and percentage of shared information on the dissemination of unshared information during group discussion. *Journal of Personality and Social Psychology, 53,* 81–93.

Stürmer, S., & Simon, B. (in press). Collective action: Towards a dual-pathway model. *European Review of Social Psychology.*

Tajfel, H., & Turner, J. C. (1986). The social identity theory of intergroup behavior. In S. Worchel & W. Austin (Eds.), *Psychology of intergroup relations* (pp. 7–24). Chicago: Nelson-Hall.

Tindale, R. S., & Kameda, T. (2000). Social sharedness as a unifying theme for information processing in groups. *Group Processes and Intergroup Relations, 3,* 123–140.

Tindale, R. S., Meisenhelder, H. M., Dykema-Engblade, A. A., & Hogg, M. A. (2001). Shared cognitions in small groups. In M. A. Hogg & R. S. Tindale (Eds.), *Blackwell handbook in social psychology: Group processes* (pp. 1–30). Oxford: Blackwell Publishers.

Tindale, R. S., Smith, C. M., Thomas, L. S., Filkins, J., & Sheffey, S. (1996). Shared representations and asymmetric social influence processes in small groups. In E. Witte & J. Davis (Eds.), *Understanding group behavior: Consensual action by small groups* (Vol. 1, pp. 81–103). Mahwah, NJ: Erlbaum.

Turner, J. C. (1991). *Social influence.* Milton Keynes, UK: Open University Press.

Turner, J. C., Hogg, M. A., Oakes, P. J., Reicher, S. D., & Wetherell, M. S. (1987). *Rediscovering the social group: A self-categorization theory.* Oxford, UK: Blackwell.

Turner, J. C., & Oakes, P. J. (1989). Self-categorization and social influence. In P. B. Paulus (Ed.), *The psychology of group influence* (2nd ed., pp. 233–275). Hillsdale, NJ: Erlbaum.

Tyler, T. R. (1997). The psychology of legitimacy: A relational perspective on voluntary deference to authorities. *Personality and Social Psychology Review, 1,* 323–345.

van Knippenberg, D., & Hogg, M. A. (2003). A social identity model of leadership in organizations. In R. M. Kramer & M. Staw (Eds.), *Research in organizational behavior* (Vol. 25, pp. 243–295). Greenwich, CT: JAI Press.

Wenzel, M., Mummendey, A., Weber, U., & Waldzus, S. (2003). The ingroup as pars pro toto: Projection from the ingroup onto the inclusive category as a precursor to social discrimination. *Personality and Social Psychology Bulletin, 29,* 561–473.

Wheelan, S. A. (Ed.). (in press). *Handbook of group research and practice.* Thousand Oaks, CA: Sage.

Wittenbaum, G. M., Hubbell, A., & Zuckerman, C. (1999). Mutual enhancement: Toward an understanding of the collective preference for shared information. *Journal of Personality and Social Psychology, 77,* 967–978.

8

Organizations as Intergroup Contexts: Communication, Discourse, and Identification

Neil Paulsen
Phil Graham
Elizabeth Jones
Victor J. Callan
Cindy Gallois

Research that focuses on the identification of employees with their employing organization has a long tradition. Over the last decade or more, major advances in this area have derived their impetus from social identity theory (SIT, Abrams & Hogg, 1990; Hogg & Terry, 2000; Tajfel & Turner, 1979, 1986). SIT provides a robust framework for examining employee identification in organizations, and for an intergroup perspective on employee and organizational outcomes (Haslam, 2004). While research that adopts this perspective in organizational contexts is on the increase, work that examines organizational *communication* processes from an intergroup perspective is limited (Gardner, Paulsen, Gallois, Callan, & Monaghan, 2001).

In this chapter, we briefly review the application of SIT to organizational contexts and suggest areas of organizational communication research in which an intergroup perspective can potentially contribute. Further, we maintain that alternative approaches for theorizing the formation of groups and group identities, such as discourse theory, are relatively less developed in organizational contexts. We outline the complementarities between SIT and critical discourse analysis (CDA) for more successful and comprehensive investigation of identity, identification, and intergroup communication in organizational studies. SIT and CDA offer perspectives on organizational communication that combine the delicate qualitative linguistic depth of CDA with the rigorous quantitative methods developed in SIT for comprehending the significance of "multimodal" meaning choices typically made by people from different social groups.

Organizations as Dynamic Intergroup Contexts

Individuals in organizations relate to and communicate with one another in an essentially intergroup context. While structural and functional arrangements are designed to achieve organizational goals, such arrangements also set the boundaries for a highly differentiated social system (Scott, 1998; Trice & Beyer, 1993). As Hogg and Terry (2000) suggest, organizations are "internally structured groups that are located in complex networks of intergroup relations characterized by power, status, and prestige differentials" (p. 123). Within such a system, individuals are differentiated from each other through membership of departments, work units or teams, ranks or levels of management, or specialized roles with specific skill sets. While such groups often represent different and competing interests, they nevertheless help employees to define themselves and their social relationships within the organization. Within this social milieu, issues related to control, power and influence, status, competition for scarce resources, and contested group boundaries are inevitably present.

Within the interdependent nature of organizational arrangements, organizational actors do not simply act as individuals but also as members of the organizational groups to which they belong (Paulsen, 2003). Kramer (1991) conceptualizes the individual in organizations "not as an independent or socially isolated decision maker, but rather as a *social* actor embedded in a complex network of intra- and intergroup relationships" (p. 195). Individuals in organizations relate to one another as members of groups, and interpersonal communication encounters are, thus, in most cases, intergroup encounters (Gallois, Giles, Jones, Cargile, & Ota, 1995). Consequently, the behavior of individuals can be understood in the context of relevant group memberships, the system within which groups are embedded, the power relations that exist between groups, and the permeability of the boundaries that define group memberships (Alderfer, 1987).

A number of changes within contemporary organizations highlight the importance of intergroup processes. As organizations move toward organic or network structures with an increased reliance on taskforces and cross-functional project teams, the importance of groups and intergroup communication in organizations has never been more apparent. Intergroup activity increases as individuals are required to "represent their own group to other groups or must interact as a group with others in order to achieve goals" (Hartley, 1996, p. 398). Furthermore, organizational capabilities are increasingly developed through intensely social and communicative processes, and these may not be directly tied to physical resources or locations (Galunic & Eisenhardt, 2001; Panteli, 2003; Wiesenfeld, Raghuram, & Garud, 2001). In addition, the increased diversity within organizations means that communication must occur across age, cultural, and professional boundaries (Nkomo & Cox, 1996). In the context of strategic alliances, strategic positioning within industries, and joint ventures or partnerships, intergroup issues arise at the organizational level (Swaminathan, 2001; von Corswant, Dubois, & Fredriksson, 2003). In the international business context, interorganizational relations can become more complex as cultural identities become salient. In fact, it is hard to imagine the contemporary organization as anything other than a context in which organizing and communication processes are essentially intergroup in nature.

Social Identity Theory and Organizations

The construct of identification is not new to the organizational literature (e.g., Foote, 1951; Tolman, 1943). Notions of employee involvement and loyalty to the organization are prominent in many formulations (e.g., the cosmopolitan-local construct developed by Gouldner, 1957). Simon (1947) included a chapter examining the implications of identification (defined as organizational loyalty) for employee decision-making (see also March & Simon, 1958). Other studies were informed by Kelman's (1958) influence theory. For example, in an extensive study of the Tennessee Valley Authority, Patchen (1970) conceptualized organizational identification as a multifaceted construct, involving loyalty, solidarity, and perceived similarity with the organization. The study examined various antecedents of identification and entertained the notion of employee identification with subunits of the organization.

Other studies examined the conditions that encourage employee identification (Brown, 1969), creativity and targets of identification (Rotondi, 1975a, 1975b), socialization (Schein, 1968), and tenure (Hall & Schneider, 1972; Hall, Schneider, & Nygren, 1970; Schneider, Hall, & Nygren, 1971). Cheney (1983a) provides a detailed list of studies that link identification constructs to a range of organizational concerns and employee outcomes. These works presume that employee identification leads to a range of benefits such as commitment to organizational goals and their achievement, quality of performance, and job satisfaction. This line of investigation did not continue at the same pace in the following years. However, given that conceptualizations of the identification construct included employee acceptance of the values and goals of the organization (e.g., Schneider et al., 1971), it is not surprising to find these researchers pursuing lines of research in organizational culture, including service culture (Schein, 1991; Schneider, 1990; Schneider, Gunnarson, & Niles Jolly, 1994).

In North America, scholarship in organizational identity constructs revived when Albert and Whetten (1985) and Ashforth and Mael (1989) published their seminal papers, although Brown and his colleagues were already developing applications of SIT in organizational contexts (e.g., Brown, 1978; Brown, Condor, Mathews, Wade, & Williams, 1986; Oaker & Brown, 1986). Since then, SIT has been used to theorize many aspects of organizational life (Whetten & Godfrey, 1998) and has been applied as an explanatory framework for a range of different employee and organizational outcomes (Haslam, 2004). A corpus of research is now emerging, and the field remains open to fruitful areas of research (Albert, Ashforth, & Dutton, 2000; Hogg & Terry, 2000, 2001).

Details of the history and development of SIT and its key tenets can be found in a number of sources (this volume, Hogg & Abrams, 1999; Hogg & Williams, 2000; Robinson, 1996; Turner, 1999). The core of SIT can be summarized as: a) individuals are motivated to achieve or maintain positive self-esteem; b) individuals' self esteem is based partly on their social identity derived from group memberships; and c) the quest for a positive social identity enhances the need for positive evaluations of the ingroup relative to relevant outgroups. For these assumptions to hold, identification with a group must occur. The relevance or salience of particular group memberships will vary across social contexts (adapted from van Dick, 2001).

Through categorization processes, individuals identify themselves as members of particular groups, and as nonmembers of others, and group identification occurs as this process becomes self-referential (Pratt, 1998). Tyler and Blader (2001) favor a definition of identification that emphasizes the "cognitive intermingling of self and group" (p. 211). At the level of social categorization, individuals identify themselves *as* members of one group or another. It is the affective dimension or attachment to that group that defines an individual's strength of identification *with* that group (van Dick, 2001). Hence, at one level, an individual might see herself or himself as a member of a group or category, but the importance of that membership can vary from individual to individual. Furthermore, it is the contextual salience of that group membership that is likely to trigger perceptions and behavior that favor the group. Organizations and the subgroups within them can become sources of employee identification (Ashforth & Mael, 1989; Dutton, Dukerich, & Harquail, 1994; Paulsen, 2003). In other words, organizational identification is a specific form of social identification. As a means of focusing attention on intergroup contexts, we outline research that examines sources of identification in organizations, and research that focuses on organizational *communication* issues.

Sources of Identification in Organizational Contexts

Individuals in organizations can access a range of possible sources of identification. Kramer (1991) represents the individual self at different levels of categorization, which are similar to, and adapted from, the levels of self-definition described by Turner et al. (1987, p. 45). At the interpersonal level, individuals differentiate themselves from others at the level of personal identity—a self-conception based on those attributes that establish individual uniqueness. At the intergroup level, individuals perceive themselves (and others) as members of particular categories (groups or subgroups) within the organization. Attributes that are common to members of one group serve to identify them as a group, but also help to distinguish them from members of other groups.

In a recent review, van Dick (2001) identifies a number of primary sources of identification for employees. The work of a number of researchers (e.g., Ellemers, de Gilder, & van den Heuvel, 1998; Roccas,

2003; Roccas & Brewer, 2002; van Knippenberg & van Schie, 2000) suggests that employees can feel attached to different work-related entities at the same time (e.g., career, work unit or team, the organization as a whole, occupational or professional group), and Morgan et al. (2004) report evidence of the influence of extra-organizational sources of employee identification. It is the salience of the source of identification in a particular social context that is likely to trigger group-related perceptions and behavior, including communication.

Researchers have investigated the role of professional group (and subgroup) identity in the nursing profession (Millward, 1995; Oaker & Brown, 1986; Skevington, 1981; van Knippenberg & van Oers, 1984) and in journalism (Russo, 1998). Studies have investigated the relationship between professional identity at work and the proportional representation of women in senior management (Ely, 1994), and the role of occupational (or professional) identification in moderating the relationship between work assignment and organizational commitment (Witt, 1993). Once again, salience is a critical issue. In some contexts, professional identity rather than the work unit or team can be the primary target of identity (Millward, 1995; Oaker & Brown, 1986; Skevington, 1981; van Knippenberg & van Oers, 1984). Research has also examined the impact of identification with multiple groups (Morgan et al., 2004; Roccas, 2003; Scott, 1997, 1999; Scott et al., 1999). The ways in which employees resolve the degree of overlap, congruence, or conflict between potentially competing identities is a rich source of future research.

In presenting a case for the primacy of intergroup level categorization in organizations, Kramer (1991) argues that most employees interact within and across primary organizational groups (usually work units). The interdependence of tasks, coupled with a preference among employees for proximal interaction reinforces the importance of this level of categorization (Ashforth & Mael, 1989). Research supports the assertion that the work unit is a primary target of identification (Barker & Tompkins, 1994; Lembke & Wilson, 1998; Shute, 1997; van Knippenberg & van Schie, 2000). Haslam (2001) argues that this is because: a) employees are "more likely to make comparisons between different work groups than between different organizations, and b) sub-organizational identities allow employees to feel that their in-group is in some way 'special' or distinct from others" (p. 110) (see also Mueller & Lawler, 1999). Individuals are more likely to identify with smaller groups (Brewer, 1991), are likely to have more in common with their work unit than the organization as a whole, and spend most of their organizational life in their work units or teams (van Knippenberg & van Schie, 2000). Furthermore, individuals in organizations are more likely to be approached as members of their work unit rather than as members of the organization, and to encounter members of other units rather than members of other organizations (although see research on boundary spanning activities Bartel, 2001; Cross, Yan, & Louis, 2000; Yan & Louis, 1999). van Knippenberg and van Schie (2000) found that employees in two separate organizations identified more strongly with their work unit than the organization as a whole and that work unit identification was a significant predictor of job satisfaction, job involvement, and intention to remain in the organization.

Three important observations arise from the research cited above. First, an understanding of the salience of particular categories is critical for assessing the influence of group identifications on employee outcomes and for an intergroup perspective on communication. For example, in one context, professional identifications can be particularly salient (e.g., in a hospital); in another context, identification with functional units might be the most salient source of identification (e.g., in a manufacturing environment). The impact of multiple group identifications in organizational contexts and their influence on communication processes is an underdeveloped area of research. Such a focus provides great possibilities for the development of new insights into the effectiveness of communication processes in organizations, such as supervisor-subordinate communication, communication in and between groups and teams, as well as the communication of organizational change. The challenge for researchers examining organizational communication is to ascertain those groups that are salient to employees, and to assess the group boundaries that effective communication must cross.

Second, one of the striking features of the research conducted to date is the limited attention paid to intergroup perspectives in the context of organizational change. The work on organizational restructuring, mergers, and acquisitions is one exception (e.g., Jetten, O'Brien, & Trindall, 2002; Terry, 2001; Terry, Carey, & Callan, 2001;

Terry & O'Brien, 2001; van Knippenberg & van Leeuwen, 2001). Organizational life is characterized by change processes, including the introduction of new systems, mergers and acquisitions, takeovers, downsizing, or restructuring. As new structures and working arrangements are created, individuals are required to form new groups and teams, as well as different reporting lines or lines of authority. Such changes rearrange the existing order and the connections between units, modify the ways in which each unit is differentiated from others, and alter how individuals and groups relate to each other in the organization. As new groups form during the change process, one of the many challenges for employees in adjusting to the change is to renegotiate their identification with and within the new organization (Chreim, 2002). There is still little research that examines the impact of organizational change from an intergroup perspective and the extent to which employees who identify with different groups feel that details of change are communicated effectively to them (Lewis & Seibold, 1998). Again, an intergroup perspective that evaluates the impact of multiple and sometimes competing identities on the communication and implementation of organizational change shows great promise for further contributions to organizational studies (Hogg & Terry, 2001).

Third, it is worth noting that the research discussed above focuses primarily on the identification of employees *with* the organization. Other lines of research focus on the identity *of* the organization. Albert and Whetten (1985) conceptualized organizational identity as the enduring, central characteristics that distinguish an organization from others in the environment. The approach examines how organizations present an external identity to key stakeholders, and the mechanisms that shape the identities negotiated internally (see Bouchikhi et al., 1998). While the approach continues to produce interesting lines of research (e.g., Foreman & Whetten, 2002; Hatch & Schultz, 2002; Whetten & Mackey, 2002), it focuses primarily on the making of *organizational* identity as significant stakeholders might perceive it (Scott & Lane, 2000) rather than the making of *individual* identities. The processes of employee identification with salient groups and the ways in which individuals enact their identities both have major implications for an intergroup perspective on communication.

SIT and Intergroup Communication

A number of researchers have investigated organizational communication from an intergroup perspective. For instance, in a case involving strategic technological change in a service organization, Hutt, Walker, and Frankwick (1995) analyzed cross-functional barriers to change as an intergroup communication issue involving functional unit identification. In another line of research, Suzuki (1998) has demonstrated that workers' level of identification is related to the perceived adequacy of their communication with both their ingroup and outgroup. Researchers have investigated the role of communication and perceived social support in developing organizational identity among virtual workers (Wiesenfeld, Raghuram, & Garud, 1999; Wiesenfeld et al., 2001). Scott and his colleagues (1999) have investigated the role of communication perceptions and multiple identification targets on intent to leave the organization, concluding that identifications do influence turnover intent (see also Abrams, Ando, & Hinkle, 1998; Scott & Timmerman, 1999). While other studies have investigated the relationship between group identification and communication processes in organizations (Postmes, Tanis, & de Wit, 2001; Scott et al., 1999; Wiesenfeld et al., 1999), more work is needed to investigate this relationship.

If identification in the organization helps us explain organizational dynamics, then it is surprising that relatively few studies have conceptualized the role of organizational and group identification in organizational communication and change processes (Chreim, 2002). As we have argued elsewhere (Gardner et al., 2001), organizational communication research, in general, has not been driven by an integrated, multilevel theoretical framework that incorporates an intergroup level of analysis. The research instead focuses mainly on interpersonal and organizational levels of analysis. In the next section, we suggest a number of areas of organizational communication research that could benefit from a theoretical framework that adopts an intergroup perspective on organizational dynamics in order to focus research attention on communication at the intergroup level of analysis.

Areas for Further Research

An intergroup approach informed by SIT can provide insights into conflict management and communication difficulties in and between diverse and cross-functional teams (e.g., Lovelace, Shapiro, & Weingart, 2001) and can potentially contribute to effective strategies for maximizing the benefits of multidisciplinary and diverse teams. The role of intergroup dynamics in virtual teams and computer-mediated communication in groups is an open area of research, although the work of Lea, Spears and colleagues is one exception (e.g., Lea, Spears, & de Groot, 2001).

Applications of network theory to interorganizational communication have been developed (e.g., Taylor & Doerfel, 2003, on relationship building among non-governmental organizations). Strong ties to other organizations can mitigate the impact of uncertainty during change and promote adaptation by increasing communication and information sharing (Kraatz, 1998). Further, networks can enhance the social learning of adaptive responses rather than less productive forms of interorganizational imitation (Kenis & Knoke, 2002). However, these approaches do not consider the identification dynamics in interorganizational relationships and the influence of these on communication and information flow within networks. An intergroup perspective provides a different focus for this research effort.

New work arrangements such as the casualization of the workplace and the increased use of temporary employees can potentially change the psychological contract that employees have with an organization. The identification of *permanent* vs. *temporary* workers with their employing organization and their work units will influence employee attitudes, and this has implications for the study of communication and other organizational processes (Chattopadhyay & George, 2001; Garsten, 2003). Of further interest is the role of telecommuting and the boundary between home and work, particularly the degree to which individuals can differ in the ability to separate and effectively manage their identities as individuals and as organizational members (e.g., Nippert-Eng, 2003).

Knowledge processes in organizations are a major focus in organizational theory and practice (Alvesson, 2000, 2001). Research on the management and transfer of knowledge, and the role of technology and social networks in this process, can be theorized from an intergroup perspective. More research is required to examine the impact of employee identification on effective knowledge transfer. An organization's interaction with external stakeholders (Bhattacharya & Mitra,

1998) involves intergroup interactions. Similarly, interorganizational communication in strategic alliances, networks, and boundary spanning activities (e.g., Bartel, 2001) are intergroup phenomena and further research in these areas would benefit from an intergroup perspectives.

Our contention is that organizational research can benefit greatly from an increased focus on intergroup dynamics and the application of insights derived from perspectives such as SIT. Along with Singelis (1996), we foresee a robust future for the continued application of intergroup perspectives on organizational communication research (Gardner et al., 2001). Furthermore, we see the benefit of integrating alternative theories and methodologies with SIT to provide an enhanced understanding of intergroup dynamics in organizations. As one example of this, we explore the value of discourse theory for developing fresh insights into identities, identification, and intergroup communication.

Identities, Discourse, and Intergroup Communication
SIT provides a useful theoretical framework for improving our understanding of organizational communication from an intergroup perspective. However, it is essentially a theory of intergroup relations and not a communication theory *per se*. Singelis (1996) argues that research in intergroup communication needs greater consideration of context, an integration of levels of analysis, and an expansion of methodologies. While SIT can provide a useful framework for achieving these goals, communicative interaction is a complex and dynamic system that SIT cannot adequately address on its own. Consequently, it would be instructive to integrate SIT with insights derived from other communication theories and methodologies in order to better understand the dynamics of intergroup communication. Applications using an integrative framework such as communication accommodation theory are an example of this effort (e.g., Gardner & Jones, 1999).

As a cognitive approach, SIT generally conceives of collective identities in terms of shared conceptions of a group in the minds of group members. Another way to think about how groups represent their identities is to examine the ways in which group members represent themselves based on their talk, conversations, or production of texts (e.g., Morgan et al., 2004). Discursive approaches conceive of collective identity as a discursive object embodied in talk and other forms of text rather than as a cognitively-held belief (Hardy, Lawrence, & Grant, in press). Such approaches do not focus primarily on the attentions and attitudes of individuals, rather they focus on observable linguistic practices and the effects of these on social relationships and action (Ainsworth & Hardy, 2004). Collective identity is situated in the language in use among members rather than in a degree of convergence across the minds of individuals (Hardy et al., in press). A focus on the role of discourse in the construction of identities allows researchers to examine ways in which discourse frames intergroup communication. The role of language and discourse in identity construction has been well established, although applications of these perspectives to organizational contexts are more recent. The analysis of organizational discourse provides an avenue to investigate the construction of organizational identities and the interdependence of communication in organizational contexts (Grant, Keenoy, & Oswick, 1998).

As we have argued above, a significant amount of communication in organizations can be considered as intergroup communication. It is important to recognize that when individuals interact, they also interact as group members, and in so doing represent the interests of their groups. An examination of the language in use or the texts produced in the acts of communicating can reveal power and status relationships between groups, the extent to which group memberships frame the discourse between individuals and groups, and detect referents used in the construction of meanings. Communication is a reflexive process of meaning making that helps to define and redefine our experiences and the way we relate to one another. The ways in which people make meaning also define and delineate the multiple social domains or discourse communities that they both inhabit and produce (Graham & Paulsen, 2002). As a result, communication reflects, shapes, and reshapes our identities. The discourse we use and the discursive strategies we adopt are a clue to the ways in which we define our group memberships and ourselves.

In recent years, organizational scholars have begun to draw on discursive approaches for expanding the study of organizational identities and identification (Grant, Hardy, Oswick, & Putnam, 2004; Putnam & Fairhurst, 2001). The literature contains a wide diversity of discourse analytic approaches, and a number of reviews of the application of discursive processes to organizational contexts have been conducted (Alvesson & Kärreman, 2000; Fairhurst & Putnam, 2004; Grant et al., 2004; Iedema & Wodak, 1999; Putnam & Fairhurst, 2001). While discursive approaches to studying organizational identification have been developed (e.g., Ainsworth & Hardy, 2004; Cheney, 1983b; Fairhurst & Cooren, 2004; Fiol, 2002; Iedema, Degeling, Braithwaite, & White, 2004; Scott et al., 1999), there is relatively little research in the area that utilizes critical discourse analysis (CDA: Fairclough, 1995) in particular. In the next section, we examine the ways in which CDA can complement SIT approaches for the analysis of group identities and intergroup communication.

Critical Discourse Analysis as a
Tool for Social Identity Analysis

CDA is a sociolinguistic endeavor. For the most part, it has its foundations in anthropologically developed, functionalist theories of language. CDA has developed as an interdisciplinary approach for examining discourse within its historical, social, and political contexts. The primary focus in CDA is the interaction between "language/discourse/speech and social structure ... (and) in uncovering ways in which social structure impinges on discourse patterns ... in the form of power relations, ideological effects, and so forth" (Blommaert & Bulcaen, 2000, p. 449). CDA articulates a framework for the analysis of (spoken or written) language texts, analysis of discourse practice (processes of text production, distribution, and consumption), and analysis of discursive events as instances of sociocultural practice (Fairclough, 1995). At the heart of CDA is an assumption that human social organizations are constituted, coordinated, maintained, and changed by meaning (meant here as a verb). Social systems of all sorts are seen as meaning systems, and groups of people are recognizable as such primarily by the way they represent themselves and others, or, to put it another way, how they represent their group (ingroup) in contradistinction to another (outgroup). At the most subtle and fundamental levels, the way people speak both organizes and expresses their realities and those of the groups they inhabit. CDA can, therefore, provide a useful and complementary suite of tools for the analysis of social identities.

While it would be misleading to present CDA as a "unified church," we can identify key theoretical assumptions that are identical with those of SIT: that human social systems of all sorts are comprised of subsystems, each of which is key in the development of identity and identification; that these subsystems, or groups, can be antithetically or sympathetically related, and the character of groups' relatedness changes according to internal and external influences; that the constitution of groups is both contextual and historical; that the character of relatedness between groups is also an essential part of identity formation; that relative power and status between groups is a determining factor in how those groups relate; that the effects of proximity and intensity upon group interactions are unpredictable; and that group identity is manifest in the attitudes, behaviors, and understanding expressed by group members.

The clearest theoretical disjunction between CDA and SIT is in the directionality of analysis into the relationship between social and individual phenomena. Being primarily psychological in its provenance, SIT places empirical emphasis on the individual, beginning and returning to that sociological point as an anchor (although this was not the intention of early SIT theorists, see Hogg & Williams, 2000). Conversely, with its provenance in critical social science and anthropology, CDA typically privileges the social unit over the individual and moves inward and outward from that point in its analytical trajectories. While there are fundamental differences between SIT and CDA, it is not our purpose to discuss those here. We wish to emphasize complementarities rather than tensions between SIT and CDA, and we see the disjunctions identified above as much as potential points of departure for the development of complementary syntheses between SIT and CDA as potential sources of perceived incompatibilities.

The complementarities between SIT and CDA are both theoretical and methodological. First, CDA is ethnographic, dynamic, internalist (or "immanent"), and concerned with seeing text-in-context (here we use "text" in its broadest sense). As a dynamic perspective on the social implications of meaning making, CDA is useful for seeing manifestations of organizational change, the attitudes expressed therein, potentials for successful interventions in potentially destructive situations, and potential spaces for change in organizational relations. Second, CDA is explicitly concerned with discerning relations of power and how these affect social dynamics, an essential focus for any study of organizations in a global context characterized by rapid changes in power relations. Third, CDA is concerned with identifying the historical layering of intergroup interactions—it is a historicized, contextualized, and grounded approach to understanding how groups of people historically constitute themselves. It, therefore, provides ways of seeing processes of identification (and disidentification) between and within groups over time.

Methodologically, SIT and CDA are also complementary. For example, each group (re)creates itself through unique means of expression, by engaging in more or less regular patterns of actions and by deploying unique combinations of modes of speech. This "texture of experience" is precisely what gives groups their unique qualities (Silverstone, 1999, p. 11–12). These complex combinations of expression, actions, and modes manifest themselves in the particular patterns through which groups and organizations quite literally reproduce and transform themselves while remaining quite recognizably themselves. Organizations maintain their social identity through the generic texturing of their members' experiences (Lemke, 1995, p. 31–32). Applying notions such as these can assist SIT researchers to complement, balance, and bridge the psychological dimension with the social, if and when necessary. It can also add a distinctly qualitative dimension to analysis.

Whereas SIT might be criticized for a tendency to under-theorize social context from the strong historical and socially grounded perspective of CDA, CDA can be criticized from a SIT perspective for its lack of rigor in sampling, measurement, and significance testing. While some SIT theorists see the potential for systemic functional linguistic approaches to the analysis of social identity, there is an overwhelming reliance on quantitative methods to capture identification constructs in SIT (e.g., experimental manipulation of group membership, self-report measurement of identification). Both SIT and CDA have much to gain from each other in offsetting these methodological differences. The "thick" descriptions provided by qualitative methods, combined with the discipline of measurement required by quantitative approaches, provides a sound basis for grounding research in the "real life" context of organizations.

How might CDA assist the conceptual and methodological development of SIT and the study of intergroup communication? One way in which CDA might assist these endeavors is an approach based on the work of Lemke (1995), though numerous other models might be equally as effective. The theoretical model emphasizes the sociality of discourse; its socially delineating, transformative, and (re)productive force; and the force of the social group in preserving knowledge, recruiting some persons and rejecting others, subtly imposing ways of seeing, being, and representing upon its members. As outlined elsewhere, the approach is organized around the concepts of *presentational*, *orientational*, and *organizational* meaning (Lemke, 1995). An analysis of texts can reveal how a specific community typically describes and relates elements of its world (presentational meaning), how members of a discourse community evaluate their world (orientational meaning), and that which provides a text with coherence (organizational meaning). These three different aspects of meaning happen at once in any given instance of meaning making, and are best seen as interdependent conveniences for analysis. The approach can reveal key values that inform the actions and meanings of actors, as well as the ways in which particular groups or discourse communities shape meaning and define their memberships.

Just as these dimensions of meaning can help anchor SIT's individual more firmly to social contexts, the inverse theoretical move entailed by SIT in the course of analysis—the move from individual to group to individual—can help CDA to better explain social change by more clearly specifying the role of individual creativity in the transformation of social identity (Ellemers, 1993; Tajfel & Turner, 1979). In fact, the synthesis of CDA and SIT provides extra theoretical dimensions to the concept of social identity. SIT's theoretical orientation allows CDA to see group identities manifested in the activities of particular persons as they move through their dynamic complex of group contexts. CDA's emphasis on the primacy of the social allows analysis of group identity at the group level. This occurs not as a theoretical abstraction arrived at inductively from observing the actions of individuals that constitute a given group, but as a concrete system of actions that is realized through the patterned actions of people. These people are, in turn, socialized and written upon by their groups to the degree that they literally embody their group membership. Such a synthesis permits a view of polysemic personalities alongside the polysemic groups of people who constitute ever-changing organizations. It, therefore, permits an especially dynamic view of social dynamics at the intergroup level.

Conclusion

A theoretical and methodological synthesis of SIT and CDA offers a powerful approach to understanding intergroup communication in organizations. Despite fundamental paradigmatic tensions, we argue that these approaches complement each other without subordinating or reducing one approach to the other. By combining the analytical movements peculiar to each approach, intergroup communication researchers can achieve fine-grained analyses of reproductive and transformative practices within organizations. CDA offers rigorous tools for identifying the qualitative aspects of group membership but has been criticized for its seeming arbitrariness in text selection and other sampling issues. Conversely, SIT has developed rigorous statistical tools for modeling quantitative expressions of identity and intergroup communication. Taken together, SIT and CDA offer a powerful combination of analytical tools and theoretical advances that neither abolishes nor discounts either group or individual agency. These two perspectives can potentially combine qualitative and quantitative methods to comprehend past, present, and future dynamics in intergroup communication contexts such as organizations.

Our understanding of organizational communication has much to gain from insights informed by an intergroup perspective. Research has often approached communication issues at the individual or organizational level of analysis, often at the expense of the intergroup level. We have outlined complementarities between SIT and critical discourse analysis (CDA) for more successful investigation of identity, identification, and intergroup communication. The insights developed from SIT and CDA provide researchers with different "ways in" to investigate organizational communication issues from an intergroup perspective. New insights will continue to emerge as researchers recognize the importance of an intergroup analysis of organizational communication processes.

References

Abrams, D., Ando, K., & Hinkle, S. (1998). Psychological attachment to the group: Cross-cultural differences in organizational identification and subjective norms as predictors of workers' turnover intentions. *Personality and Social Psychology Bulletin, 24*, 1027–1039.

Abrams, D., & Hogg, M. A. (1990). *Social identity theory: Constructive and critical advances.* London: Harvester Wheatsheaf.

Ainsworth, S., & Hardy, C. (2004). Discourse and identities. In D. Grant, C. Hardy, C. Oswick & L. L. Putnam (Eds.), *The SAGE handbook of organizational discourse* (pp. 153–174). London: Sage.

Albert, S., Ashforth, B. E., & Dutton, J. E. (2000). Organizational identity and identification: Charting new waters and building new bridges. *Academy of Management Review, 25*, 13–17.

Albert, S., & Whetten, D. A. (1985). Organizational identity. In L. L. Cummings & B. M. Staw (Eds.), *Research in Organizational Behavior* (Vol. 7, pp. 263–295). Greenwich, CT: JAI.

Alderfer, C. P. (1987). An intergroup perspective on group dynamics. In J. W. Lorsch (Ed.), *Handbook of organizational behavior* (pp. 190–222). Englewood Cliffs, NJ: Prentice Hall.

Alvesson, M. (2000). Social identity and the problem of loyalty in knowledge-intensive companies. *Journal of Management Studies, 37*, 1101–1123.

Alvesson, M. (2001). Knowledge work: Ambiguity, image and identity. *Human Relations, 54*, 863–886.

Alvesson, M., & Kärreman, D. (2000). Varieties of discourse: On the study of organizations through discourse analysis. *Human Relations, 53*, 1125–1149.

Ashforth, B. E., & Mael, F. A. (1989). Social identity and the organization. *Academy of Management Review, 14*, 20–39.

Barker, J. R., & Tompkins, P. K. (1994). Identification in the self-managing organization. *Human Communication Research, 21*, 223–240.

Bartel, C. A. (2001). Social comparisons in boundary-spanning work: Effects of community outreach on members' organizational identity and identification. *Administrative Science Quarterly, 46*, 379–413.

Bhattacharya, C. B., & Mitra, A. (1998). Special session summary—The individual, the company, and the product. *Advances in Consumer Research, 25*, 54.

Blommaert, J., & Bulcaen, C. (2000). Critical discourse analysis. *Annual Review of Anthropology, 29*, 447–466.

Bouchikhi, H., Fiol, M., Gioia, D. A., Golden-Biddle, K., Hatch, M. J., Rao, H., Rindova, V. P., & Schultz, M. (1998). The identity of organizations. In D. A. Whetten & P. C. Godfrey (Eds.), *Identity in organizations: Building theory through conversations* (pp. 33–80). Thousand Oaks, CA: Sage.

Brewer, M. B. (1991). The social self: On being the same and different at the same time. *Personality and Social Psychology Bulletin, 17*, 475–482.

Brown, M. E. (1969). Identification and some conditions of organizational involvement. *Administrative Science Quarterly, 14*, 346–355.

Brown, R. (1978). Divided we fall: An analysis of relations between sections of a factory workforce. In H. Tajfel (Ed.), *Differentiation between social groups: Studies in the social psychology of intergroup relations* (pp. 395–429). London: Academic Press.

Brown, R., Condor, S., Mathews, A., Wade, G., & Williams, J. (1986). Explaining intergroup differentiation in an industrial organization. *Journal of Occupational Psychology, 59*, 273–286.

Chattopadhyay, P., & George, E. (2001). Examining the effects of work externalization through the lens of social identity theory. *Journal of Applied Psychology, 86*, 781–788.

Cheney, G. (1983a). On the various and changing meanings of organizational membership: A field study of organizational identification. *Communication Monographs, 50*, 342–362.

Cheney, G. (1983b). The rhetoric of identification and the study of organizational communication. *Quarterly Journal of Speech, 69*, 143–158.

Chreim, S. (2002). Influencing organizational identification during major change: A communication-based perspective. *Human Relations, 55*, 1117–1137.

Cross, R. L., Yan, A., & Louis, M. R. (2000). Boundary activities in "boundaryless" organizations: A case study of a transformation to a team-based structure. *Human Relations, 53*, 841–868.

Dutton, J. E., Dukerich, J. M., & Harquail, C. V. (1994). Organizational images and member identification. *Administrative Science Quarterly, 39*, 239–263.

Ellemers, N. (1993). The influence of socio-structural variables on identity management strategies. In W. Stroebe & M. Hewstone (Eds.), *European Review of Social Psychology* (Vol. 4, pp. 27–57). Chichester, UK: Wiley.

Ellemers, N., de Gilder, D., & van den Heuvel, H. (1998). Career-oriented versus team-oriented commitment and behavior at work. *Journal of Applied Psychology, 83*, 717–730.

Ely, R. J. (1994). The effects of organizational demographics and social identity on relationships among professional women. *Administrative Science Quarterly, 39*, 203–238.

Fairclough, N. (1995). *Critical discourse analysis.* Harlow: Longman.

Fairhurst, G. T., & Cooren, F. (2004). Organizational language in use: Interaction analysis, conversation analysis and speech act schematics. In D. Grant, C. Hardy, C. Oswick, & L. L. Putnam (Eds.), *The SAGE handbook of organizational discourse* (pp. 131–152). London: Sage.

Fairhurst, G. T., & Putnam, L. L. (2004). Organizations as discursive constructions. *Communication Theory, 14*, 5–26.

Fiol, C. M. (2002). Capitalizing on paradox: The role of language in transforming organizational identities. *Organization Science, 13*, 653–666.

Foote, N. N. (1951). Identification as the basis for a theory of motivation. *American Sociological Review, 16*, 14–21.

Foreman, P., & Whetten, D. A. (2002). Members' identification with multiple-identity organizations. *Organization Science, 13*, 618–635.

Gallois, C., Giles, H., Jones, E., Cargile, A. C., & Ota, H. (1995). Accommodating intercultural encounters: Elaborations and extensions. In R. L. Wiseman (Ed.), *Inter-*

cultural communication theory (pp. 115–147). Thousand Oaks, CA: Sage.

Galunic, D. C., & Eisenhardt, K. M. (2001). Architectural innovation and modular corporate forms. *Academy of Management Journal, 44*, 1229–1249.

Gardner, M. J., & Jones, E. (1999). Communication and miscommunication in the workplace: Beliefs of superiors and subordinates. *International Journal of Applied Linguistics, 9*, 185–206.

Gardner, M. J., Paulsen, N., Gallois, C., Callan, V. J., & Monaghan, P. G. (2001). Communication in organizations: An intergroup perspective. In W. P. Robinson & H. Giles (Eds.), *The new handbook of language and social psychology* (2nd ed., pp. 561–584). Chichester, UK: Wiley.

Garsten, C. (2003). Colleague, competitor, or client: Social boundaries in flexible work arrangements. In N. Paulsen & T. Hernes (Eds.), *Managing boundaries in organizations* (pp. 244–261). Basingstoke, UK: Palgrave.

Gouldner, A. W. (1957). Cosmopolitans and locals: Toward an analysis of latent social roles—1. *Administrative Science Quarterly, 2*, 281–306.

Graham, P., & Paulsen, N. (2002). Third sector discourses and the future of (un)employment: Skilled labour, new technologies, and the meaning of work. *Text: An interdisciplinary journal for the study of discourse, 22*, 443–467.

Grant, D., Hardy, C., Oswick, C., & Putnam, L. L. (Eds.). (2004). *Handbook of organizational discourse*. London: Sage.

Grant, D., Keenoy, T., & Oswick, C. (Eds.). (1998). *Discourse and organization*. London: Sage.

Hall, D., & Schneider, B. (1972). Correlates of organizational identification as a function of career pattern and organizational types. *Administrative Science Quarterly, 17*, 340–350.

Hall, D., Schneider, B., & Nygren, H. T. (1970). Personal factors in organizational identification. *Administrative Science Quarterly, 15*, 176–190.

Hardy, C., Lawrence, T. B., & Grant, D. (in press). Discourse and collaboration: The role of conversations and collective identity. *Academy of Management Review*.

Hartley, J. F. (1996). Intergroup relations in organizations. In M. A. West (Ed.), *Handbook of work psychology* (pp. 397–422). London: Wiley.

Haslam, S. A. (2001). *Psychology in organizations: The social identity approach*. London: Sage.

Haslam, S. A. (2004). *Psychology in organizations: The social identity approach* (2nd ed.). London: Sage.

Hatch, M. J., & Schultz, M. (2002). The dynamics of organizational identity. *Human Relations, 55*, 989–1018.

Hogg, M. A., & Abrams, D. (1999). Social identity and social cognition: Historical background and current trends. In D. Abrams & M. A. Hogg (Eds.), *Social identity and social cognition* (pp. 1–25). Oxford: Blackwell.

Hogg, M. A., & Terry, D. J. (2000). Social identity and self-categorization processes in organizational contexts. *Academy of Management Review, 25*, 121–140.

Hogg, M. A., & Terry, D. J. (Eds.). (2001). *Social identity processes in organizational contexts*. Philadelphia, PA: Psychology Press.

Hogg, M. A., & Williams, K. D. (2000). From "*I*" to "*We*": Social identity and the collective self. *Group Dynamics: Theory, Research, and Practice, 4,* 81–97.

Hutt, M. D., Walker, B. A., & Frankwick, G. L. (1995). Hurdle the cross-functional barriers to strategic change. *Sloan Management Review, 36(3),* 22-30.

Iedema, R., Degeling, P., Braithwaite, J., & White, L. (2004). "It's an interesting conversation I'm hearing": The doctor as manager. *Organization Studies, 25,* 15–33.

Iedema, R., & Wodak, R. (1999). Introduction: Organizational discourses and practices. *Discourse and Society, 10,* 5–19.

Jetten, J., O'Brien, A., & Trindall, N. (2002). Changing identity: Predicting adjustment to organizational restructure as a function of subgroup and superordinate identification. *British Journal of Social Psychology, 41,* 281–297.

Kelman, H. C. (1958). Compliance, identification, and internalization: Three processes of attitude change. *Journal of Conflict Resolution, 2,* 51-60.

Kenis, P., & Knoke, D. (2002). How organizational field networks shape interorganizational tie-formation rates. *Academy of Management Review, 27,* 275–293.

Kraatz, M. S. (1998). Learning by association? Interorganizational networks and adaptation to environmental change. *Academy of Management Journal, 41,* 621–643.

Kramer, R. M. (1991). Intergroup relations and organizational dilemmas: The role of categorization processes. *Research in Organizational Behavior, 13,* 191–228.

Lea, M., Spears, R., & de Groot, D. (2001). Knowing me, knowing you: Anonymity effects on social identity processes within groups. *Personality and Social Psychology Bulletin, 27,* 526–537.

Lembke, S., & Wilson, M. G. (1998). Putting the "team" into teamwork: Alternative theoretical contributions for contemporary management practice. *Human Relations, 51,* 927–944.

Lemke, J. L. (1995). *Textual politics: Discourse and social dynamics.* London: Taylor & Francis.

Lewis, L. K., & Seibold, D. R. (1998). Reconceptualizing organizational change implementation as a communication problem. In M. E. Roloff (Ed.), *Communication Yearbook* (Vol. 21, pp. 93–151). Thousand Oaks, CA: Sage.

Lovelace, K., Shapiro, D. L., & Weingart, L. R. (2001). Maximizing cross-functional new product teams' innovativeness and constraint adherence: A conflict communications perspective. *Academy of Management Journal, 44,* 779–793.

March, J. G., & Simon, H. A. (1958). *Organizations.* New York: Wiley.

Millward, L. J. (1995). Contextualizing social identity in considerations of what it means to be a nurse. *European Journal of Social Psychology, 25,* 303–324.

Morgan, J. M., Reynolds, C. M., Nelson, T. J., Johanningmeier, A. R., Griffin, M., & Andrade, P. (2004). Tales from the fields: Sources of employee identification in agribusiness. *Management Communication Quarterly, 17(3),* 360–395.

Mueller, C. W., & Lawler, E. J. (1999). Commitment to nested organizational units: Basic principles and preliminary findings. *Social Psychology Quarterly, 62,* 325–346.

Nippert-Eng, C. (2003). Drawing the line: Organizations and the boundary work of "home" and "work." In N. Paulsen & T. Hernes (Eds.), *Managing boundaries in organizations: Multiple perspectives* (pp. 262–280). Basingstoke, UK: Palgrave.

Nkomo, S. M., & Cox, T. (1996). Diverse identities in organizations. In S. R. Clegg, C.

Hardy, & W. R. Nord (Eds.), *Handbook of Organizational Studies* (pp. 338–356). Thousand Oaks, CA: Sage.

Oaker, G., & Brown, R. (1986). Intergroup relations in a hospital setting: A further test of social identity theory. *Human Relations, 39*(8), 767–778.

Panteli, N. (2003). Virtual interactions: Creating impressions of boundaries. In N. Paulsen & T. Hernes (Eds.), *Managing boundaries in organizations: Multiple perspectives* (pp. 76–92). Basingstoke, UK: Palgrave.

Patchen, M. (1970). *Participation, achievement, and involvement on the job.* Englewood Cliffs, NJ: Prentice Hall.

Paulsen, N. (2003). "Who are we now?": Group identification, boundaries, and the (re)organizing process. In N. Paulsen & T. Hernes (Eds.), *Managing boundaries in organizations: Multiple perspectives* (pp. 14–34). Basingstoke, UK: Palgrave.

Postmes, T., Tanis, M., & de Wit, B. (2001). Communication and commitment in organizations: A social identity approach. *Group Processes & Intergroup Relations, 4,* 227–246.

Pratt, M. G. (1998). To be or not to be? Central questions in organizational identification. In D. A. Whetten & P. C. Godfrey (Eds.), *Identity in organizations: Building theory through conversations* (pp. 171–207). Thousand Oaks, CA: Sage.

Putnam, L. L., & Fairhurst, G. T. (2001). Discourse analysis in organizations: Issues and concerns. In F. M. Jablin & L. L. Putnam (Eds.), *The new handbook of organizational communication* (pp. 78–136). Thousand Oaks, CA: Sage.

Robinson, W. P. (Ed.). (1996). *Social groups and identities: Developing the legacy of Henri Tajfel.* Oxford: Butterworth-Heinemann.

Roccas, S. (2003). The effects of status on identification with multiple groups. *European Journal of Social Psychology, 33,* 297–439.

Roccas, S., & Brewer, M. (2002). Social identity complexity. *Personality and Social Psychology Review, 6,* 88–106.

Rotondi, T. (1975a). Organizational identification and group involvement. *Academy of Management Journal, 18,* 892–897.

Rotondi, T. (1975b). Organizational identification: Issues and implications. *Organizational Behavior and Human Decision Processes, 13,* 95–109.

Russo, T. C. (1998). Organizational and professional identification: A case of newspaper journalists. *Management Communication Quarterly, 12,* 72–111.

Schein, E. H. (1968). Organizational socialisation and the profession of management. *Industrial Management Review, 9,* 1–15.

Schein, E. H. (1991). What is culture? In P. J. Frost, L. F. Moore, M. Reis Louis, C. C. Lundberg, & J. Martin (Eds.), *Reframing organizational culture* (pp. 243–253). Newbury Park, CA: Sage.

Schneider, B. (1990). *Organizational culture and climate.* San Francisco: Jossey-Bass.

Schneider, B., Gunnarson, S. K., & Niles Jolly, K. (1994). Creating the climate and culture of success. *Organizational Dynamics, 23,* 17–29.

Schneider, B., Hall, D., & Nygren, H. T. (1971). Self-image and job characteristics as correlates of changing identification. *Human Relations, 24,* 397–416.

Scott, C. R. (1997). Identification with multiple targets in a geographically dispersed organization. *Management Communication Quarterly, 10,* 491–522.

Scott, C. R. (1999). The impact of physical and discursive anonymity on group members' multiple identifications during computer-supported decision-making. *Western Journal of Communication, 63,* 456–487.

Scott, C. R., Connaughton, S. L., Diaz-Saenz, H. R., Maguire, K., Ramirez, R., Richardson, B., Shaw, S. P., & Morgan, D. (1999). The impacts of communication and multiple identifications on intent to leave: A multimethodological exploration. *Management Communication Quarterly, 12,* 400–435.

Scott, C. R., & Timmerman, C. E. (1999). Communication technology use and multiple workplace identifications among organizational teleworkers with varied degrees of virtuality. *IEEE Transactions on Professional Communication, 42,* 240–260.

Scott, S. G., & Lane, V. R. (2000). A stakeholder approach to organizational identity. *Academy of Management Review, 25,* 43–62.

Scott, W. R. (1998). *Organizations: Rational, natural, and open systems* (4th ed.). Upper Saddle River, NJ: Prentice Hall.

Shute, R. H. (1997). Multidisciplinary teams and child health care: Practical and theoretical issues. *Australian Psychologist, 32,* 106–113.

Silverstone, R. (1999). *Why study the media?* London: Sage.

Simon, H. A. (1947). *Administrative behavior.* New York: Free Press.

Singelis, T. M. (1996). The context of intergroup communication. *Journal of Language and Social Psychology, 15,* 360–371.

Skevington, S. (1981). Intergroup relations and nursing. *European Journal of Social Psychology, 11,* 43–59.

Suzuki, S. (1998). In-group and out-group communication patterns in international organizations: Implications for social identity theory. *Communication Research, 25,* 154–182.

Swaminathan, A. (2001). Resource partitioning and the evolution of specialist organizations: The role of location and identity in the U.S. wine industry. *Academy of Management Journal, 44,* 1169–1185.

Tajfel, H., & Turner, J. C. (1979). An integrative theory of intergroup conflict. In W. G. Austin & S. Worchel (Eds.), *The social psychology of intergroup relations* (pp. 33–47). Monterey, CA: Brooks-Cole.

Tajfel, H., & Turner, J. C. (1986). The social identity theory of intergroup behavior. In S. Worchel & W. G. Austin (Eds.), *Psychology of intergroup relations* (2nd ed., pp. 7–24). Chicago: Nelson-Hall.

Taylor, M., & Doerfel, M. L. (2003). Building interorganizational relationships that build nations. *Human Communication Research, 29,* 153–181.

Terry, D. J. (2001). Intergroup relations and organizational mergers. In M. A. Hogg & D. J. Terry (Eds.), *Social identity processes in organizational contexts* (pp. 229–247). Philadelphia, PA: Psychology Press.

Terry, D. J., Carey, C. J., & Callan, V. J. (2001). Employee adjustment to an organizational merger: An intergroup perspective. *Personality and Social Psychology Bulletin, 27,* 267–280.

Terry, D. J., & O'Brien, A. T. (2001). Status, legitimacy, and ingroup bias in the context of an organizational merger. *Group Processes & Intergroup Relations, 4,* 271–289.

Tolman, E. C. (1943). Identification and the post-war world. *Journal of Abnormal and*

Social Psychology, 38, 141–148.

Trice, H. M., & Beyer, J. M. (1993). *The cultures of work organizations*. Englewood Cliffs, NJ: Prentice-Hall.

Turner, J. C. (1999). Some current issues in research on social identity and self-categorization theories. In N. Ellemers, R. Spears, & B. Doosje (Eds.), *Social identity: Context, commitment, content* (pp. 6–34). London: Blackwell.

Turner, J. C., Hogg, M. A., Oakes, P. J., Reicher, S. D., & Wetherell, M. S. (1987). *Rediscovering the social group: A self-categorization theory*. Oxford: Blackwell.

Tyler, T. R., & Blader, S. L. (2001). Identity and cooperative behavior in groups. *Group Processes & Intergroup Relations, 4*, 207–226.

van Dick, R. (2001). Identification in organizational contexts: Linking theory and research from social and organizational psychology. *International Journal of Management Reviews, 3*, 265–283.

van Knippenberg, A., & van Oers, H. (1984). Social identity and equity concerns in intergroup perceptions. *British Journal of Social Psychology, 23*, 351–361.

van Knippenberg, D., & van Leeuwen, E. (2001). Organizational identity after a merger: Sense of continuity as the key to postmerger identification. In M. A. Hogg & D. J. Terry (Eds.), *Social identity processes in organizational contexts* (pp. 249–264). Philadelphia, PA: Psychology Press.

van Knippenberg, D., & van Schie, E. C. (2000). Foci and correlates of organizational identification. *Journal of Occupational and Organizational Psychology, 73*, 137–147.

von Corswant, F., Dubois, A., & Fredriksson, P. (2003). Organizing activities in industrial networks: The case of Volvo S80. In N. Paulsen & T. Hernes (Eds.), *Managing boundaries in organizations* (pp. 129–146). Basingstoke, UK: Palgrave.

Whetten, D. A., & Godfrey, P. C. (Eds.). (1998). *Identity in organizations: Building theory through conversations*. Thousand Oaks, CA: Sage.

Whetten, D. A., & Mackey, A. (2002). A social actor conception of organizational identity and its implications for the study of organizational reputation. *Business and Society, 41*(4), 393–414.

Wiesenfeld, B. M., Raghuram, S., & Garud, R. (1999). Communication patterns as determinants of organizational identification in a virtual organization. *Organization Science, 10*, 777–790.

Wiesenfeld, B. M., Raghuram, S., & Garud, R. (2001). Organizational identification among virtual workers: The role of need for affiliation and perceived work-based social support. *Journal of Management, 27*, 213–229.

Witt, L. A. (1993). Reactions to work assignment as predictors of organizational commitment: The moderating effect of occupational identification. *Journal of Business Research, 26*, 17–30.

Yan, A. M., & Louis, M. R. (1999). The migration of organizational functions to the work unit level: Buffering, spanning, and bringing up boundaries. *Human Relations, 52*, 25–47.

9
Social Identity Theory and Mass Communication Research

Jake Harwood
Abhik Roy

Social identity theory (SIT: Tajfel & Turner, 1986) suggests that social group memberships constitute crucial elements of the self and that they combine with societal intergroup dynamics to influence thoughts and actions. Little research has linked SIT (or other intergroup theory) with mass communication research (cf. Husband, 1977; Mastro, 2003; Reid, Giles, & Abrams, 2004). Media research that considers intergroup processes has not been integrated into a coherent theory. We will illustrate the ways in which an intergroup approach illuminates mass communication processes at the individual and institutional level.

This chapter draws on three traditions. First, it incorporates a uses and gratifications (U&G) framework that claims that media consumers actively seek out messages that provide particular gratifications (Rosengren, Wenner, & Palmgreen, 1985). These gratifications tend to be conceived at the individual level (e.g., seeking entertainment, gathering information; Blumler, 1985). The attempts to examine broader social influences on gratification seeking have not become mainstays in the relevant literature (Blumler, 1985; Harwood, 1997; 1999a, 1999b; Johnstone, 1974; Katz, Gurevitch, & Haas, 1973; Roe, 1985), and when scholars have focused on identity, they have usually studied *personal* identity (e.g., Blumler, 1979; von Feilitzen, 1976; McQuail, Blumler, & Brown, 1972). Our approach supports the U&G conceptualization of the media consumer as active; however, it takes the position that some gratifications can be usefully conceptualized at the *group* level.

One problem with U&G theory is its assumption that media use is always related to gratifications. This fails to consider the fact that people who are dissatisfied with media messages might respond by creatively reinterpreting or "reading" the messages (Ang, 1995). Such issues have been explored by scholars in the British cultural studies perspective, which is the second main influence on this chapter. These scholars (e.g., Hebdige, 1981; Hodge & Tripp, 1986) examine how racial, ethnic, class, and gender groups oppose media messages from the dominant system, while creating their own style and identities (Kellner, 1995). According to Fiske (1987a), cultural studies research focuses on how subcultures resist and struggle with the dominant media's hegemony. Hall's (1980) encoding/decoding model argues that people interpret media messages in different ways, and group affiliations such as social class influence these interpretations. For those in the cultural studies tradition, audiences' interpretations of messages reflect a negotiation between individuals and media texts.

Third, our chapter builds on content analytic work that has examined media portrayals of groups. This work has often been atheoretical, although some has been associated with traditions such as cultivation theory (e.g., Gerbner, Gross, Signorielli, & Morgan, 1980). Herein, we provide a broader SIT-based justification of such work. We suggest that the intergroup arena provides good theoretical reasons for examining the quantity and quality of groups' media portrayals, but that the theoretical rationale for such research has remained largely implicit to this point (Abrams, Eveland, & Giles, 2003; Harwood & Anderson, 2002).

The body of this chapter focuses on five propositions concerning the relationship between various media phenomena and intergroup processes. These provide different lenses through which to understand intergroup perspectives on the media. They are interrelated and symbiotic in that they consider processes that can occur simultaneously at different levels of the media production and consumption process.

Media Ownership and Content Are
Important Elements of the Intergroup Environment

This proposition encompasses issues of both *ownership* and *content* as central to an understanding of intergroup structural dynamics. First, we argue that control over media production and dissemination is a crucial dimension of group vitality (see Harwood, Giles, & Palomares, this volume, and also below; Giles, Bourhis, & Taylor, 1977), and that media ownership and control can function as a means to support the subordination of disadvantaged groups. In the United States, recent discussion in the Federal Communications Commission (FCC) and among political groups (e.g., the National Association for the Advancement of Colored People—NAACP; the National Organization for Women—NOW) has reflected the intensifying political battle over media ownership. While the FCC appears to be leaning toward consolidation, there is concern among those who advocate for the underrepresented that consolidation will reduce opportunities for different voices to be heard, particularly those of disadvantaged groups. NOW's president, Kim Gandy, recently commented:

> Women and people of color already own less than five percent of broadcast media outlets… The new FCC rules threaten to shut out women and people of color from top-level participation in the media industry… the free marketplace of ideas will suffer as the already small number of independent voices in the media wither under concentrated ownership (NOW, 2003).

Numerous scholars have written extensively about American mainstream media as a vehicle of political manipulation. They argue that American media propagate the dominant class's hegemonic ideology in order to gain the consent of the subordinate classes to a system that perpetuates their subordination. This power is reflected in the media's concentrated and ethnically homogenous ownership (Jakubowicz, 1995) that does not allow them to function as a viable forum for advocating alternative political ideologies. Opposing viewpoints are covered only in alternative media with limited budgets and, hence, seldom get disseminated to wide audiences (Lull, 1995).

Clearly, battles over media ownership reflect broader concerns with group status in society, and are reflected in arguments concerning intergroup equity, as well as arguments about the link between ownership and content. From our perspective, media ownership is a crucial element of group *vitality* in terms of the specific status implications of holding positions of power (Giles et al., 1977). Hence, by applying SIT, we can see that studies of media ownership help us understand the underlying intergroup dynamic. Beyond ownership, the intergroup dynamic will also be revealed by examining the degree to which groups are represented as creative talent, producers, management, and the like. The NAACP is particularly concerned with minority involvement in "green lighting" network television shows (i.e., approving shows for production: NAACP, 1999, 2000).

Studies of the impact of ownership and control are wide ranging. An extreme example of the power of ownership can be found in the use of media for promoting ethnic hate (e.g., racist individuals using media channels that they own to express and incite support for racism; Zickmund, 1997). According to Jakubowicz (1995), the hegemonic power of the dominant media in the United States has had serious consequences for Native Americans. Daley and James (1992) examined the introduction of television to rural Alaskan Native Americans in the 1980s. The Native American communities' attempt at having their own indigenous television programming that would reflect and protect their culture and community was subordinated to the economic interests of the dominant commercially-driven media. Similarly, Henningham's (1992) study revealed similar negative effects of media hegemony on Hawaiian Natives, including the destruction of the Hawaiian language. He notes that during the 1990s, commercial broadcasters dominated the media, and native Hawaiian cultural development was restricted to (little-watched) public access TV.

In addition to the ownership issues discussed above, media *content* also reflects important intergroup issues. First, much content analysis research examining the media presence of minority cultural groups, women, older adults, and the like has demonstrated that such groups are not receiving a "fair" portrayal (Dixon & Linz, 2000; Greenberg & Brand, 1994; Harwood & Anderson, 2001, 2002; Mastro & Greenberg, 2000; Roy & Harwood, 1997). Such studies compare the representation of particular groups in the television population with the "real" population to evaluate their degree of overrepresentation (for dominant groups) or under-representation (for marginalized groups). Recently, Abrams et al. (2003) and Harwood and Anderson (2002) have argued that the extent to which groups are represented on television is a fundamental element of their objective vitality (i.e., their group's strength in the intergroup context). Part of the original conceptualization of the vitality construct concerned institutional representation (Giles et al., 1977), including the media.

The *quality* of group portrayals in the media is as important as their quantity. This informs us about prevailing societal representations of groups and illustrates how cognitive representations of those groups might be perpetuated. For instance, Bird (1999) examines media images of Native Americans. She notes a shift over time toward less "savage" portrayals, but fundamentally unrealistic and demeaning depictions are still retained. Similarly, Merskin (2001) found that advertising almost always depicted American Indians in stereotypical ways. Such biased representation "denies that they are human beings, and presents them as existing only in the past and as single, monolithic Indians" (p. 167). Other similar work has examined the low levels of sexual activity in older adults on television (Harris & Feinberg, 1977), the lack of family involvement of African Americans (Harwood & Anderson, 2001), the over-coverage of criminal activity among Blacks and Latinos (Dixon & Linz, 2000) and the low employment status of women (Ferrante, Haynes, & Kingsley, 1988). Moreover, research findings consistently affirm that the American media represent African Americans in narrowly defined stereotypical roles (Dates & Barlow, 1990; Diamond, 1991; Matabane & Merritt, 1996).

Explanations for biased representations include a general ethnic blame discourse (Romer, Jamieson, & De Coteau, 1998), or biases based on unconscious stereotypes (e.g., Dixon & Linz, 2000). Indeed, such biases can be displayed in very subtle linguistic differentiations that almost certainly operate below the level of explicit control (Maass, Corvino, & Arcuri, 1994). From an SIT perspective, Husband (1977) notes that race and culture are rendered problematic by the ways in which White British reporters use linguistic terms in their coverage of ethnic and racial issues. Such findings illustrate group inequities, and, thus, content analytic work constitutes an effective way to map tolerance or prejudice concerning particular groups.

Beyond the presence and portrayal of groups, an intergroup focus forces consideration of *diversity* in media content. In the United States context, we might look at availability of TV offerings such as BET (Black Entertainment Television) and Spanish-language channels, newspapers published in languages other than the local dominant language, or culture-specific radio programming. The presence of these media indicates respect and tolerance for different groups and provides public support for those groups' vitalities. A diverse media environment can also reflexively influence other media (e.g., in the

United States, a successful Spanish language newspaper might drive an established English language paper to cater better to a Latino audience).

Finally, an intergroup perspective leads us to consider how media content reflects current intergroup dynamics. For instance, media styles often originate within particular groups and come to express the nature of that group and its identity (e.g., jazz or hip-hop for African Americans, punk for young people around 1978). When this occurs, outgroup influence and appropriation can be viewed as a threat and deliberately excluded. For instance, the distinction between authentic and inauthentic productions is crucial in the hip-hop community, and this distinction is drawn, in part, on whether the product emerges from the White or Black community. "Authenticity" can become a valuable marketing device, and can emerge as an attractive feature for the dominant group (e.g., Whites want to be seen listening to "authentic" hip hop, not an inauthentic imitation; McLeod, 1999; cf. Coupland, 2003). In turn, the original community of production might develop new forms or styles that maintain differentiation from the dominant group. For instance, a number of developments in jazz can be understood in terms of African American attempts to reclaim the music from Whites who were appropriating the music (e.g., moves away from traditional harmonic and melodic patterns; incorporation of African instruments and rhythms; Kofsky, 1970). The extent to which groups protect "their" cultural products from outgroup influence is an indication of the value of those products for their ingroup identities (Frith, 1981; Lull, 1987). Thus, the content of media represents important turf and identity battles between particular groups. It is clear that media content reflects group status and vitality (via the presence and nature of portrayals), conveys societal values concerning diversity (via the offerings available focused on specific groups), and serves as a barometer of intergroup relations.

Individuals' Group Identification Levels
Influence Their Relationships with the Media

In this section, we argue that group identification is central to media consumers' selection and cognitive processing of messages. We approach selection practices from a SIT perspective, focusing particularly on the ways in which media selection can constitute a social creativity strategy for identity support. Tajfel and Turner (1986) outline a range of *social creativity* strategies, which are all ways to improve an individual's perceptions of the intergroup status quo without actually improving the position of the group within the hierarchy. Harwood (1997, 1999a, 1999b) describes social creativity in media selection by focusing on the role of social identification. This work builds on U&G theory by considering the ways in which group memberships structure the resources that individuals bring to their media interpretations and the gratifications they derive (e.g., Ang, 1996; Morley, 1992). Using experimental and survey methods, Harwood (1997) has demonstrated that individuals prefer shows featuring ingroup members, even when the content is controlled (an identical show is preferred if the star is an ingroup as opposed to an outgroup member). Viewing data support this contention, demonstrating that individuals consistently prefer to view shows featuring members of their own culture (Greenberg & Atkin, 1982), age (Harwood, 1997), and gender groups (von Feilitzen & Linne, 1975). Similarly, work has demonstrated that membership in the same social groups (e.g., gender groups) is crucial in determining children's personal identification with television characters (Cohen, 2001; Hoffner, 1996) and that ingroup characters are perceived as more similar to the self than outgroup characters (von Feilitzen & Linne, 1975; Greenberg, 1972; Hoffner & Cantor, 1991; Sprafkin & Liebert, 1978). Viewers also tend to select messages featuring values and attitudes consistent with their group memberships (Atkin, 1985).

In SIT terms, people are creatively dealing with the media in ways that make their *personal* viewing profile considerably more supportive of their group identity than it would be otherwise (see earlier discussion of the overall demographics of the television world). Perhaps most notable from this work is that gratifications grounded in group identification (e.g., "I watch television because I enjoy watching people who are like me") account for significant *unique* variance in television viewing and are empirically distinct from other gratifications (e.g., escape, information; Harwood, 1999a, 1999b). In other words, we have empirical grounds to claim that social identity influences media selection in ways that go beyond traditional U&G theory.

New technologies can enhance the ability to engage in social creativity strategies of identity-based selectivity. Gillespie (1989) has shown the ways in which Asian Indians in Britain use video to show Indian media that are not available through traditional channels. Developments such as digital video recorders and digital cable make such selection even easier. An elaborated discussion of social creativity and the media is provided by Reid et al. (2004) who expand on the precursors to social creativity and also note the role that new media can play in such processes.

In addition to the selectivity issues above, viewers' social identifications also influence the ways in which they process and understand media. Audience analysis research has focused on different groups' radically different readings of media texts. Hall (1980) examined this phenomenon through his theory of "preferred reading," which suggests that audiences use three positions to decode media messages. The *dominant reading* is produced when an individual accepts the dominant ideology and interprets the media messages in line with the intentions of the writers and producers. Most audiences, however, read media messages by producing what Hall calls *negotiated readings*, which "accord the privileged position to the dominant definitions of events while reserving the right to make a more negotiated application to local conditions" (1980, p. 137). Third, *oppositional readings* occur when the individual understands the aims of the writer or producer but directly opposes the message. Here, the individual "retotalizes the message within some alternative framework of reference," which results in direct opposition to the dominant ideological message (p. 138). As argued by Morley (1992), social groups provide the resources and narratives within which individuals understand the media. The extent to which an individual identifies with a group will determine the extent to which that person processes media messages in group-related ways.

Radway (1984), for instance, describes the ways in which women's readings of romance novels function to support their gender identities, despite what might be construed as demeaning portrayals of women in the books (e.g., at the most basic level, these are books for women, by women, and primarily about women—the romantic hero is often a fairly peripheral character). Romance novels provide escape from the mundane patterns and pressures of daily life, and provide a way of reinterpreting women's roles in relationships (Radway, 1983). Similarly, Morley (1992) has shown that trade unionists question the basic economic assumptions underlying a news story, whereas others are broadly accepting of those assumptions (see also Tate & Surlin, 1976; Vidmar & Rokeach, 1974). From a different (and more centrally intergroup) perspective, Mastro (2003) demonstrates ingroup-favoring interpretations of television portrayals of ethnic ingroups vs. outgroups. For instance, White respondents viewed criminal behavior by a Latino perpetrator in a television show as less justified than the same behavior by a White perpetrator.

Oppositional readings support group identity, but do not explicitly challenge the status quo (Tajfel & Turner, 1986)—they are not *social competition* in the original sense (Harwood et al., this volume). Radway (1984) makes this point very well:

> Women's domestic role in patriarchal culture… is left virtually intact by her leisure-time withdrawal. Although in restoring a woman's depleted sense of self romance reading may constitute tacit recognition that the current arrangement of the sexes is not ideal for her emotional well-being, it does nothing to alter a woman's social situation, itself very likely characterized by those dissatisfying patterns. In fact, this activity may very well obviate the need or desire to demand satisfaction in the real world because it can be so successfully met in fantasy (p. 212).

In other words, Radway suggests that *social creativity* strategies in media consumption can satisfy the impulses that might otherwise find expression in a search for genuinely improved intergroup relations. In line with Ang (1996), we suggest that "audiences appropriate television in ways suitable to their situated practices of living… [but] that this appropriative power of the audience is the power of the weak… not to change or overturn imposed structures, but to negotiate the potentially oppressive effects of those structures where they cannot be overthrown, where they have to be lived with" (p. 8; see also Fiske, 1987b).

Media Content Influences Intergroup Cognitions

First, media messages influence *identification* in a number of ways. This can occur most dramatically in the context of national events. Wars and international sporting events are often associated with ethnocentric media coverage which, in turn, is likely to result in enhanced nationalism for some (Horak, 2003). Pedic (1989) demonstrates that nationalistic appeals in advertising can protect the collective self-esteem of individuals who identify strongly with their nation, and that nationalistic appeals are more effective for strongly identifying individuals (Pedic, 1989; Sloan, 1979). Gillespie's (1989) work indicates that immigrant Indian communities in Britain use video as a source of cultural connection to the past, as a means of maintaining identity, and as a tool to transmit cultural norms and language (i.e., identity) to younger generations. In the extreme, media organizations and politicians might manipulate information in order to maintain support for political leaders and the status quo (Giles et al., 1977; Horkheimer and Adorno, 1972). This might be particularly likely when the dominant group perceives a threat to their position (Sachdev & Bourhis, 1985, 1991). For instance, US media coverage of the (first) Gulf War was constructed in ways that encouraged support for the war and discouraged dissent (Chomsky, 2002).

Second, media can influence intergroup *attitudes*. Branscombe and Wann (1994) demonstrated that exposure to a scene from *Rocky IV* in which Rocky loses to a Russian boxer results in high levels of derogation of Russians as a group—the media portrayal serves as an intergroup threat. Similar work has demonstrated correlations between sex-role attitudes and exposure to stereotypical television content (Ross, Anderson, & Wisocki, 1982). Kimball (1986) demonstrated that children's attitudes became significantly more sex-typed *after* the introduction of television to a previously television-free town. Similarly, experimental evidence shows that exposure to media featuring comic stereotypes of African Americans results in negative effects. Ford (1997) showed that White viewers of such material are likely to judge a Black target as more guilty of a crime than a White target (Ford, 1997). Similarly, Tan and Tan (1979) provide correlational evidence that exposure to stereotypical portrayals has harmful consequences for African Americans' self esteem. Husband (1977) has shown that the specifics of individuals' language use is influenced by the media— for instance, some of the precise words used in everyday conversations about immigration reflect those used in news reporting (van Dijk, 1987). In other words, the media can provide a means by which stereotypes are transmitted and perpetuated for majority and minority group members (Fryberg, 2003). Interestingly, some groups might be happy with inaccurate presentations and the ensuing effects. For instance, Perlmutter (2000) discusses the ways in which the police might, at times, endorse and seek media images that downplay the duller aspects and play up the more exciting and sensationalist side of their work.

Third, group portrayals influence *perceptions of group vitality*. Television presence is an immediate element of objective group vitality (see earlier section). To this extent, given the relatively close links between objective and subjective vitality, the presence or absence of group members in media presentations (e.g., as TV characters) will influence *subjective group vitality* (Abrams et al., 2003; Bourhis, Giles, & Rosenthal, 1981). Abrams (2003) demonstrates that African American viewers who seek television to fulfill identity gratifications also experience elevated estimates of group vitality. Extensive viewing of shows featuring small numbers of older adults is also associated with reduced perceptions of older adults' demographic vitality (Gerbner et al., 1980). There is overlap here with the ideas presented earlier concerning objective vitality, however it is useful to distinguish, as the vitality literature does, between the objective macro-manifestations of objective vitality, and the micro-level subjective vitality representations.

Finally, the media influence perceptions of *cognitive alternatives* to the intergroup situation. Minority media might do this explicitly by encouraging social protest or pointing out and labeling injustices (Song, 1997). Mainstream media can provide such messages in a more subtle fashion. While programs such as *The Cosby Show* have been criticized as providing unrepresentative portrayals (Gates, 1989), they, nonetheless, provide examples of alternatives to the status quo (Innis & Feagin, 2002; Lewis, 1991). The Cosbys were respected members of their community, a world featuring upper-middle-class Black families. In effect, they illustrated an alternative way of being for the Black community (albeit one to which access might currently be blocked by prejudice). Interestingly, the show was criticized at times for being too "White" and, subsequently, the show incorporated more elements of Black culture (Gray, 1989). Likewise, Graves (1999) discusses the role of *Sesame Street* in modeling positive interracial relationships, and the power this has to change children's attitudes concerning such relationships. Hence, it is clear that media have the power to influence group identities, attitudes, perceptions of diversity, and perceptions of alternatives to the current intergroup status quo.

Group Processes Driven by Identification
Influence the Media Environment

In this section, we argue that identity-driven group processes influence established media organizations and also that those same processes influence creation of *new* media production organizations. A common media-related strategy of social competition is for interest groups to challenge dominant media to alter their content. For instance, the NAACP (1999, 2000) has criticized the lack of African Americans in primetime network programming. In a 1999 press release, the association accused the networks of a "whitewash" of primetime television, suggesting legal action to remedy the absence of African Americans in lead roles. Similar activities occur with regard to other levels in the media industry (e.g., campaigning for radio licenses to be granted to minorities; Napoli, 1999). Buxton (1991) describes complex negotiations between ACT UP (a prominent AIDS activist group) and TV production companies concerning a network drama's AIDS story line. Buxton's is a detailed account of the ways in which oppressed groups can engage in *social competition* with the mainstream media to resist negative, and encourage positive, portrayals.

The above strategies are focused on actions that might be taken by the minority or oppressed group. Dominant groups might also use these strategies when they experience threats to their position. As an example, Giles (personal communication, July 7, 2003) suggests that violent pornography, particularly that based on rape myths, might be in part a response to the growth of feminism. As women's power in society grows and explicit discrimination against them becomes less acceptable, so men seek out more covert means of undermining the growing threat to their own dominance (for instance, by accentuating women's supposed desire for that dominance). The growth of unapologetically right-wing news media in the United States (and more recent attempts to begin left-wing responses) might well be captured within a similar theoretical lens. Reid et al. (2004) describe similar processes, focusing on how media can facilitate social change.

An alternative to challenging established media for greater and improved portrayal is for groups to take control of media production. Thus, programming on BET (which was founded by Robert Johnson, an African American) is largely produced by and oriented toward a

Black audience. Access to such programming renders the quantity and quality of African Americans in broadcast programming less relevant and, hence, less of a source of an identity threat to African American audiences. Similar points can be made with regard to Spanish language television programming, ethnic newspapers, and the like. We treat this as a *social creativity* response to social inequity because it does not directly affect the status quo (Tajfel & Turner, 1986). However, these media have the capacity to undermine the power of mainstream media by taking audiences away. Also, they offer the potential to subvert dominant channels by criticizing them, and they can mobilize social competition beyond the media arena by publicizing and encouraging participation in protest or endorsing minority-friendly political candidates (Michaels, 1987). For instance, the Rodney King case in Los Angeles in the early 1990s was represented very differently in the African American vs. the mainstream media. The former challenged mainstream interpretations and educated their readers to be critical consumers of "facts" concerning the case and the subsequent riots (Song, 1997). Having an ingroup voice is not an end in itself, but provides an outlet for messages that challenge outgroup domination, question outgroup depictions of intergroup relations, and support activism by marginalized groups. It is important, however, to understand the complexity underlying some "ethnic" media. For instance, some prominent "minority" media networks in the United States are owned and operated by large mainstream conglomerates (Pearlstein, 2003). If these media become successful, they become targets for the big media conglomerates, and as a result, they can become part of the mainstream (e.g., Viacom's acquisition of BET in 2000).

A different (and more local) approach to ingroup media production can be found in the garage band phenomenon. When groups of (generally) young males get together to write and perform their own music, this suggests a dissatisfaction with current media offerings and a desire to create something more original. Such bands often constitute the core of a broader subcultural construction of youth identity (Frith, 1981; Lull, 1987). The production of music as an expression of youth identity has received considerable attention (McQuail, 1997; Hebdige, 1981; Roe, 1992), although little from social identity scholars.

Media Serve as the Locus for Group Identifications

At times, media become central to the development of group identities and, indeed, group identity can derive from a shared connection with specific media messages. As far back as 1969, Carey described a "centrifugal force" of the modern media environment. He argued that the increasingly specialized media environment has led to the formation of groups *defined by* media rather than national identity. That is, the act of viewing the same television show, visiting the same Web sites or listening to the same band can create a shared identity that, in turn, can influence existing intergroup dynamics and tensions.

Jenkins' (1986) study of highly active *Star Trek* fans revealed the powerful influence of groups in understanding and appreciating this show. The fans, especially the females, published fantasy stories in newsletters and fanzines concerning the lives of the show's characters, even developing their own "language." These allowed the development of a distinctive group identity in spite of the fans' geographical dispersion (Penley, 1997). According to Fiske (1987b), this kind of group activity helps "promote and circulate gossip within a community that is defined not geographically but by a commonality of taste, deriving from a shared social situation" (p. 80). Similarly, Hobson (1982) explored the way female audiences sought pleasure in watching the popular British television soap opera *Crossroads*. Her ethnographic research revealed that female viewers of the show applied norms and values to evaluate it based on conversations with other viewers. This kind of "group talk" helped the viewers to bring out the "meanings that 'work' for a particular audience group…. In this way, solitary viewing can be experienced as group viewing, because the viewer knows well that other members of her or his group are viewing at the same time" (Fiske, 1987b, p. 80). This is also a way in which the group can achieve a "collaborative reading" of the show—an interpretation that is grounded in the group and represents the group ideology.

These are examples of situations in which media messages united individuals and provided a locus for their group identification (Baym, 1999)—situations in which the media created novel groups that crossed traditional geographic boundaries (Carey, 1969). Additional research in this area might examine individuals who (literally) follow musical groups (e.g., "Deadheads"; followers of the band *Phish*), individuals playing online interactive computer games, or devotees of reality TV shows. In general, we feel there are some very useful links to be explored between work on *fandom* (e.g., Penley, 1997) and social identity processes (see also Leets, de Becker, & Giles, 1995).

Conclusion and Research Agenda

First, research should examine portrayals on television shows popular among different groups. For instance, since elderly characters are portrayed less *frequently* in shows preferred by younger viewers (Harwood, 1997), it could be expected that elderly characters are portrayed more *negatively* in those same shows. Surprisingly, there is little work examining links between the nature of ingroup and outgroup portrayals and viewership data that would reveal viewers' group memberships. We know little about whether minority-owned media criticize the dominant media or encourage collective action against the dominant group. Indeed, we do not even know much about minority portrayals on "minority media" (e.g., are African Americans portrayed more positively on BET than other cable or broadcast networks?), or the extent to which minority viewers critically consume those images. Likewise, the relationship between consumption of minority media and social protest against the dominant group is unclear: Does minority media consumption result in social activism? Relatedly, research tends to focus on group portrayals as positive or negative, with an implied preference for the former. However, it is important to note that *diverse* portrayals of groups can be important for encouraging perceptions of group *variability* (which are crucially important: Harwood & Anderson, 2001; Hewstone & Hamberger, 2000). The availability of group portrayals that vary in significant ways from one another can also be valuable for *ingroup* members. For instance, Mares and Cantor (1992) demonstrate that lonely older adults prefer *negative* portrayals of the ingroup and feel better after viewing such portrayals (presumably because of the greater opportunity for achieving positive *individual level* comparisons with the media character in such situations).

Second, more examination of the *effects* of group portrayals is warranted, especially whether positive portrayals of ingroup members are associated with increased group identification (Branscombe & Wann, 1994; Mares & Cantor, 1992). Similarly, what are the consequences for viewers who cannot access ingroup portrayals no matter how "selectively" they seek them (Harwood, 1997; Harwood & Anderson, 2002)? Given the limits to individuals' capacity to creatively interpret texts (Condit, 1994), we might expect that people will seek alternative media (e.g., Gillespie, 1989) that are increasingly available via technologies such as video, satellite television, and the Internet (Mitra, 1997). Of course, some of those media are also making hate speech more accessible (Leets, 2001). Finally, the absolute extent to which media are important in influencing intergroup processes (relative to other forms of socialization) should be examined more carefully.

Third, intergroup media industry politics deserve more attention. Many constituencies exert pressure on producers with respect to group portrayals. The extent to which these campaigns are effective and the ways in which they are received within media organizations deserves more attention. How can social groups effectively campaign for more and better representation? To which appeals do media organizations respond positively?

We have presented a conceptual map with which media and intergroup scholars might approach the intersection of the two areas. At its broadest, this map deals with two levels: A macro-level of media ownership, objective indices of media content, and the societal manifestations of intergroup dynamics (e.g., objective vitality); and a micro-level of intergroup cognitions (subjective vitality, identity, group-related attitudes). These levels intersect at numerous points (e.g., content influencing attitudes, perceptions of ingroup under-representation leading to campaigns to change media ownership, etc.). Such a map is conceptually consistent and complementary with Reid et al.'s (2004) social identity model of media usage and effects. It attempts to cover a little more ground, and, in doing so, it remains somewhat more abstract than the Reid et al. model. However, the essence of both frameworks is the same: Individuals' interactions with the media are often intergroup interactions and need to be considered as such.

Placing such a diverse array of media research into a social identity framework does a number of things. It provides a deeper understanding of the *social* (in the broad sense) functions of media. SIT integrates knowledge about individual viewing and processing, media influence on intergroup relations, and group-related processes in media organizations. The chapter also illustrates that apparently unrelated literatures are operating in complementary ways. For instance, from an SIT perspective, industry-level examinations of media ownership are quite closely related to individual examinations of viewing gratifications in that both focus on understanding the ways in which intergroup dynamics are played out in the media context. Likewise, SIT provides some insight on Hall's notions of negotiated and oppositional readings, demonstrating that even *oppositional* readings might not always be strategies aimed at social change. The SIT approach reveals how mass media serve as a locus of group struggle (Hall, 1980; Fiske, 1987b; Kellner, 1995). While entertainment remains the most common reason for media use, group memberships and identifications influence the ways in which people process and react to media messages, and provide a foundation for examining such issues in the changing media environment of the future.

In closing, we return to the three strands of work from which this chapter derives. Work in cultural studies has set the stage for the understanding of audiences' careful and multiple interpretations of texts, and the role that group memberships (particularly class and gender) play in those interpretations. However, the epistemological orientation of cultural studies is largely inconsistent with that of SIT. Our chapter has more metatheoretical commonality with U&G, which describes an active, interpretive audience whose activity is somewhat predictable based on measurable predispositions. Finally, this chapter provides a theoretical framework for previous content analytic work. The quantity and quality of media portrayals can now be conceived as a crucial element in understanding intergroup dynamics concerning vitality (Abrams et al., 2003). That said, audiences are not consuming a television diet that resembles the results of these content analyses. Rather, viewing patterns are influenced by group memberships and identifications. Indeed, to return to the fundamental goal of this chapter, we have illustrated that understanding the process of mass communication, from creation to consumption, is aided by taking an intergroup perspective.

Author Note

The authors express their appreciation to Yan Bing Zhang for her comments.

References

Abrams, J. (2003). *The role of television on African American subjective vitality.* PhD dissertation: University of California, Santa Barbara.

Abrams, J. R., Eveland, W. P., & Giles, H. (2003). The effects of television on group vitality: Can television empower nondominant groups? In P. J. Kalbfleisch (Ed.), *Communication Yearbook 27* (pp. 193–219). Mahwah, NJ: Erlbaum.

Ang, I. (1995). The nature of the audience. In J. Downing, A. Mohammadi, & A. Sreberny-Mohammadi (Eds.), *Questioning the media* (pp. 207–220). Thousand Oaks, CA: Sage.

Ang, I. (1996). *Living room wars: Rethinking media audiences for a postmodern world.* New York: Routledge.

Atkin, C. K. (1985). Informational utility and selective exposure to entertainment media. In D. Zillman & J. Bryant (Eds.), *Selective exposure to communication* (pp. 63–92). Hillsdale, NJ: Erlbaum.

Baym, N. (1999). *Tune in, log on : Soaps, fandom, and on-line community.* Thousand Oaks, CA: Sage.

Bird, S. E. (1999). Gendered construction of the American Indian in popular media. *Journal of Communication, 49,* 61–83.

Blumler, J. G. (1979). The role of theory in uses and gratifications studies. *Communication Research, 6,* 9–36.

Blumler, J. G. (1985). The social character of media gratifications. In K. E. Rosengren, L. A. Wenner, & P. Palmgreen (Eds.), *Media gratifications research* (pp. 41–60). Beverly Hills, CA: Sage.

Bourhis, R. Y., Giles, H., & Rosenthal, D. (1981). Notes on the construction of a "Subjective Vitality Questionnaire" for ethnolinguistic groups. *Journal of Multilingual and Multicultural Development, 2,* 144–155.

Branscombe, N., & Wann, D. L. (1994). Collective self-esteem consequences of outgroup derogation when a valued social identity is on trial. *European Journal of Social Psychology, 24,* 641–658.

Buxton, R. (1991). "After it happened...": The battle to present AIDS in a television drama. *The Velvet Light Trap, 27,* 37–47.

Carey, J. W. (1969). The communication revolution and the professional communicator. In P. Halmos (Ed.), *The sociology of mass media communicators* (pp. 23–38). Keele, UK: Keele University Press.

Chomsky, N. (2002). *Understanding power: The indispensable Chomsky.* New York: The New Press.

Cohen, J. (2001). Defining identification: A theoretical look at the identification of audiences with media characters. *Mass Communication and Society, 4,* 245–264.

Condit, C. M. (1994). The rhetorical limits of polysemy. In H. Newcomb (Ed.), *Television: The critical view* (5th ed., pp. 426–447). New York: Oxford University Press.

Coupland, N. (2003). Sociolinguistic authenticities. *Journal of Sociolinguistics, 7,* 417–456.

Daley, P., & James B. (1992). Ethnic broadcasting in Alaska. The failure of a participatory model. In S. H. Riggins (Ed.), *Ethnic minority media: An international perspec-*

tive (pp. 26–42). Newbury Park, CA: Sage.

Dates, J., & Barlow, W. (1990). *Split image: African Americans in the mass media*. Washington, DC: Howard University Press.

Diamond, E. (1991). *The media show: The changing face of the news, 1985–1990*. Cambridge, MA: MIT Press.

Dixon, T. L., & Linz, D. (2000). Overrepresentation and underrepresentation of African Americans and Latinos as lawbreakers on television news. *Journal of Communication, 50,* 131–154.

Ferrante, C. L., Haynes, A. M., & Kingsley, S. M. (1988). Image of women in television advertising. *Journal of Broadcasting and Electronic Media, 32,* 231–237.

Fiske, J. (1987a). British cultural studies and television. In R. C. Allen (Ed.), *Channels of discourse reassembled* (pp. 284–326). Chapel Hill, NC: University of North Carolina Press.

Fiske, J. (1987b). *Television culture*. London/New York: Routledge.

Ford, T. E. (1997). Effects of stereotypical television portrayals of African-Americans on person perception. *Social Psychology Quarterly, 60,* 266–275.

Frith, S. (1981). *Sound effects*. New York: Pantheon.

Fryberg, S. A. (2003). Really? You don't look like an American Indian: Social representations and social group identities. *Dissertation Abstracts International: Section B: The Sciences & Engineering, 64(3–B),* 1549.

Gates, H. L. (1989, November 12). TV's Black world turns—but stays unreal. *New York Times*, p. H1.

Gerbner, G., Gross, L., Signorielli, N., & Morgan, M. (1980). Aging with television: Images on television drama and conceptions of social reality. *Journal of Communication, 30,* 37–48.

Giles, H., Bourhis, R. Y., & Taylor, D. M. (1977). Towards a theory of language in ethnic group relations. In H. Giles (Ed.), *Language, ethnicity, and intergroup relations* (pp. 307–348). London: Academic Press.

Gillespie, M. (1989). Technology and tradition: Audio-visual culture among South Asian families in West London. *Cultural Studies, 3,* 226–239.

Graves, S. B. (1999). Television and prejudice reduction: When does television as a vicarious experience make a difference. *Journal of Social Issues, 55,* 707–725.

Gray, H. (1989). Television, Black Americans, and the American dream. *Critical Studies in Mass Communication, 6,* 376–387.

Greenberg, B. S. (1972). Children's reactions to TV Blacks. *Journalism Quarterly, 49,* 5–14.

Greenberg, B. S., & Atkin, C. (1982). Learning about minorities from television: A research agenda. In G. Berry & C. Mitchell-Kernan (Eds.), *Television and the socialization of the minority child* (pp. 215–243). New York: Academic Press.

Greenberg, B. S., & Brand, J. (1994). Minorities and the mass media: 1970s to 1990s. In J. Bryant & D. Zillman (Eds.), *Media effects: Advances in theory and research* (pp. 273–314). Hillsdale, NJ: Erlbaum.

Hall, S. (1980). Encoding/decoding. In S. Hall, D. Hobson, A. Lowe, & P. Willis (Eds.), *Culture, media, language* (pp. 128–138). London: Hutchinson.

Harris, A., & Feinberg, J. (1977). Television and aging: Is what you see what you get?

The Gerontologist, 17, 464–468.

Harwood, J. (1997). Viewing age: Lifespan identity and television viewing choices. *Journal of Broadcasting and Electronic Media, 41,* 203–213.

Harwood, J. (1999a). Age identification, social identity gratifications, and television viewing. *Journal of Broadcasting and Electronic Media, 43,* 123–136.

Harwood, J. (1999b). Age identity and television viewing preferences. *Communication Reports, 12,* 85–90.

Harwood, J., & Anderson, K. (2001). Social group membership and family involvement on prime-time TV. *Electronic Journal of Communication, 11(1).* Retrieved, August 27, 2001 from *http://www.cios.org/www/ejc/v11n101.htm*

Harwood, J., & Anderson, K. (2002). The presence and portrayal of social groups on prime-time television. *Communication Reports, 15,* 81–98.

Hebdige, D. (1981). *Subculture: The meaning of style.* New York: Routledge.

Henningham, J. (1992). Flaws in the melting pot: Hawaiian media. In S. H. Riggins (Ed.), *Ethnic minority media: An international perspective* (pp. 149–161). Newbury Park, CA: Sage.

Hewstone, M., & Hamberger, J. (2000). Perceived variability and stereotype change. *Journal of Experimental Social Psychology, 36,* 103–124.

Hobson, D. (1982). *Crossroads: The drama of a soap opera.* London: Methuen.

Hodge, R., & Tripp, D (1986). *Children and television.* Cambridge, UK: Polity Press.

Hoffner, C. (1996). Children's wishful identification and parasocial interaction with favorite television characters. *Journal of Broadcasting and Electronic Media, 40,* 389–402.

Hoffner, C., & Cantor, J. (1991). Perceiving and responding to mass media characters. In J. Bryant & D. Zillman (Eds.), *Responding to the screen: Reception and reaction processes* (pp. 63–102). Hillsdale, NJ: Erlbaum.

Horak, R. (2003). Sport space and national identity. *American Behavioral Scientist, 46,* 1506–1518.

Horkheimer, M., & Adorno, T. (1972). *Dialectic of enlightenment.* New York: Herder & Herder.

Husband, C. (1977). News media, language and race relations: A case study in identity maintenance. In H. Giles (Ed.), *Language, ethnicity and intergroup relations* (pp. 211–240). London: Academic Press.

Innis, L. B., & Feagin, J. R. (2002). The Cosby Show: The view from the Black middle class. In R. M. Coleman (Ed.), *Say it loud! African-American audiences, media, and identity* (pp. 187–204). New York: Routledge.

Jakubowicz, A. (1995). Media in multicultural nations: Some comparisons. In J. Downing, A. Mohammadi, & A. Sreberny-Mohammadi (Eds.), *Questioning the media* (pp. 165–183). Thousand Oaks, CA: Sage.

Jenkins, H. (1986). Star Trek rerun, reread, rewritten: Fan writing as textual poaching. *Critical Studies in Mass Communication, 5,* 85–107.

Johnstone, J. W. C. (1974). Social integration and mass media use among adolescents: A case study. In J. G. Blumler & E. Katz (Eds.), *The uses of mass communications: Current perspectives on gratifications research* (pp. 35–48). Beverly Hills, CA: Sage.

Katz, E., Gurevitch, M., & Haas, H. (1973). On the use of the mass media for important things. *American Sociological Review, 38,* 164–181.

Kellner, D. (1995). Cultural studies, multiculturalism and media culture. In G. Dines & J. M. Humez (Eds.), *Gender, race and class in media* (pp. 5–17). Thousand Oaks, CA: Sage.

Kimball, M. M. (1986). Television and sex-role attitudes. In T. M. Williams (Ed.), *The impact of television* (pp. 265–301). Orlando, FL: Academic.

Kofsky, F. (1970). *Black nationalism and the revolution in music.* New York: Pathfinder Press.

Leets, L. (2001). Responses to Internet hate sites: Is speech too free in cyberspace? *Communication, Law, and Policy, 6,* 287–318.

Leets, L., de Becker, G., & Giles, H. (1995). FANS: Exploring expressed motivations for contacting celebrities. *Journal of Language and Social Psychology, 14,* 102–124.

Lewis, J. (1991). *Ideological octopus: An exploration of television and its audience.* New York/London: Routledge.

Lull, J. (Ed.). (1987). *Popular music and communication.* Newbury Park, CA: Sage.

Lull, J. (1995). *Media, communication, culture: A global culture.* New York: Columbia University Press.

Maass, A., Corvino, P., & Arcuri, L. (1994). Linguistic intergroup bias and the mass media. *Revue de Psychologie Sociale, 1,* 31–43.

Mares, M. L., & Cantor, J. (1992). Elderly viewers' responses to televised portrayals of old age. *Communication Research, 19,* 459–478.

Mastro, D. (2003). A social identity approach to understanding the impact of television messages. *Communication Monographs, 70,* 98–113.

Mastro, D., & Greenberg, B. (2000). The portrayal of racial minorities on prime-time television. *Journal of Broadcasting and Electronic Media, 44,* 690–703.

Matabane, P., & Merritt, B. (1996). African American on television: Twenty-five years after Kerner. *Howard Journal of Communications, 7,* 329–337.

McLeod, K. (1999). Authenticity within hip-hop and other cultures threatened with assimilation. *Journal of Communication, 49,* 134–150.

McQuail, D. (1997). *Audience analysis.* Thousand Oaks, CA: Sage.

McQuail, D., Blumler, J. G., & Brown, J. W. (1972). The television audience, a revised perspective. In D. McQuail (Ed.), *Sociology of mass communication* (pp. 135–164). Harmondsworth, UK: Penguin.

Merskin, D. (2001). Winnebagos, Cherokees, Apaches, and Dakotas: The persistence of stereotyping of American Indians in American advertising brands. *Howard Journal of Communications, 12,* 159–169.

Michaels, E. (1987). *For a cultural future: Francis Jupurrla makes TV at Yuendumu.* Melbourne, Australia: Artspace.

Mitra, A. (1997). Virtual commonality: Looking for India on the Internet. In S. G. Jones (Ed.), *Virtual culture: Identity and communication in cyberspace* (pp. 55–79). Thousand Oaks, CA: Sage.

Morley, D. (1992). *Television, audiences, and cultural studies.* New York: Routledge.

NAACP (1999). *NAACP blasts TV networks' fall season whitewash.* Retrieved, June 13th, 2000 from http://www.naacp.org/press1999.asp

NAACP (2000). *Cable television grade is "C" on NAACP report card.* Retrieved, June 13th,

2000 from http://www.naacp.org/cable.html

Napoli, P. M. (1999). Deconstructing the diversity principle. *Journal of Communication,* *49,* 7–34.

NOW (2003). *New FCC rules threaten to shut out women and people of color.* Retrieved, June 9, 2003 from http://www.now.org/press/06–03/06–04.html

Pearlstein, S. (2003, July 15). Are Hispanics a distinct market? FCC to decide. *Tucson Citizen,* p. B1.

Pedic, F. (1989). Effect on social self-esteem of nationalistic appeals in corporate image advertisements. *Australian Journal of Psychology, 41,* 37–47.

Penley, C. (1997). *NASA/Trek: Popular science and sex in America.* New York: Verso.

Perlmutter, D. D. (2000). *Policing the media: Street cops and public perceptions of law enforcement.* Thousand Oaks, CA: Sage.

Radway, J. (1983). Women read the romance: The interaction of text and context. *Feminist Studies, 9,* 53–78.

Radway, J. (1984). *Reading the romance: Woman, patriarchy, and popular culture.* Chapel Hill, NC: University of North Carolina Press.

Reid, S., Giles, H., & Abrams, J. (2004). A social identity model of media effects. *Zeitschrift für Medienpsychologie, 16,* 17–25.

Roe, K. (1985). Swedish youth and music: Listening patterns and motivation. *Communication Research, 12,* 353–362.

Roe, K. (1992). Different destinies—different melodies: School achievement, anticipated status, and adolescents' tastes in music. *European Journal of Communication, 7,* 335–358.

Romer, D., Jamieson, K. H., & De Coteau, N. J. (1998). The treatment of persons of color in local television news: Ethnic blame discourse or realistic group conflict. *Communication Research, 25,* 268–305.

Rosengren, K. E., Wenner, L. A., & Palmgreen, P. (Eds.). (1985). *Media gratifications research: Current perspectives.* Beverly Hills, CA: Sage.

Ross, L., Anderson, D. R., & Wisocki, P. A. (1982). Adult television viewing and sex-role attitudes. *Sex Roles, 8,* 589–592.

Roy, A., & Harwood, J. (1997). Underrepresented, positively portrayed: Older adults in television commercials. *Journal of Applied Communication Research, 25,* 39–56.

Sachdev, I., & Bourhis, R. Y. (1985). Social categorization and power differentials in group relations. *European Journal of Social Psychology, 15,* 415–434.

Sachdev, I., & Bourhis, R. Y. (1991). Power and status differentials in minority and majority group relations. *European Journal of Social Psychology, 21,* 1–24.

Sloan, L. R. (1979). The function and impact of sports for fans. In J. H. Goldstein (Ed.), *Sports, games, and play* (pp. 219–262). Hillsdale, NJ: Erlbaum.

Song, K. (1997). *Two tales of an American city: Portrayal of African-American and Korean-American relations in two ethnic newspapers between 1991 and 1993, the "Los Angeles Sentinel" and the "Korea Times."* Unpublished Doctoral Dissertation, University of Kansas, DAI, 59, no. 09A: 3269.

Sprafkin, J. N., & Liebert, R. M. (1978). Sex-typing and children's television preferences. In G. Tuchman, A. K. Daniels, & J. Benet (Eds.), *Hearth and home: Images of women in the mass media* (pp. 228–239). New York: Oxford University Press.

Tajfel, H., & Turner, J. C. (1986). The social identity theory of intergroup behavior. In S. Worchel & W. C. Austin (Eds.), *Psychology of intergroup relations* (pp. 7–24). Chicago: Nelson Hall.

Tan, G., & Tan A. S. (1979), Television use and self-esteem of Blacks. *Journal of Communication, 29,* 129–135.

Tate, E., & Surlin, S. (1976). Agreement with opinionated TV characters across culture. *Journalism Quarterly, 53,* 199–203.

Vidmar, N., & Rokeach, M. (1974). Archie Bunker's bigotry: A study in selective perception and exposure. *Journal of Communication, 24,* 35–47.

Van Dijk, T. A. (1987). *Communicating racism: Ethnic prejudice in thought and talk.* Newbury Park, CA: Sage.

von Feilitzen, C. (1976). The functions served by the mass media. In R. Brown (Ed.), *Children and television* (pp. 90–115). London: Collier-Macmillan.

von Feilitzen, C., & Linne, O. (1975). Identifying with television characters. *Journal of Communication, 25,* 51–55.

Zickmund, S. (1997). Approaching the radical other: The discursive culture of cyber-hate. In S. G. Jones (Ed.), *Virtual culture: Identity and communication in cyberspace* (pp. 185–205). Thousand Oaks, CA: Sage.

10
Intergroup Dimensions of the Internet

Tom Postmes
Nancy Baym

Intergroup boundaries of nationality, race, language, and ideology are called into question whenever new opportunities for intergroup contact arise. The Internet questions these boundaries like no other communication medium before it, because of its capacity to serve any (mediated) communication needs from interpersonal to mass broadcasting, because of its worldwide reach, and because of its access within and across a wide variety of groups and cultures (Hoffman & Novak, 1998; Katz, Rice, & Aspden, 2001).

There are indications that this gradually alters the fabric of society and institutions (Castells, 1996), and the Internet has undoubtedly transformed the nature of intergroup contact in three regards. First, it facilitates intergroup communication, offering the potential of reducing prejudicial attitudes (Pettigrew, 1998). Second, it facilitates intragroup communication, pivotal to the development of intragroup consensus, stereotypes of in- and outgroups, and pathways to collective action (Haslam, 1997; Postmes, Haslam, & Swaab, in press). Third, the Internet provides new paradigms for intergroup conflict and cooperation itself, for symbolic and nonphysical confrontations and collective action (Postmes & Brunsting, 2002). A major factor moderating the influence of these factors is that communications over the Internet can be relatively anonymous and that users tend to be isolated from each other.

In theory, the Internet can shift power relations between groups, with possibilities for emancipation and mobilization (Herring, 1996; Spears & Lea, 1994; Zuboff, 1988). Indeed, the Internet spawned a wide variety of emancipatory integrationist initiatives (see e.g., www.idealist.org). Less positively, the Internet is a showcase of

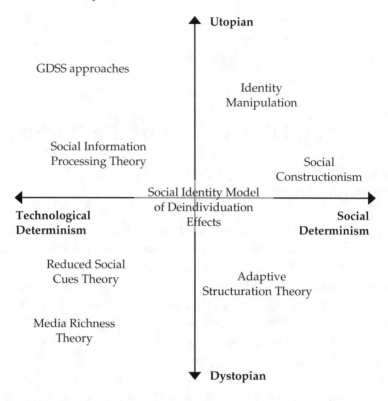

Figure 1: *A Taxonomy of Theories about the Social Effects of Communication Technology*

intergroup prejudices, and can facilitate oppression and inequity (Leets, 2001; Zickmund, 1997), including racism (e.g., the Hate Directory, www.bcpl.net/~rfrankli/hatedir.htm), sexism, and classism, and more subtle cultural prejudices. The Internet is a forum for a range of intergroup (collective) actions under the umbrella of anticorporatism and antiglobalization, and even online extensions of "real" wars (e.g., the virtual Intifadah). These collective actions can take forms such as defacements, virtual blockades, sit-ins, denial of service attacks, or site hijacking. Not only do these developments have intrinsic importance and interest, but they also provide inroads to studying novel or traditionally covert aspects and forms of intergroup behavior.

However, despite intense research into the social effects of the Internet, we know little about its consequences for intergroup relations. One reason for this is a lack of systematic empirical research on the topic. A second cause is the neglect of intergroup relations in theories of computer-mediated communication (CMC). This chapter argues that this neglect is unfortunate because it ignores an important dimension of online life and hinders our understanding of CMC's interpersonal and intragroup effects. The first part of the chapter classifies perspectives on social influence of technological mediation in metatheoretical terms. The second part then identifies the limitations of these approaches and traces these to the metatheories of self and identity in which they are grounded. The third part explores how a social identity approach can inform our understanding of the implications of technological mediation for intergroup relations.

Theoretical Perspectives

In the past 30 years, various theories have considered communication technology's social consequences. A general taxonomy taking metatheoretical assumptions of different approaches into account distinguishes two dimensions (Spears, Postmes, Wolbert, Lea, & Rogers, 2000). The *first* is to see technological change as positive or negative in general, providing "utopian" and "dystopian" perspectives on technology (Kling, 1996; Spears & Lea, 1994). The *second* is whether social change is attributed to characteristics of technology (technological determinism), or whether technology and technology use are driven by social factors (social determinism). Crossing these two dimensions results in a four-fold taxonomy of approaches (see Figure 1). In order to illustrate each of the quadrants, we briefly outline some important perspectives.

Theories of Technological Determinism

On the left-hand side of Figure 1 are located some early theories about the social impact of communication technology, developed in the *protodigital era* when audioconferencing first became available, and computer-mediated communication appeared on the horizon. These theories have been reviewed extensively elsewhere (Baym, 2002; Postmes & Lea, 2000; Spears & Lea, 1992; Spears, Lea, & Postmes, 2001), so we can be brief here. They tend to predict that medium characteristics have certain static effects on individuals, usually to make their inter-action less "social." The "social" consequences here are essentially restricted to characteristics of positive interpersonal relationships (e.g., friendliness, sociability, and warmth). Because the Internet lacks the nonverbal means by which such feelings tend to be conveyed in face-to-face interaction, the idea is that the Internet is, therefore, so-cially impoverished (e.g., Cummings, Butler, & Kraut, 2002; Kraut et al., 1998). Theories following this logic are, among others, reduced social cues theory (Kiesler, Siegel, & McGuire, 1984) and media rich-ness theory (Daft & Lengel, 1984). These perspectives usually paint a bleak picture of the social consequences of the Internet (i.e., they are dystopian). More recently, the social information processing model (SIP: Walther, 1992) also emphasized CMCs limitations in terms of *speed* of relational development.

However, in keeping with a utopian tradition of viewing science and technology as progress (Segal, 1986), in some cases social impov-erishment was identified as a blessing. A good example of this is the literature on group decision support systems (GDSS). Here, social in-fluence is seen as an obstacle to effective group decision-making and performance (cf., Buys, 1978). If technological systems remove the ca-pacity for sociability, this will therefore improve group performance (Jessup, Connolly, & Tansik, 1990; Valacich, Jessup, Dennis, & Nuna-maker, 1992). Similarly, the inability to see gender, race, or other so-cial cues can render them irrelevant, undermining status and power differentials and fostering equality in online groups (e.g., Dubrovsky, Kiesler, & Sethna, 1991). This idea can be extended to intergroup rela-tions more generally, where the Internet could exert a democratizing influence through obscuring traditional group distinctions and em-powerment (cf. Bakardjieva, 2002; Mantovani, 1994).

Across these distinct approaches, the underlying assumption is invariably that *social* effects are due to technology reducing the *indi-vidual's* capacity to encode or decode social signals (see also Hay-thornthwaite, 2002). Perhaps due to this inherent individualism, the empirical and theoretical concerns of these theories have tended to be interpersonal (and to a lesser extent intragroup) processes, with little attention on intergroup relations. Nonetheless, the implications of these approaches for intergroup relations are straightforward. Where social influences are seen as obstacles for intergroup relations, these theories are positive: technology could be used to reduce stereotyping and prejudice that is triggered by direct face-to-face contact, and it could increase equality (Dubrovsky et al., 1991). Conversely, technology's influence is negative where social influence would benefit intergroup relations (e.g., where an absence of social regulation would encourage "flaming": cf. Douglas & McGarty, 2001; Lea, O'Shea, Fung, & Spears, 1992; O'Sullivan & Flanagin, 2003).

The main problem of these determinist theories is the huge variety of social effects that communication technologies have (Baym, 2002). The Internet is hardly a Mecca of equality and tolerance (Bakardjieva, 2002; Douglas & McGarty, 2001; Mantovani, 1994), although there are pockets where such goals are pursued with vigor (Brunsting & Postmes, 2002; Postmes & Brunsting, 2002). Likewise, communication technologies have hardly made the workplace more egalitarian and open across the board (Iacono & Kling, 2001; Micklethwait & Wooldridge, 1996; Zuboff, 1988). Also in field studies of group decision support, adverse effects have been noted especially in international settings (Espinosa, Cummings, Wilson, & Pearce, 2003; Lyytinen, Maaranen, & Knuuttila, 1993). Finally, descriptive studies of Internet use have declared that it leads to reduced social involvement and poorer psychological well being (Kraut et al., 1998)—only to report reverse effects a few years later (Kraut et al., 2002).

Even in the more controlled environments of laboratory experiments, the contradictory effects of communication technology abound. With regard to intergroup relations, for example, Walther (1997) failed to find support for SIP in a study of cross-national student collaboration over CMC. Studies of multicultural and multinational GDSS sessions have observed no major beneficial effects of mediation (Daily & Steiner, 1998). Studies of online gender differences also produce more complex results than initially envisaged (Flanagin, Tiyaamornwong, O'Connor, & Seibold, 2002; Jackson, Ervin, Gardner, & Schmitt, 2001; Thomson & Murachver, 2001).

In response to this diversity of effects, many theorists have dismissed technological determinism. This has fuelled an equally one-sided countermovement, which assumes that technologies are principally determined by their social uses.

Social Determinism

The original opposition to technological determinism was inspired by social constructionists' argument that social practices and discourses shape social reality (Berger & Luckman, 1966). From this perspective, social practices within groups and organizations could be a major determinant of technology use (Baym, 2002; Fulk, 1993; Haythornthwaite, 2002), and social context and technology could mutually influence the "adaptive structuration" of technology (Contractor & Seibold, 1993; Orlikowski, Yates, Okamura, & Fujimoto, 1995; Poole & DeSanctis, 1990).

Despite their theoretical sophistication, theories of adaptive structuration and constructionism have been critiqued for remaining rather indeterminate and vague (Baym, 1995; Rice, 1993), and this is arguably their very purpose (Gergen, 1985). Moreover, they deemphasize the extent to which technology restrains practice. Even when they acknowledge the importance of technological constraints, as in adaptive structuration theory, they consistently fail to specify *how* technology limits the extent to which users can construct their own uses of technology, in contrast to the straightforward and strong role of social norms and internal systems of the group. Thereby, these theories ultimately convey the message that social factors are the key to understanding technology use and, in that sense, that they can be termed social determinist (Postmes, Spears, & Lea, 2000; Spears et al., 2000).

The individual is granted rather more agency and control in postmodern approaches arguing that the Internet offers a realm for reinventing identity (Myers, 1987; Poster, 1990; Turkle, 1995). However, this perspective suffers from the (opposite) problem of sliding into relativism and even voluntarism (i.e., indeterminate individualism). For example, postmodern perspectives have suggested that the Internet would be "neutral"—a blank social space users are free to decorate as they choose. This has obvious implications for intergroup relations, creating a somewhat utopian perspective that the social identities inscribed to stigmatized and powerless groups offline would become irrelevant online, ultimately perhaps even erasing those divisions in offline contexts (Haraway, 1990; see also McKenna & Bargh, 1998; McKenna & Bargh, 2000; Turkle, 1996).

The prime problem is that most people value their (social) identities, warts and all. Research examining the use of identity online confirms that people generally present and develop their "true" selves online. Rutter and Smith (1999) studied more than 17,000 messages in an online newsgroup and found that the use of fantasy selves was rare. Rather than inventing identities online, people appear most concerned with using the Internet to extend and enrich their "real" (i.e., offline social and individual) selves, questioning the distinction between virtual and real (see also Bargh, McKenna, & Fitzsimons, 2002).

More generally, social determinist approaches also have tended to ignore the intergroup dimension of the Internet—being overly concerned with predicting consequences of technology for individual users and for groups of decision makers. As we shall see shortly, however, intergroup communications introduce a different set of constraints, which, for example, seem to make norm formation in online communities less voluntaristic than social constructivists would tend to argue (Postmes et al., 2000).

In sum, reacting against the shortcomings of technological determinism, social determinist theories have sometimes embraced "anything goes" relativism. Although this might be a reasonable response given that technological determinist research clearly demonstrated that effects of technology are varied, it ignores that technology is *not* neutral. Whatever its effects, technological mediation influences the content and consequences of communication. Moreover, where technological determinism has had problems explaining the variability of these effects, social determinism faces the opposite conundrum of explaining *invariances* of technological innovation. At the individual and interpersonal level, technologies transform the properties and modes of interaction. At the group level, technology such as GDSS has relatively predictable effects on certain aspects of group processes (Benbasat & Lim, 1993; McLeod, 1992; Postmes & Lea, 2000; but see Chun & Park, 1998, for a different approach). At the macrosocial level, technology has not revolutionized social structures, society, or work on any large scale but has typically kept existing social orders intact (Iacono & Kling, 2001). And with regard to the theme of this volume, the Internet by and large has not changed existing intergroup relations but has provided a new forum for the perpetuation and accentuation of familiar forms of racism and sexism (Douglas & McGarty, 2001; Nakamura, 2002; Postmes, Spears, & Lea, 1998).

Putting Groups Back into the Frame

So far, we have discussed theories whose primary concern is with the "internal system of the group," that is with interpersonal and intragroup processes (Baym, 2002). This neglect of the (inter)group dimensions in theories of mediated communication has had unfortunate consequences. It has led to a state of affairs where intergroup distinctions are reduced to interpersonal properties, for example, where status is considered a personal attribute (Dubrovsky et al., 1991; Sproull & Kiesler, 1991) or an intragroup distinction (Espinosa et al., 2003; Nunamaker, Briggs, Mittleman, Vogel, & Balthazard, 1997), ignoring the possibility that status can transform interpersonal and intragroup situations into an intergroup one (e.g., as in the white-blue collar distinction). It can also be felt in studies of cross-national workgroups focusing on relational and interpersonal development rather than intergroup dynamics (Walther, 1997; Walther, Slovacek, & Tidwell, 2001).

There are limitations to such interpersonal analyses where social behavior is informed by factors that are not reducible to individual or interpersonal influences, but that are best understood as characteristics of the group as an entity—i.e., social norms or social identities (e.g., Baym, 1995; Postmes et al., 1998). These problems are apparent in both technological and social determinist perspectives, although in slightly different ways for each.

Technological Determinism and the Group

In the case of technological determinist theories, the emphasis on interpersonal and intragroup processes is grounded in analyses of how mediation influences the *individual's cognitive processing* of information. The problem here is that characteristics of the medium might influence both how messages and cues are perceived and interpreted, and influence relations to ingroup members and outgroup members, for reasons unrelated to the cognitive processing of messages or cues *per se*, and to slightly different effects (Lea & Spears, 1991, 1995; Spears & Lea, 1992). In intergroup interactions, for example, a greater sense of distance and anonymity might exacerbate the operation of stereotypes and prejudices—influencing perceptions and behaviors *independently* of the actual interactions (Spears, Lea, & Lee, 1990).

The problems for technological determinism can be illustrated by the "equalization phenomenon." This describes the idea that status differences would be less influential when group members are anonymous, as is sometimes the case in CMC. Indeed, some research has shown that group members participate more equally when they are anonymous (Dubrovsky et al., 1991). Paradoxically, however, similar studies have found opposite effects that status persists despite anonymity (Hollingshead, 1996; Scott & Easton, 1996) or even that anonymity amplifies status effects (Weisband, 1994; Weisband, Schneider, & Connolly, 1995).

The key to understanding these contradictory results is that anonymity does not operate as a "switch" to turn status and other aspects of identity "on or off" (cf. Valacich, Dennis, & Nunamaker, 1991, p. 344)—rather, it has multiple effects on multiple levels of social abstraction (Tanis, 2003). It is important to differentiate multiple aspects of status—status can be a (visible) personal attribute, but it is also a relevant intergroup distinction that ties in with people's *social identity* as either high- or low-status group members. Where signs of status might be rendered invisible by medium characteristics, status can persist as a relevant factor in the interaction irrespective of its visibility simply by virtue of its *known* existence and *social relevance*, and by its personal relevance as internalized part of one's social identity (Spears & Lea, 1994). Furthermore, anonymity can be used as a means to (strategically) manifest valued stigmatized social identities (McKenna & Bargh, 1998) or even to display highly stereotyped racial or gendered identities, as when men assume identities as outrageously sexy women or whites assume identities as Rastafarian or gangsta black men. In each of these cases, anonymity becomes a resource for self-stereotyping, or the stereotypical treatment of others, in ways that alter the balance of power between the groups involved (Nakamura, 2002).

Social Determinism and Intergroup Context
Neglecting intergroup processes has presented social determinism with a rather different set of problems. In general, these stem from failures to define the "social context" to which it attributes such prominence (Lea, O'Shea, & Fung, 1995). Although social determinism devotes considerable attention to the group, it fails to consider

what the group *is* in any systematic and theoretical analysis of how it relates to its wider social context. Once again, a key factor is that the intergroup dimension is ignored but, in contrast to technological determinism, the resulting problem is one of indeterminism. In particular, without considering the intergroup consequences of group process, it becomes difficult if not impossible to predict the form and direction that social influence might take (Turner, 1991).

One reason for this is that in the complete absence of any specific intergroup context, the processes of norm formation (social construction, structuration, or identity formation) are likely to be dictated by factors of an individual and interpersonal nature, such as group composition (Postmes et al., in press). Factors involved here are so diverse that any systematic theoretical analysis is likely to end with oblique and inconsequential references to the importance of taking into account characteristics of the individual and history of the group, without being able to specify in what way these will influence norm formation (DeSanctis & Poole, 1994; Fulk, Schmitz, & Steinfield, 1990).

This problem is compounded by the fact that, in intragroup contexts, the social demands to behave normatively are usually quite mild. It is when groups are engaged in some intergroup dynamic that normative behavior becomes truly important and deviance becomes punishable. In the Second World War, for example, severe punishments and hefty fines were administered for relatively mild offenses such as overcharging and petty theft (Thomas, 2003). Indeed, it has been argued that situations without a clear intergroup dynamic are perhaps not "group" contexts at all but are better understood as interpersonal in nature (Tajfel, 1978; Turner, 1982).

Thus, when theorists argue that online communities are best characterized as networks of interpersonal relationships or ties (Haythornthwaite, 2002; Wellman et al., 1996), they might, inadvertently, create a problem of removing essential elements of group behavior from their analysis. Interpersonal ties are not always *all* that matter. In many online contexts, as in offline ones, group processes can also occur at a different level of abstraction, such as when groups have a shared fate or experience intergroup conflict. Individual behavior in such cases is motivated not just by individual calculations but also by group-level considerations, such as a desire to express social identity and maintain or create a perceived social reality of "us" and "them" through self-stereotyping (Tajfel, 1978). Interpersonal analyses fall short of understanding what motivates actions in the many contexts that are explicitly intergroup in nature (i.e., when issues of race, class, gender, or any other social identity come into play). They also prevent us from considering that individuals' actions can be shaped by group-level processes even when the group under consideration would not appear to be in conflict with another, and when no common social identity can easily be identified.

As we will explore in the next section, the engagement with other groups severely restricts the individual's freedom to engage in identity play. Users usually are far from "free" to construct and structure technology almost boundlessly. This is only possible in unthreatened intragroup contexts that afford a liberty that does not exist to the same extent in intergroup contexts. Thus, the indeterminism and voluntarism of social determinist perspectives can be overcome by broadening our perspective on the wider social context within which a group operates. It is the exclusive focus on intragroup and interpersonal contexts that gives rise to the conclusion that "it depends."

Putting Group and Individual Back Together: Reconstructing Identity

The argument above suggests that technological and social determinist approaches differ in their underlying assumptions about who the "user" of technology is. Technological determinists approach the user as a psychologist would—as an individual with cognitive capacities geared to processing input and generating output. Most social determinists see users more as sociologists would—as a network or structure of actors in which individuals are considered mainly as products of social structure. The shortcomings of each approach become apparent when examining these conceptions of "group" and "individual" more closely, and when challenging the dualism that is assumed to exist between individual and structural factors (cf. Giddens, 1984; Turner & Oakes, 1986).

An alternative approach to studying effects of mediated communication begins with the realization that both individual and structural factors (comprising characteristics of technology, as well as wider social contexts) are essential to understanding the coordinated human activity of mediated communication. In order to overcome the dualism, the social identity approach postulates that the social is not external to the self, but that it is internalized through a *social identity* (Haslam, 2001; Tajfel & Turner, 1979; Turner, 1985, 1999). These social identities are not merely individual conceptions of a group, social category, or organization. They are—to some extent at least—*socially shared* conceptions of what the defining features and boundaries of these structures are. This definition implies that, although social identities are represented in individual cognition, they are simultaneously properties of the group itself because they could not exist without some degree of consensus among those who share this identity. Between the individual and the social there is reciprocal interaction—to ask about cause and effect is futile.

Social identities can be derived from common perspectives on group history and a sense of future direction, but importantly, they are formed to a large extent through comparison and differentiation from relevant outgroups (Oakes, Haslam, & Turner, 1994). This can occur online. In their analysis of the Internet in Trinidad, for example, Miller and Slater (2000) have shown that Trinidadians' social identity is amplified by the discovery that most of their interlocutors, especially North Americans, do not know where or even what Trinidad is. Also important for online behavior is that social identities incorporate group *norms*—that is, a group-specific set of conventions, rules, and possible sanctions. A social identity (and the norms associated with it) can shape individual thought and action through the twin processes of self-categorization and social identification. The categorization of oneself as a member of a social group is in part dependent on the salience of categories, and this can be aroused by specific features of the social context, and (importantly) is not dependent on the *actual presence* of other members of the group (McGarty, 1999; Oakes, 1987).

Social identification goes beyond the cognitive knowledge of being a group member: it describes the affective consequences of (aspirant) group membership. Thus strong identification with a certain social group increases the likelihood that the group's social identity is self-defining. Both processes of categorization and identification—the first tending to be more situationally and contextually determined, the latter more enduring and long term—enhance the likelihood that individuals will come to define themselves in terms of a certain social identity (Haslam, 2001). If this is the case, then the norms and properties that are commonly ascribed to the social group become internalized; they become subjectively interchangeable with personal norms, influencing thought and guiding action.

This social identity approach provides the ingredients for a reanalysis of some of the contradictory effects observed in studies of technology adopting a technological determinist perspective (Spears & Lea, 1992). This perspective (formalized in the social identity model of deindividuation effects, or SIDE) argues for a distinction between cognitive and strategic effects of communication media. Cognitively, different media might make personal and social attributes more or less visible, and thereby influence the relative importance of (inter)personal and (inter)group differences in users' perceptions and in group processes more generally (Reicher, Spears, & Postmes, 1995; Spears & Lea, 1992). In addition, users and groups can seize upon characteristics of media, such as anonymity, as a (strategic) instrument in making intergroup challenges and changes more or less feasible (Postmes & Brunsting, 2002; Reicher, 2001; Spears & Lea, 1994; Spears, Lea, Corneliussen, Postmes, & Ter Haar, 2002) and to influence one's self-presentation toward the ingroup (Barreto & Ellemers, 2000; Douglas & McGarty, 2002).

Thus, according to SIDE, technology neither has one specific effect on how messages are processed, nor does it have any effect whatsoever (in the sense of being neutral). Rather, SIDE argues that technology can have a variety of effects and that this variability is at least partially explained by the specific aspects of identity (personal or social) that are involved in and invoked through its usage. Where anonymity might indeed serve to make person perceptions *less* articulate and refined (thereby potentially decreasing a sense of "presence") it might thereby render the underlying social dimensions *more* visible, in the same way that ceasing to treat a group as individuals named "Rose, Emma, and Iris" might enhance the likelihood of seeing them as a group of women (Tanis, 2003).

To illustrate this point, Tanis and Postmes (2003) conducted three studies examining online impression formation. These studies showed, on the one hand, that individual identifiability has straightforward and considerable effects on impression formation. When targets were individuated by means of portrait pictures or short biographies, they were perceived more distinctly and evaluated more posi-

tively. Conversely, anonymous targets were not perceived as positively nor were person perceptions as well developed. Interestingly,
however, this lack of individuating capacity resulted in a proportion-
ally greater reliance on group memberships when it came to choosing
partners for future collaboration: ingroup others were perceived as
considerably more attractive collaborators, despite an equally negative and unrefined person perception. In other words, in the absence
of individuating information, the social identity of targets and perceiver becomes more relevant (see also Sassenberg & Postmes, 2002).

Such effects of individual identifiability are not just restricted to
the cognitive realm of salience of individual or social identity. Importantly, there are also strategic consequences of identifiability: characteristics of technology such as anonymity and physical isolation can
provide power and opportunity to oppose and counter a particular
outgroup from a safe distance (Postmes & Brunsting, 2002; Reicher et
al., 1995; Spears & Lea, 1994).

These strategic effects of anonymity were illustrated in two recent
studies examining the prediction that CMC can provide channels of
social support fostering resistance (Spears et al., 2002). In study 1, the
availability of CMC provided students with the means to resist authority. Specifically, when CMC was available as a means of intragroup communication, students felt empowered to express opinions that were normative for their group but punishable by the outgroup (faculty). In study 2, a direct manipulation of the amount of
perceived social support within CMC led to an increased willingness
to express normative attitudes against outgroup interests. Thus, when
students perceived that others would support them via CMC, they
were more likely to endorse punishable statements in the face of potential outgroup punishment.

Another study has examined the potential for the Internet to support collective action (Brunsting & Postmes, 2002). A survey examining actual and intended protest-related behaviors among different
groups of environmental activists and nonactivist control groups
showed that the Internet plays an increasingly central role in collective action efforts, in particular in its use as a mass communication
device for mobilization. Moreover, the Internet was found to facilitate
movements in their efforts to involve peripheral group members and
attract new members. Together, these studies reveal the importance of

CMC as a medium for communicating and coordinating the social support central to collective action (see McCaughey & Ayers, 2003, for other work on social activism and the Internet).

Going beyond these effects of technology on aspects of identity, however, there are also clear reasons why intergroup contexts should be taken into account as factors that influence the processes with which social determinists are primarily concerned: those of construction of social norms and structuration. There are three reasons why intergroup contexts restrict users' freedom to do as they please.

The first reason is that an intergroup context transforms the interaction from an interpersonal one to an intergroup context (Tajfel, 1978; Turner, 1985). For instance, Miller and Slater (2000), report that Trinidadians' social identity is made so salient by the inherently outgroup nature of the Internet that they even fill their personal homepages with links to national Trinidadian sites. This not only has effects on how we present the self but also on how we perceive the self in relation to others. The intergroup context triggers an (implicit) social comparison, transforming our perceived relationship to others from an unstructured and undifferentiated mass of stronger and weaker "links" into a clearly structured perception of "us" and "them." The consequence is that personal identity and its idiosyncratic needs and motives are pushed to the background. Instead, different aspects of self become relevant. Prominent among these is social identity—that aspect of self that is derived from a particular social group membership (Turner, Hogg, Oakes, Reicher, & Wetherell, 1987). The salience of social identity has marked consequences for intragroup relations, for example, in terms of attraction (shifting from interpersonal to group-based, Hogg, 1992; see Hogg & Tindale, this volume) or in terms of social cognition and social perceptions (these become homogenized and consensualized, leading to shared cognition, Haslam, 1997; Postmes et al., in press).

The second reason is that intergroup contexts activate stereotyped conceptions of in- and outgroup (Oakes et al., 1994; Turner, 1985). These stereotypes influence our relations with others, making us more susceptible to prejudice. However, they also influence our perceptions of ourselves, in that they foster self-stereotyping in thought and action (Spears, Doosje, & Ellemers, 1997; Turner et al., 1987). Thus, merely activating gender stereotypes has been shown to affect the use of

228 • Postmes & Baym

technology: women tend to self-stereotype and perceive themselves as technologically incompetent when attention is drawn to their femaleness and the stereotypes of females (Brouwer, Kawakami, Rojahn, & Postmes, 1997; Postmes & Spears, 2002).

Third, the intergroup dimension affects the processes of social construction and structuration (Postmes et al., in press), giving them a sense of predictability which is sorely lacking in the social determinist tradition. When considering the processes by which a group forms a social identity, a group derives its purposes to a certain degree from implicit and explicit comparisons with relevant outgroups (Oakes et al., 1994; Turner et al., 1987) and from interactions with that outgroup in an ongoing intergroup dynamic (Drury & Reicher, 2000; Reicher, 1996). More specifically, the social construction of a group normative position is likely to produce a consensus that captures the prevailing sentiment within the group *while at the same time seeking to contrast itself from relevant outgroups* (Haslam et al., 1998; Turner, 1991).

To put this more plainly, we "construct" or "structure" our group to be about that which defines us best in comparison to relevant outgroups. Postmes, Spears, and Lea (2002) sought to demonstrate this in two studies of intergroup interaction via the Internet. One study examined interaction between groups in England and the Netherlands over several weeks. These groups had online discussions on several political topics. Half the groups conducted these discussions anonymously, which is known to have a depersonalizing effect on perceptions of self and other in- and outgroup members (Lea, Spears, & de Groot, 2001; Sassenberg & Postmes, 2002). In half the groups, in contrast, members were identifiable and individuated.

When group members were individuated, intergroup divisions did not emerge, despite the fact that the topics could give rise to differences of opinion. As can be seen in Figure 2, when group members were individuated during the discussion, they converged on a common perspective over time. When group members were depersonalized, however, the subgroups polarized such that they came to occupy distinct positions. Crucially, these normative positions were occupied right from the start of the intergroup discussions (in week 2), and little change over time occurred from that moment on. Thus, when personal identities were less salient within the context of the interaction, the normal processes of construction of a normative

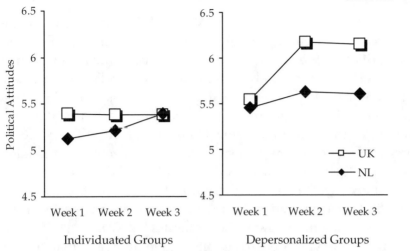

Figure 2: *Attitude Polarization Occurring in International Groups During Longitudinal Discussions over the Internet by Conditions of Individuation or Depersonalization*

position were disrupted, and stereotypic intergroup divisions occurred right from the start.

Such convergence processes do not *require* the explicit salience of the intergroup frame, however. In one study, we examined the communications of students who participated in a statistics course (Postmes et al., 2000). In addition to their regular classes, they could participate in an online statistics tutorial, which let them send e-mails to the course instructor. As it transpired, participants also used this facility to send each other e-mails, and these messages were subsequently analyzed by us. We analyzed the content of messages, in an attempt to chart the emergence of social norms. Using network analysis, we identified groups of students. Results showed that over time each group converged in both content (i.e., their use of humor) and stylistic form (i.e., punctuation and capitalization) of their messages, but group communication also became distinctive in that the aspects of communication that were accentuated were those that distinguished each group relative to the others. Thus, each group effectively displayed a form of group polarization that served to develop a particular identity as a group in an *implicit comparison* with the wider group context.

A similar process can be seen in Mitra's (1997) analysis of the discussion group "soc.culture.indian," where Indian immigrants define their identities as Indians in opposition to other Indian subcultures, rather than defining themselves as members of a collective and common Indian diaspora. Mitra writes that "the large range of discussions about the merits of Hinduism, the problems with Pakistan, and evaluation of the newly emerging Hindu party in India all become manifestations and concretizations of the fundamental contradictions between the different social, cultural, and political blocs that make up post-Independence India." Furthermore, this polarization is accomplished "in languages and styles that are often bigoted, suggestive of violence, and sometimes low-level harangues" (p. 71).

In sum, we have proposed an alternative approach that seeks to integrate aspects of technological and social determinist theories. It seeks to overcome the limitations of technological determinism by considering the social implications of communication technology at individual as well as social levels of identity. It has many things in common with social determinist theories but seeks to define the "social context" that shapes intragroup processes by taking into account the role of relevant outgroups. It is in the intergroup dynamic that group behavior acquires its purpose and direction and is, therefore, crucial to understanding the processes of structuration and construction.

Conclusion

To conclude, traditional theories of computer-mediated communication have tended to ignore intergroup relations in favor of interpersonal and group effects. Parallel to this, intergroup effects of the Internet have been seriously understudied. Ironically, we argue, it is the neglect of the intergroup dimension of the Internet that has rendered the analysis of its social effects on interpersonal relations and within groups powerless. It is by appreciating the intergroup dimension of our social life that we see the conditions where individuals internalize the group into the self. This internalized social identity ultimately helps us resolve the false dualism of agency/structure.

Despite the critique, however, both technological and social determinism have made clear contributions. Technological determinism acknowledges that the medium does have an impact and that technology is not neutral. Indeed, the characteristics of media should *a priori* assume a central role in our theories about technology's consequences. Social determinism's prime contribution has been to show that social norms (or culture or structure) play a key role in shaping the individual's medium usage. In addition to individual cognition and medium characteristics, the community of users cannot be ignored.

However, each of these approaches is too much anchored in one specific level of analysis to be versatile enough to avoid reducing technological effects to causes at an individual, interpersonal, social, or technological level. In order to achieve this, we need to develop an approach that tries to avoid falling into any one of the four quadrants of Figure 1—a more interactionist metatheory. The final sections of this chapter can be read as our attempt to provide such a starting point with the SIDE model. This model emphasizes that the uses and effects of the Internet are co-determined by technological features and social factors (identities, social relations, and social practices) rather than being (ultimately) reducible to either.

From this approach, and on the basis of the research it inspired, we come to a tentative conclusion about the implications of the Internet for intergroup relations. Although it is undoubted that the Internet produces a marked increase in contact opportunities, it remains to be seen whether this will lead to noticeable improvements in intergroup contact. The research conducted so far suggests that the effects of this contact are moderated by the conditions under which it takes place—technology is not neutral. Importantly, in cases where intergroup divisions are marked and salient, and where individual users are rendered anonymous and depersonalized, contact is likely to increase intergroup divides rather than bridge them for reasons both strategic and cognitive. People need social structures, and they re-create and create them in the virtual world even if this results in intergroup conflict. It is, perhaps, for this reason that, despite the apparent individualism of CMC, the Internet remains a most social and political space.

References

Bakardjieva, M. (2002). Community technology and democratic rationalization. *Information Society, 18*, 181–192.

Bargh, J. A., McKenna, K. Y. A., & Fitzsimons, G. M. (2002). Can you see the real me?

Activation and expression of the "true self" on the Internet. *Journal of Social Issues, 58*, 33–48.

Barreto, M., & Ellemers, N. (2000). You can't always do what you want: Social identity and self-presentational determinants of the choice to work for a low-status group. *Personality and Social Psychology Bulletin, 26*, 891–906.

Baym, N. K. (1995). The emergence of community in computer-mediated communication. In S. Jones (Ed.), *Cybersociety: Computer-mediated community and communication* (pp. 138–163). Thousand Oaks, CA: Sage.

Baym, N. K. (2002). Interpersonal life online. In S. Livingstone & L. Lievrouw (Eds.), *The handbook of new media* (pp. 62–76). London: Sage.

Benbasat, I., & Lim, L. H. (1993). The effects of group, task, context, and technology variables on the usefulness of group support systems: A meta-analysis of experimental studies. *Small Group Research, 24*, 430–462.

Berger, P. L., & Luckman, T. (1966). *The social construction of reality*. Harmondsworth, UK: Penguin.

Brouwer, J., Kawakami, J., Rojahn, K., & Postmes, T. (1997). De effecten van de (on)zichtbaarheid van sekse op zelf-stereotypering [The effects of gender (in)visibility on self-stereotyping]. In C. K. W. De Dreu, N. K. de Vries, D. Van Knippenberg, & C. Rutte (Eds.), *Fundamentele sociale psychologie* (Vol. 11, pp. 150–157). Tilburg, The Netherlands: Tilburg University Press.

Brunsting, S., & Postmes, T. (2002). Social movement participation in the digital age: Predicting offline and online collective action. *Small Group Research, 33*, 525–554.

Buys, C. J. (1978). Humans would do better without groups. *Personality and Social Psychology Bulletin, 4*, 123–125.

Castells, M. (1996). *The information age: Economy society and culture, Vol. 1: The network society*. Oxford: Blackwell.

Chun, K. J., & Park, H. K. (1998). Examining the conflicting results of GDSS research. *Information and Management, 33*, 313–325.

Contractor, N. S., & Seibold, D. R. (1993). Theoretical frameworks for the study of structuring processes in group decision support systems: Adaptive structuration theory and self-organizing systems theory. *Human Communication Research, 19*, 528–563.

Cummings, J. N., Butler, B., & Kraut, R. (2002). The quality of online social relationships. *Communications of the ACM, 45*, 103–108.

Daft, R. L., & Lengel, R. H. (1984). Information richness: A new approach to managerial behavior and organizational design. *Research in Organizational Behavior, 6*, 191–233.

Daily, B. F., & Steiner, R. L. (1998). The influence of group decision support systems on contribution and commitment levels in multicultural and culturally homogeneous decision-making groups. *Computers in Human Behavior, 14*, 147–162.

DeSanctis, G., & Poole, M. S. (1994). Capturing the complexity in advanced technology use: Adaptive structuration theory. *Organization Science, 5*, 121–147.

Douglas, K. M., & McGarty, C. (2001). Identifiability and self-presentation: Computer-mediated, communication and intergroup interaction. *British Journal of Social Psychology, 40*, 399–416.

Douglas, K. M., & McGarty, C. (2002). Internet identifiability and beyond: A model of the effects of identifiability on communicative behavior. *Group Dynamics: Theory Research and Practice, 6*, 17–26.

Drury, J., & Reicher, S. (2000). Collective action and psychological change: The emergence of new social identities. *British Journal of Social Psychology, 39*, 579–604.

Dubrovsky, V. J., Kiesler, S., & Sethna, B. N. (1991). The equalization phenomenon: Status effects in computer-mediated and face-to-face decision-making groups. *Human Computer Interaction, 6*, 119–146.

Espinosa, J. A., Cummings, J. N., Wilson, J. M., & Pearce, B. M. (2003). Team boundary issues across multiple global firms. *Journal of Management Information Systems, 19*, 157–190.

Flanagin, A. J., Tiyaamornwong, V., O'Connor, J., & Seibold, D. R. (2002). Computer-mediated group work: The interaction of member sex and anonymity. *Communication Research, 29*, 66–93.

Fulk, J. (1993). Social construction of communication technology. *Academy of Management Journal, 36*, 921–950.

Fulk, J., Schmitz, J., & Steinfield, C. W. (1990). A social influence model of technology use. In J. Fulk & C. Steinfield (Eds.), *Organizations and communication technology* (pp. 117–140). Newbury Park: Sage.

Gergen, K. J. (1985). The social constructionist movement in modern psychology. *American Psychologist, 40*, 266–275.

Giddens, A. (1984). *The constitution of society: Outline of the theory of structuration.* Cambridge, UK: Polity.

Haraway, D. (1990). A manifesto for cyborgs: Science, technology, and socialist feminism in the 1980s. In L. J. Nicholson (Ed.), *Feminism / Postmodernism* (pp. 190–233). London: Routledge.

Haslam, S. A. (1997). Stereotyping and social influence: Foundations of stereotype consensus. In R. Spears, P. J. Oakes, N. Ellemers, & S. A. Haslam (Eds.), *The social psychology of stereotyping and group life* (pp. 119–143). Oxford, UK: Blackwell.

Haslam, S. A. (2001). *Psychology in organizations: The social identity approach.* London: Sage.

Haslam, S. A., Turner, J. C., Oakes, P. J., Reynolds, K. J., Eggins, R. A., Nolan, M., & Tweedie, J. (1998). When do stereotypes become really consensual? Investigating the group-based dynamics of the consensualization process. *European Journal of Social Psychology, 28*, 755–776.

Haythornthwaite, C. (2002). Strong, weak, and latent ties and the impact of new media. *Information Society, 18*, 385–401.

Herring, S. C. (1996). Gender and democracy in computer-mediated communication. In R. Kling (Ed.), *Computerization and controversy* (2nd ed., pp. 476–489). San Diego: Academic Press.

Hoffman, D. L., & Novak, T. P. (1998). Bridging the racial divide on the Internet. *Science, 280*, 390–391.

Hogg, M. A. (1992). *The social psychology of group cohesiveness: From attraction to social identity.* Hemel Hempstead, UK: Harvester Wheatsheaf.

Hollingshead, A. B. (1996). Information suppression and status persistence in group decision-making: The effects of communication media. *Human Communication Research, 23,* 193–219.

Iacono, S., & Kling, R. (2001). Computerization movements: The rise of the Internet and distant forms of work. In J. Yates & J. Van Maanen (Eds.), *Information technology and organizational transformation: History, rhetoric, and practice* (pp. 93–136). Thousand Oaks, CA: Sage.

Jackson, L. A., Ervin, K. S., Gardner, P. D., & Schmitt, N. (2001). Gender and the Internet: Women communicating and men searching. *Sex Roles, 44,* 363–379.

Jessup, L. M., Connolly, T., & Tansik, D. A. (1990). Toward a theory of automated group work: The deindividuating effects of anonymity. *Small Group Research, 21,* 333–348.

Katz, J. E., Rice, R. E., & Aspden, P. (2001). The Internet, 1995–2000: Access, civic involvement, and social interaction. *American Behavioral Scientist, 45,* 405–419.

Kiesler, S., Siegel, J., & McGuire, T. W. (1984). Social psychological aspects of computer-mediated communication. *American Psychologist, 39,* 1123–1134.

Kling, R. (1996). Hopes and horrors: technological utopianism and anti-utopianism in narratives of computerization. In R. Kling (Ed.), *Computerization and controversy* (2nd ed., pp. 40–58). San Diego: Academic Press.

Kraut, R., Kiesler, S., Boneva, B., Cummings, J., Helgeson, V., & Crawford, A. (2002). Internet paradox revisited. *Journal of Social Issues, 58,* 49–74.

Kraut, R., Patterson, M., Lundmark, V., Kiesler, S., Mukopadhyay, T., & Scherlis, W. (1998). Internet paradox: A social technology that reduces social involvement and psychological well-being? *American Psychologist, 53,* 1017–1031.

Lea, M., O'Shea, T., & Fung, P. (1995). Constructing the networked organization: Content and context in the development of electronic communications. *Organization Science, 6,* 462–478.

Lea, M., O'Shea, T., Fung, P., & Spears, R. (1992). "Flaming" in computer-mediated communication: observations, explanations, implications. In M. Lea (Ed.), *Contexts of computer-mediated communication* (pp. 30–65). Hemel Hempstead, UK: Harvester Wheatsheaf.

Lea, M., & Spears, R. (1991). Computer-mediated communication, de-individuation and group decision-making. *International Journal of Man Machine Studies, 34,* 283–301.

Lea, M., & Spears, R. (1995). Love at first Byte? Building personal relationships over computer networks. In J. T. Wood & S. Duck (Eds.), *Understudied relationships: Off the beaten track.* (pp. 197–233). Beverly Hills: Sage.

Lea, M., Spears, R., & de Groot, D. (2001). Knowing me, knowing you: Anonymity effects on social identity processes within groups. *Personality and Social Psychology Bulletin, 27,* 526–537.

Leets, L. (2001). Response to Internet hate sites: Is speech too free in cyberspace? *Communication, Law and Policy, 6,* 287–317.

Lyytinen, K., Maaranen, P., & Knuuttila, J. (1993). Unusual business or business as usual: An investigation of meeting support requirements in multilateral diplomacy. *Accounting, Management and Information Technologies, 4,* 97–119.

Mantovani, G. (1994). Is computer-mediated communication intrinsically apt to enhance democracy in organizations? *Human Relations, 47*, 45–62.

McCaughey, M., & Ayers, M. D. (2003). *Cyberactivism: Online activism in theory and practice*. London: Routledge.

McGarty, C. (1999). *Categorization in social psychology*. London: Sage.

McKenna, K. Y. A., & Bargh, J. A. (1998). Coming out in the age of the Internet: Identity "demarginalization" through virtual group participation. *Journal of Personality and Social Psychology, 75*, 681–694.

McKenna, K. Y. A., & Bargh, J. A. (2000). Plan 9 from cyberspace: The implications of the Internet for personality and social psychology. *Personality and Social Psychology Review, 4*, 57–75.

McLeod, P. L. (1992). An assessment of the experimental literature on electronic support of group work: Results of a meta-analysis. *Human Computer Interaction, 7*, 257–280.

Micklethwait, J., & Wooldridge, A. (1996). *The witch doctors: Making sense of the management gurus*. New York: Random House.

Miller, D., & Slater, D. (2000). *The Internet: An ethnographic approach*. Oxford: Berg.

Mitra, A. (1997). Virtual commonality: Looking for India on the Internet. In S. Jones (Ed.), *Virtual culture* (pp. 55–79). Newbury Park, CA: Sage.

Myers, D. (1987). "Anonymity is part of the magic": Individual manipulation of computer-mediated communication contexts. *Qualitative Sociology, 10*, 251–266.

Nakamura, L. (2002). *Cybertypes: Race, ethnicity, and identity on the Internet*. New York: Routledge.

Nunamaker, J. F. Jr., Briggs, R. O., Mittleman, D. D., Vogel, D. R., & Balthazard, P. A. (1997). Lessons from a dozen years of group support systems research: A discussion of lab and field findings. *Journal of Management Information Systems, 13*, 163–207.

O'Sullivan, P. B., & Flanagin, A. J. (2003). Reconceptualizing "flaming" and other problematic messages. *New Media and Society, 5*, 69–94.

Oakes, P. J. (1987). The salience of social categories. In J. C. Turner, M. A. Hogg, P. J. Oakes, S. Reicher, & M. S. Wetherell (Eds.), *Rediscovering the social group: A self-categorization theory* (pp. 117–141). Oxford: Basil Blackwell.

Oakes, P. J., Haslam, S. A., & Turner, J. C. (1994). *Stereotyping and social reality*. Oxford: Blackwell.

Orlikowski, W. J., Yates, J., Okamura, K., & Fujimoto, M. (1995). Shaping electronic communication: The metastructuring of technology in the context of use. *Organization Science, 6*, 423–444.

Pettigrew, T. F. (1998). Intergroup contact theory. *Annual Review of Psychology, 49*, 65–85.

Poole, M. S., & DeSanctis, G. (1990). Understanding the use of group decision support systems: the theory of adaptive structuration. In J. Fulk & C. Steinfield (Eds.), *Organizations and Communication Technology* (pp. 173–193). Newbury Park: Sage.

Poster, M. (1990). *The mode of information: Poststructuralism and social context*. Chicago: Polity.

Postmes, T., & Brunsting, S. (2002). Collective action in the age of internet: Mass communication and online mobilization. *Social Science Computer Review, 20*, 290–

301.

Postmes, T., Haslam, S. A., & Swaab, R. (in press). Social identity and social influence in small groups: Communication, consensualization and socially shared cognition. *European Review of Social Psychology, 15*.

Postmes, T., & Lea, M. (2000). Social processes and group decision-making: Anonymity in group decision support systems. *Ergonomics, 43*, 1252–1274.

Postmes, T., & Spears, R. (2002). Contextual moderators of gender differences and stereotyping in computer-mediated group discussions. *Personality and Social Psychology Bulletin, 28*, 1073–1083.

Postmes, T., Spears, R., & Lea, M. (1998). Breaching or building social boundaries? SIDE-effects of computer-mediated communication. *Communication Research, 25*, 689–715.

Postmes, T., Spears, R., & Lea, M. (2000). The formation of group norms in computer-mediated communication. *Human Communication Research, 26*, 341–371.

Postmes, T., Spears, R., & Lea, M. (2002). Intergroup differentiation in computer-mediated communication: Effects of depersonalization. *Group Dynamics, 6*, 3–16.

Reicher, S. (1996). "The Battle of Westminster:" Developing the social identity model of crowd behavior in order to explain the initiation and development of collective conflict. *European Journal of Social Psychology, 26*, 115–134.

Reicher, S. (2001). Social identity definition and enactment: A broad SIDE against irrationalism and relativism. In T. Postmes, R. Spears, M. Lea, & S. Reicher (Eds.), *SIDE effects centre stage: Recent developments in studies of de-individuation in groups*. Amsterdam: Elsevier.

Reicher, S., Spears, R., & Postmes, T. (1995). A social identity model of deindividuation phenomena. In W. Stroebe & M. Hewstone (Eds.), *European Review of Social Psychology* (Vol. 6, pp. 161–198). Chichester, UK: Wiley.

Rice, R. E. (1993). Using network concepts to clarify sources and mechanisms of social influence. In W. Richards Jr. & G. Barnett (Eds.), *Progress in communication sciences: Advances in communication network analysis* (pp. 43–52). Norwood, NJ: Ablex.

Rutter, J., & Smith, G. W. H. (1999, December). *Presenting the offline self in an everyday, online environment.* Paper presented at the Identities in Action conference, University of Wales, Aberystwyth. Retrieved August 14, 2004 from http://les1.man.ac.uk/cric/Jason_Rutter/papers/Self.pdf

Sassenberg, K., & Postmes, T. (2002). Cognitive and strategic processes in small groups: Effects of anonymity of the self and anonymity of the group on social influence. *British Journal of Social Psychology, 41*, 463–480.

Scott, C. R., & Easton, A. C. (1996). Examining equality of influence in group decision support system interaction. *Small Group Research, 27*, 360–382.

Segal, H. P. (1986). The technological utopians. In J. J. Corn (Ed.), *Imagining tomorrow* (pp. 188–201). Cambridge, MA: MIT Press.

Spears, R., Doosje, B., & Ellemers, N. (1997). Self-stereotyping in the face of threats to group status and distinctiveness: The role of group identification. *Personality and Social Psychology Bulletin, 23*, 538–553.

Spears, R., & Lea, M. (1992). Social influence and the influence of the "social" in computer-mediated communication. In M. Lea (Ed.), *Contexts of computer-mediated communication* (pp. 30–65). Hemel Hempstead, UK: Harvester Wheatsheaf.

Spears, R., & Lea, M. (1994). Panacea or panopticon? The hidden power in computer-mediated communication. *Communication Research, 21*, 427–459.

Spears, R., Lea, M., Corneliussen, R. A., Postmes, T., & Ter Haar, W. (2002). Computer-mediated communication as a channel for social resistance: The strategic side of SIDE. *Small Group Research, 33*, 555–574.

Spears, R., Lea, M., & Lee, S. (1990). De-individuation and group polarization in computer-mediated communication. *British Journal of Social Psychology, 29*, 121–134.

Spears, R., Lea, M., & Postmes, T. (2001). Social psychological theories of computer-mediated communication: Social gain or social pain? In H. Giles & P. Robinson (Eds.), *New handbook of language and social psychology* (pp. 601–624). Chichester, UK: Wiley.

Spears, R., Postmes, T., Wolbert, A., Lea, M., & Rogers, P. (2000). *Social psychological influence of ICT's on society and their policy implications*. Amsterdam: Infodrome. http://www.infodrome.nl/publicaties/domeinen/03_spears.html

Sproull, L., & Kiesler, S. (1991). *Connections: New ways of working in the networked organization*. Cambridge, MA: MIT Press.

Tajfel, H. (1978). Interindividual behavior and intergroup behavior. In H. Tajfel (Ed.), *Differentiation between groups: Studies in the social psychology of intergroup relations* (pp. 27–60). London: Academic Press.

Tajfel, H., & Turner, J. C. (1979). An integrative theory of intergroup conflict. In S. Worchel & W. G. Austin (Eds.), *The psychology of intergroup relations* (pp. 33–47). Monterey, CA: Brooks-Cole.

Tanis, M. (2003). *Cues to identity in CMC: The impact of person perception and subsequent interaction outcomes*. Unpublished PhD Thesis, University of Amsterdam.

Tanis, M., & Postmes, T. (2003). Social cues and impression formation in CMC. *Journal of Communication, 53*, 676–693.

Thomas, D. (2003). *An underworld at war: Spivs, deserters, racketeers and civilians in the second world war*. London: John Murray.

Thomson, R., & Murachver, T. (2001). Predicting gender from electronic discourse. *British Journal of Social Psychology, 40*, 193–208.

Turkle, S. (1995). *Life on the screen: Identity in the age of the Internet*. New York: Simon & Schuster.

Turkle, S. (1996). Parallel lives: Working on identity in virtual space. In D. Grodin & T. R. Lindlof (Eds.), *Constructing the self in a mediated world* (pp. 156–175). Thousand Oaks, CA: Sage.

Turner, J. C. (1982). Towards a cognitive redefinition of the group. In H. Tajfel (Ed.), *Social identity and intergroup relations* (pp. 15–40). Cambridge: Cambridge University Press.

Turner, J. C. (1985). Social categorization and the self-concept: A social cognitive theory of group behavior. In E. J. Lawler (Ed.), *Advances in group processes: Theory and research* (Vol. 2, pp. 77–122). Greenwich, CT: JAI Press.

Turner, J. C. (1991). *Social influence*. Milton Keynes, UK: Open University Press.

Turner, J. C. (1999). Some current issues in research on social identity and self-categorization theories. In N. Ellemers, R. Spears, & B. Doosje (Eds.), *Social identity: Context, commitment, content* (pp. 68–89). Oxford: Basil Blackwell.

Turner, J. C., Hogg, M. A., Oakes, P. J., Reicher, S., & Wetherell, M. S. (1987). *Rediscovering the social group: A self-categorization theory*. Oxford: Basil Blackwell.

Turner, J. C., & Oakes, P. J. (1986). The significance of the social identity concept for social psychology with reference to individualism, interactionism and social influence. *British Journal of Social Psychology, 25*, 237–252.

Valacich, J. S., Dennis, A. R., & Nunamaker, J. F. Jr. (1991). Electronic meeting support: The groupsystems concept. *International Journal of Man Machine Studies, 34*, 261–282.

Valacich, J. S., Jessup, L. M., Dennis, A. R., & Nunamaker, J. F. Jr. (1992). A conceptual framework of anonymity in group support systems. *Group Decision and Negotiation, 1*, 219–241.

Walther, J. B. (1992). Interpersonal effects in computer-mediated interaction: A relational perspective. *Communication Research, 19*, 52–90.

Walther, J. B. (1997). Group and interpersonal effects in interpersonal computer-mediated communication. *Human Communication Research, 23*, 342–369.

Walther, J. B., Slovacek, C. L., & Tidwell, L. C. (2001). Is a picture worth a thousand words? Photographic images in long-term and short-term computer-mediated communication. *Communication Research, 28*, 105–134.

Weisband, S. P. (1994). Overcoming social awareness in computer-supported groups: Does anonymity really help? *Computer-Supported Cooperative Work, 2*, 285–297.

Weisband, S. P., Schneider, S. K., & Connolly, T. (1995). Computer-mediated communication and social information: Status salience and status differences. *Academy of Management Journal, 38*, 1124–1151.

Wellman, B., Salaff, J., Dimitrova, D., Garton, L., Gulia, M., & Haythornthwaite, C. (1996). Computer networks as social networks: Collaborative work, telework, and virtual community. *Annual Review of Sociology, 22*, 213–238.

Zickmund, S. (1997). Approaching the radical other: The discursive culture of cyberhate. In S. Jones (Ed.), *Virtual culture: Identity and communication in cybersociety* (pp. 185–205). Thousand Oaks, CA: Sage.

Zuboff, S. (1988). *In the age of the smart machine*. New York: Basic Books.

PART 3

Epilogue

11

A Self-Categorization Perspective on Communication and Intergroup Relations

Scott A. Reid
Howard Giles
Jake Harwood

Since the early 1970s, work on the interface of language, social identity, and intergroup relations has escalated. While such an interface might now seem apposite, this has not always been the case. Language and communication have generally been considered to be of *relevance* to intergroup relations, but their treatment as theoretically central constructs is a quite recent development. Language received its first sustained treatment in the group dynamics tradition throughout the 1950s and 1960s (e.g., Bales, 1956; Festinger, 1950; see Hogg & Tindale, this volume). In fact, the rich data that was produced from real groups in interaction was pivotal in the development of social comparison and dissonance theories, work that continues to be central to social psychology. However, the group dynamics tradition was concerned almost exclusively with interpersonal and intragroup relations, and language was rarely treated as anything more than a vehicle for psychological process. It was not until the late 1960s that intergroup relations and social identity were given the theoretical and empirical attention they deserved (see Tajfel, 1969; Israel & Tajfel, 1972). With this shift in emphasis, social identity theory (SIT) assimilated the insights of the previous work (e.g., social comparison theory) and extended it into the intergroup realm (see Gudykunst & Ting-Toomey, 1990). These ideas were quickly developed and adapted by Giles and colleagues into speech (now communication) accommodation theory (CAT: Giles & Coupland, 1991; Shepard, Giles, & Le Poire, 2001), ethnolinguistic identity theory (Giles & Johnson, 1981, 1987), and later by Gudykunst and colleagues' anxiety/uncertainty reduction theory (Gudykunst, 1995). These theories stand as background models for an array of phenomena, a sampling of which is described in this volume. Much has happened since the initial development of the social identity approach. There has been the development of social cognition, the arrival of the discourse analytic approach, and the almost independent development of self-categorization theory (SCT), which articulates the social cognitive underpinnings of social identity (Turner, 1987).

The roots of social cognition can be perhaps best appreciated as a development of the group dynamics tradition. On the one hand, this has been of immense value. There has been an explosion of research, particularly on attributions, stereotyping, schemata, and social influence. As a result, an entire lexicon of social cognitive processes has been described and tested across many contexts. On the other hand, language has been all but absent from social cognition (cf. Semin, 2000; Semin & Fiedler, 1992); there has been a model of the individual as a passive recipient and processor of social stimuli, rather than as a creator, negotiator, or manipulator (see Reicher & Hopkins, 1996, 2004). We are now experiencing a period where the principal elements of social cognition have been established (or refuted), social cognition has lost some vitality, and there is a sense that we are overdue for a paradigm shift. This has lent the field a fractured disposition. There has been a return to motivational processes (e.g., Aronson, 1992; Sedikides & Strube, 1995; Swann, 1990), applied work, particularly on organizations (e.g., Haslam, 2000; Hogg & Terry, 2000) and leadership (e.g., Hogg, 2001; Reid & Ng, 2004), a continued and growing body of work on social identity processes, and, in all of this, a schism between mainstream social psychology and discourse analysis (Abrams & Hogg, 1990a).

While the mainstream of social psychology all but eschewed language use, discursive social psychologists embraced it and made it central to their discussions of phenomena such as prejudice (van Dijk, 1987) and nationalism (Billig, 1996; see also Paulsen et al., this volume). If there is a central theme in discourse analysis, it is that social life is an active and constructive process lived in and through language. As yet, the idea of language use as constructive social action—despite being an obvious truth about the human condition—has yet to be assimilated by any predictive social psychological theory. Just how this will be resolved stands as one of the major challenges for the field.

This leaves us with SCT. Where SIT continues to have a disproportionate impact on the study of language and intergroup relations, SCT is yet to have the same influence. Indeed, the contributions to this book are testament to the continued influence of SIT, with each chapter putting it to creative use. There are applications to new phenomena, elaborations and extensions of the theoretical framework, and cross-fertilization with other theories. Most chapters employ SIT and, in particular, the identity management strategies described therein, as well as allied developments from ethnolinguistic identity theory and CAT. In contrast, only two chapters in this volume have focused centrally on SCT and what it can offer (Hogg & Tindale; Sachdev & Bourhis). What we will argue—and hopefully illustrate—is that SCT is overdue for an excursion into the study of language and communication phenomena.

Given the state of the field, we will depart somewhat from the standard mold for an epilogue. While there is value in considering the details of each chapter from this collection in turn, we believe the discipline might be better served by both a wider overview and discussion of the future avenues and challenges, as well as some focused theoretical attention. For this reason, we will consider what directions the field might take to address yet more phenomena. This will be partly achieved by elaborating upon how SCT can contribute to knowledge about communication, and how the study of communication will add to the social cognitive processes described by SCT.

In what follows, we open with a description of the social identity perspective (see also the first chapter of this book), describe the different theories, and outline the role of language and communication in those theories. We then consider a subsample of communicative phenomena for which a self-categorization perspective might bring insights that go beyond our current understanding.

The Social Identity Perspective

Social identity theory began as an attempt to explain macro-social patterns of prejudice and discrimination, and social changes resulting from intergroup competition for status, power, and prestige. In this, the theory was exclusively intergroup in focus, and restricted to this narrow, albeit important set of phenomena. However, this was just the beginning; in retrospect, SIT can now be seen as leading to a broader and allied set of social psychological theories—as the basis for a wider social identity perspective, or approach (Turner, 1999). A far from exhaustive list would include (as above) communication accommodation theory, ethnolinguistic identity theory, SCT, and sub-theories specific to social influence (e.g., Abrams & Hogg, 1990b; Turner, 1991), stereotyping (e.g., Oakes, Haslam, & Turner, 1994), leadership (e.g., Hogg, 2001), crowd behavior (Reicher, 1984), and computer mediated communication (Reicher, Spears, & Postmes, 1995).

The theory has not just survived, it has prospered—indeed, SIT has extended its reach in several directions, going so far as to serve as an integrative force across disciplines (sociolinguistics, communication, and social psychology come to mind). In part, this is because SIT incorporates an important and flexible, yet simple, insight. The argument is that we can understand social psychology as an interaction of individual psychological processes (social categorization, social comparison, and the search for evaluatively positive social identity) with the social context or frame of reference in which people find themselves (broadly speaking, whether intergroup relations are perceived to be cooperative or competitive) (Tajfel, 1969). Thoughts, feelings, and behaviors flow from people's (rational) social psychological engagement with their intergroup environment. With broad strokes, this "interactive metatheory" has made it possible to understand a raft of social psychological phenomena, while avoiding a series of theoretical pitfalls. The theory has served as the basis for understanding new phenomena and for the creation of new and broader theories.

The central concern of most of this work is intergroup relations, but the social identity perspective has not restricted itself to this domain. Indeed, in SCT, nothing in social psychology is off limits—interpersonal and intragroup relations are now entering the fold (see Hogg & Tindale and Sachdev & Bourhis, this volume). Indeed, intragroup phenomena cannot be logically conceived without reference to intergroup relations. On the one hand, this is a matter of simple logic; there is no "us" without "them." Perhaps more vividly, we can see that wider intergroup relations color intragroup relations. In the

United States, for example, the "war on terror" has had an effect on President Bush's approval ratings and re-election, we live with a color-coded terror alert system and witness the erosion of numerous civil liberties—all intranational phenomena articulating with international relations.

Nevertheless, there is ample opportunity for SCT to advance the study of language and communication. Sachdev and Bourhis (this volume) show that SCT can provide useful new insights on multilingual phenomena such as code-switching, and propose self-categorization as the basis for communicative shifts (see also Abrams & Hogg, 1987; Reid, Keerie, & Palomares, 2003). Similarly, Hogg and Tindale (this volume) discuss the role of self-categorization processes in the realm of intragroup relations and make a case for the role of group prototypes in influencing decision-making. However, there are some phenomena (e.g., age categorization) that continue to be difficult for SIT to address, many other phenomena (particularly in the mass-media literature) that lack credible explanation, and there are phenomena that are not easily integrated into SIT that can be better explained by SCT.

Self-Categorization Theory

In this section, we describe SCT (see also Hogg & Tindale, this volume; Turner, 1987). As our discussion unfolds, we hope that it will become apparent that we are not suggesting that SCT will overthrow SIT. To the contrary, what we are suggesting is that these theories can be best understood in concert. There is a synergy to be found in the analysis of intergroup phenomena when both theories are employed concurrently; where SIT illustrates the intergroup landscape in broad strokes, SCT explores and clarifies the details. Much like viewing a painting, too close and all we see is course lines, too far we see a blur, but at the right distance we see a detailed image spring from the canvas.

For our purposes, SCT can be understood as a social-cognitive account of identity salience. It describes what identities people are most likely to internalize, when this will happen, and why. With this information, it is a (relatively) simple matter to predict attitudes, beliefs, and behavior. The idea is that people define self in terms of categories that can be understood as contextually relevant prototypes. A prototype is a set of features that best define a category (see Rosch, 1978). The typical demonstration is to ask someone to provide a category exemplar: "bring to mind a bird." Rosch's contention is that the answer will be a representative instance of the category—the prototype—and, as such, she would predict that people will come up with prototypical instances like blackbird, sparrow, or blue jay, and not instances low in prototypicality, like penguin, dodo, or ostrich. Blackbirds and their ilk are more "birdy" birds, and the reason for this is that such prototypical birds share a set of features common to the bird category (flight, size, color, behavior, etc.), and at the same time are most distinct from other categories of animal. Another way of stating this is that prototypes are the most typical representations because they comprise the features that best define any given category in relation to background categories (they maximize the meta-contrast ratio—see Campbell, 1958). The same is of course true of human categories—nationality, gender, age, ethnicity, and so on.

But, SCT takes Rosch's static and object-oriented view of prototypes further by demonstrating that prototypes are flexible and shift with the frame of reference in which social comparisons are made. The prototypical American will differ depending upon whether she or he is being compared with the French or the Iraqis, as well as dependent upon the specific current intergroup dynamics (e.g., once war with Iraq became an inevitability, Americans may have started to see themselves as assertive, Christian, and democratic, as opposed to rich, capitalistic, and individualistic: see Haslam & Turner, 1992).

Finally, we can see that some people are more prototypical than others in any given social comparison. Just as we might think of how a prototypical Democrat differs from a prototypical Republican, we can also see that some Democrats are not highly prototypical and are, in fact, rather more like Republicans. At the same time, we can think of other nonprototypical Democrats who are even more extreme in their differences from Republicans. The upshot of this is that there is variation within groups around the prototype, and these variations can be understood only within the context of the relevant intercategory comparison. We see far left Democrats as having "extreme" views, not because there is anything inherently extreme in their views, but because their views are polarized away from those of Republicans. Should the context change, however, and the relevant comparison is between Democrats and anarchists, then the extreme Democrats will likely be perceived as quite moderate. In sum, the prototypical position shifts to best clarify the contextually relevant similarities and differences between categories.

The consequence is that people internalize self-representations that fit the contextually salient prototype. What "we" Democrats believe in contrast to "those" Republicans is the basis for identity, attitudes, beliefs, and behaviors. Depending upon the individual's position within the frame of reference, some people can be considered more or less extreme, but only within the confines of a given social comparison. Finally, as noted by Sachdev and Bourhis (this volume), the context of prototypes is not limited, it can be almost anything; indeed, it can be the language use of people in different groups in terms of multilingual choices, and the process that governs communication accommodation and differentiation (see Gallois & Callan, 1988).

Prejudice and Discrimination

The study of prejudice and discrimination has been a core of social identity research since its inception. However, there are several ways in which SCT takes the explanation of prejudice further. For example, SIT was designed to explain macro-social patterns of prejudice between groups but not individual differences in prejudice. Indeed, any evidence for individual differences was dismissed in the wake of the reductionist critique. Since then, however, SCT has explained how individuals can differ in their degrees of prejudice, but it does so in a way that is entirely consistent with the (metatheoretical) logic of SIT, and without recourse to an analysis of personality.

For example, Hajek, Abrams, and Murachver (this volume) describe the case of gay ageism. They show that *young* gay men have co-opted mainstream values of physical attractiveness, elevated them to a core ingroup norm, and then discriminated against ingroup members who do not meet the standards—"no fats, no fems, no old trolls." In other words, we have a form of intragroup discrimination. Starting with SIT, we can speculate as to where the norm came from. If we were to examine representations of gay people in (say) 1950s culture, we would first of all be struck by how few there are (there were few gay movements at the time), and we would find little information outside of the definitions common in mainstream society (the term "gay" was coined, but rarely used). In essence, we have a non-entitative group; its members exist, but are fragmented and have little collective consciousness. At most, we would probably find an effeminate stereotype but few people willing to claim membership in the category. Critically, the black movements of the 1960s gave the impetus to the gay movement—here was a clear demonstration that coordinated action could produce social change. However, rather than the social creativity of the black movements—"Black is beautiful"—what we find in the gay movement is a form of social competition. The effeminate stereotype is rejected in favor of its masculine opposite. In essence, gay men are attempting to out-compete heterosexual males on masculinity.

However, we can employ SCT to understand why this intergroup competition produces intragroup discrimination. We would argue that the result of this social competition is a tightly focused ingroup prototype. Because social competition is an attempt to reverse the status quo, the features that make gay males distinctive from heterosexual males are highly exclusive. In this context, many older gay men (among others) cannot conform to the ingroup image—by definition, many of the group are labeled deviant, and this deviance entails social ostracization, and outright discrimination (cf. the black sheep effect: Marques & Páez, 1994). Further, SCT tells us that it is those who can meet the prototype who are prejudiced in this way. Thus, wider intergroup dynamics tell us what kinds of prototypes are likely to crystallize, and by knowing who is more prototypical within the group, we can predict who is most likely to be prejudiced.

However, this situation is only likely to last for a short time. Continued intragroup differentiation will make salient alter.   y identities. Indeed, this intragroup discrimination might be   source of distinctive gay subgroups such as the "Ventura Bears" described by Hajek et al. There is an evolution of group definitions that reflect the intergroup struggle, not just for positive identity in and of itself, but in the form of staking the prototypical territory. In this case (and indeed in others, see Reid & Ng, 2004), SIT clearly and persuasively tells us what kind of intergroup landscape frames prejudice and discrimination. Quite simply, whether groups stand in cooperative or competitive relations tells us much about the likely form of people's attitudes and beliefs. However, it is SCT that tells us who within the group is mostly likely to produce discriminatory language, how this language reflects and substantiates intergroup dynamics, and when such dynamics produce new identities.

Social Categorization, Aging, and Subjective Uncertainty

A fascinating dilemma has been how we apply SIT—a theory that deals with ingroup-outgroup dichotomies—to the various phenomena of aging. Age is a continuous category, and so it raises many issues about the malleability of stereotypes. For example, Williams and Garrett (this volume) review evidence that different age cohorts perceive different age ranges for the same age categories. In addition, there is the subjective perception of aging, which Williams and Garrett capture with the Humean phrase, the "punctuated stream of experience." There is also the phenomenon of rejecting membership in the category "elderly." This has generally been seen as a self-enhancement bias—people do not wish to claim membership in a stigmatized category. Then there is evidence of *intra*category age discrimination, such as elderly people who negatively stereotype other people of the same age, and there is variation in the content of age-based stereotypes, the *old curmudgeon*, the *perfect grandparent*, and so on (Hummert, Garstka, Ryan, & Bonnesen, 2004; cf. Ryan et al., this volume).

In each case, we would argue that self- and other stereotypes are pivotal. Self-categorization theory is of benefit here because it can deal with the psychological "breaking up" of continuous data into discrete categories, the applications of these categories to self, and (rather more modestly) the content of those categories. In an attempt to address these issues, Giles and Reid (in press) have proposed a self-categorization model of aging that might prove to capture a number of these phenomena and others.

For example, it might be that we perceive aging as a series of punctuated shifts, in part, because we are compelled by our social worlds to define ourselves in terms of age-based prototypes and, at the same time, to reject others. In this model, age is represented as a series of *overlapping* normal distributions that describe the prototypical attributes of adolescents, teenagers, young adults, adults, the middle-aged, older adults, and so on (or indeed, whatever age categories might be salient). The prototypical positions will fall on the average position in all but the most extreme categories (where there is only one adjacent category to differentiate from), and there will be grey "transition areas" as we pass between the age groups. However, with time we inevitably pass through these grey areas and into the prototypical center of these age categories. Thus, we experience aging as a series of discrete events because of a push-and-pull effect of adjacent prototypes. As we pass the prototypical age of a "young adult," we feel the prototype directing our self-definition back, and this pull gets gradually stronger until reaching a zenith in the grey area between young adult and adult, where subjective uncertainty is a maximum (Berger & Bradac, 1982). At that point, the pull of the adult prototype is strong enough to break the pull of the young adult prototype—escape velocity is reached, and people re-define themselves (subjectively) as adults. With time, self-definition will grow more secure as people get closer to the core of the prototype where self-definition is distinctive and low in subjective uncertainty, only to pass though this process once again with the next transition.

Of course, the gravity of some prototypes will be especially strong, and this is likely to vary with both local psychological experience—the degree to which age happens to be a salient feature in any given individual life—and with cultural norms; all cultures place more emphasis on some transitions than on others. There might be less consistent age prescriptions, for example, for being a young adult in the United States when you are 18 years old than in most other Western countries. In terms of absolute age, an 18-year-old has much life experience, can participate in the military, is possibly undertaking higher education, and lives independent of the family. Yet drinking alcohol—which is surely a marker of young adulthood—is illegal in all states until 21 years of age (the oldest for any Western nation). Research in the US context shows that the 18- to 25-year-old period is a transition period of emerging adulthood (Arnett, 2000). In essence, the grey transition area between teen and young adult is disproportionately large compared to other transitions. The unwitting result is that drinking age laws might amplify "youthful exuberance" and lead to activities like binge drinking, drug taking, and reckless driving. Thus, one way of producing self-conceptual certainty in this transition is to engage in behavior that is normative for the young adult category—behavior that serves to differentiate self from the teen category.

If this is the case, then we can make some predictions. Cross cultural studies might show that attitudes toward drinking, alcohol consumption, and drunk driving deaths among teens vary depending upon the *consistency* of age-based laws, and the effect should be mediated by the degree of self-conceptual uncertainty that the individual experiences at the transition ages (cf. section on pluralistic ignorance below). People who feel little subjective uncertainty about being a teen are perhaps less likely to engage in binge drinking than non-prototypical teens who are in the transition to young adulthood and who are, therefore, experiencing more subjective uncertainty. Further, it would seem that cultures that have more distinctive and consistent norms or rites of passage for such transitions would be less likely to have social problems, such as binge drinking.

This process should also be evident in language. The jargon of youth is always changing, and, in part, this might be attributed to the constant generation-by-generation negotiation of distinctive self-definitions. Broadly speaking, the styles and fashions of the elders are rejected by the styles and fashions of the younger. However, should this model prove to be correct, we would predict that the very people who are most inclined to use, and indeed invent these linguistic differentiations, are those who occupy the age-transition stages where subjective uncertainty and, thus, pressure for differentiation is at its maximum.

In fact, this might be the tip of a more general communicative process. Einstein famously remarked "a person who has not made his great contribution to science before the age of thirty will never do so" (cited in Kanazawa, 2003, p. 257). Einstein's observation, though not perfectly accurate, is backed up by Kanazawa whose survey of 280 scientists evidences an "age genius curve"—a kurtosed normal distribution with the peak of male creativity between the ages of 30 and 35. This same curve is apparent for jazz musicians, painters, authors, and the distribution of crime (but see Sternberg & Lubart, 2001, for a discussion of creativity in old age). Kanazawa argues that this pattern is due to the action of evolutionarily relevant levels of testosterone, which produces competitive behavior in males. His argument for testosterone is corroborated by the observation that such competitive behavior switches off when men get married and have children, which is, in turn, associated with a decrease in testosterone. Another possibility is that optimal levels of subjective uncertainty spur creative focus—with the work being done in the transition to adulthood and being published shortly thereafter. Further, it might be that marriage with its attendant cultural norms—etched in stone—reduce uncertainty to the point where it stifles creativity (cf. Gudykunst, 1995).

If this is true, then it might be that there are shifts in creativity with age as a function of subjective uncertainty, both at the individual and cultural levels. Indeed, there is evidence that bursts of creativity co-occur with social instability and war (e.g., Hellenic Greece, Great Britain during empire growth), but are stifled when social instability is too great (e.g., during state failure). But what is it specifically about cultural certainties that are relevant? These are intimated at by Green (1989) in his introduction to the Hobbe's translation of Thucydides', *Peloponnesian war*:

> We are very near to the world of fifth-century Greece... For, strangely enough, they faced something like our problem of the mass society—a society without respect for traditional standards of birth or conduct, with few restraints in religion or mortality, with war past or war impending the most dynamic force in political life. Add to this a universal Greek rationalism— that is, the Greek's belief that he could solve the problems of the cosmos and the problems of political life by applying his brains to them (pp. ix–x).

Clearly, there are common social forces at work that make creativity a possibility, and these would seem to be the conditions where tradition has lost its irrational grip on thought.

Then there is the question of subcultural creativity. In the US black community, for example, the late 1800s to the present have spawned spirituals, blues, jazz, rock 'n' roll, and rap. Perhaps the degree to which groups are repressed produces creativity as a function of identity uncertainty. Indeed, Marris (1996) makes the case that the distribution of social status in society is essentially a distribution of social uncertainties, with a disproportionate share being allotted to lower-status groups. We might also find that creativity co-occurs with cultural norms for marriage. Cultures (or historical eras) with young marriage ages might show earlier creativity stages than contemporary North America where people are marrying later, or not at all (Castells, 1997).

In sum, we can potentially model a great number of aging phenomena by considering the identity consequences of age transition points. If we know something of the subjective uncertainty experienced by the individual, as a function of autobiographical and social factors, we can predict adherence to age-based norms, variation in linguistic differentiation, and bursts of communicative activity.

Social Identity, Self-Categorization, and the Mass-Media

If there is one area set for an explosion of work on intergroup relations it is material that has traditionally fallen within the purview of the mass-media (see Harwood & Roy, this volume). There are an array of short-range theories, phenomena, and manifestly intergroup processes in this arena and, at the same time, a dearth of integrative theory. While such an analysis has yet to gather the momentum of a full-scale invasion, it is clear that some limited range sorties have already begun, and there is much potential for more to come.

In particular, a number of phenomena investigated by media scholars beg social psychological explanation. Among others, these include the third-person effect (Davison, 1983), pluralistic ignorance (Allport, 1924), the hostile media bias (Vallone, Ross, & Lepper, 1985), the cultivation hypothesis (Gerbner & Gross, 1976), the uses and gratifications approach to media selection (Blumler & Katz, 1974), and the spiral of silence (Noelle-Neumann, 1984). With the arguable exception of the latter, all are phenomena in search of a theory. While we will not attempt to cover all of this work, it can be readily seen—as noted by others (e.g., Eveland, 2002)—that these phenomena bear more than a passing resemblance to one another and, therefore, beg a common explanation. What we propose is that SCT is one such unifying force. In what follows, we will describe the self-categorization explanations for the third-person effect and pluralistic ignorance.

The Third-Person Effect

The third-person effect is the tendency for people to perceive that they are less influenced by the media than are other people. The third-person effect has been found using a variety of media, for instance advertisements (Gunther & Thorson, 1992), anti-social music lyrics (Eveland & McLeod, 1999), news stories (Perloff, 1989), political campaigns (Cohen & Davis, 1991), pornography (Rojas, Shah, & Faber, 1996), public service announcements (Duck, Terry, & Hogg, 1998), and the miniseries *Amerika* (Lasorsa, 1989).

Relatively little research has tested theoretical explanations, but there is evidence for a number of moderating variables. The effect increases with "ego-involvement" (Perloff, 1989, 2002), which might be related to social identification (e.g., Duck, Terry, & Hogg, 1998; Price, Tewksbury, & Huang, 1998), and with self-other social distance (e.g., Cohen, Mutz, Price, & Gunther, 1988), but not always linearly (e.g., Eveland, Nathanson, Detenber, & McLeod, 1999). It also decreases with message desirability (e.g., Gunther & Thorson, 1992), and there is mixed evidence for variation due to topic knowledge, age, education level, and gender (e.g., Driscoll & Salwen, 1997; Tiedge, Silverblatt, Havice, & Rosenfeld, 1991).

Reid and Hogg (in press) have tested a self-categorization explanation for third-person perceptions that extends the work of Duck, Hogg, & Terry (1998, Duck, Terry, & Hogg, 1998). Consider the typical structure of third-person questions: how influenced are *you* by tabloid publications like the *National Enquirer*? This question is followed by an equivalent item for how influenced are *others* by the same material (both questions scored from 1 *not at all influenced*, to 7 *very influenced*). Reid and Hogg argue that to make such judgments requires three items of information. The social perceiver must (1) bring to mind a relevant comparison "other" to make a judgment, (2) consider the media in question in relation to that other (whether consumption of the particular media is normative for the comparison other), and (3) the degree of self-other (prototypical) similarity in the context where the comparison judgment is made.

Reid and Hogg (in press) asked undergraduates how similar they considered themselves to an investment banker, *trailer-trash*, and other local undergraduates. Participants were then asked to judge the influence of the *Jerry Springer Show*, *CNBC Financial News*, and *MTV* on self and each of these comparison others. The profile of influence effects is quite obvious, and followed closely with participants' judgments of the normative viewing profile of these programs. More importantly, the size of the third-person effect was moderated by perceived self-other similarity, but only for media that were normative for a given comparison other. For example, as similarity to local undergraduates increased, the greater the similarity between perceived effects of *MTV* on self and on other undergraduates (this was not true for the *Jerry Springer Show* or *CNBC Financial News*).

In a second study, Reid and Hogg (in press) asked students to judge how influential the *National Enquirer* would be on them vs. students of a local community college. Preceding this question, participants were asked to indicate their similarity to community college students (condition 1), or Stanford graduates (condition 2). By changing these similarity items, we changed the meaning of the comparison with the community college students. In condition 1, we have a simple ingroup-outgroup comparison, but it is more or less devoid of meaning. In condition 2, our participants could align themselves with Stanford graduates (they did), and, in so doing categorize themselves as members of the "college elite," and thus make a downward social comparison with the community college. Thus, we predicted, and found, a larger third-person effect in condition 2 than condition 1.

Our data suggest that third-person judgments are the result of the self-categorization process. People make third-person judgments that reflect the normative character of the social comparisons between self and others, as defined within given social contexts. Thus, third-person perceptions are not the perceptual anomaly suggested by Davison (1983). Rather, third-person perceptions are the result of a veridical social comparison process, albeit one that is normally conducted under conditions of high uncertainty—most research fails to specify exactly who the "others" are, the media is often ambiguous (e.g., "advertisements"), and the meaning of the term "influence" is often left implicit. Our analysis suggests particular strategies for social influence. Imagine you are creating a public service announcement that is designed to decrease smoking. An effective way would be to demonstrate how members of outgroups are influenced by cigarette advertisements, and that being influenced in such a way is not intelligent. In fact, the current wave of US anti-tobacco advertising uses this very technique—people who smoke are portrayed as unwitting victims of greedy, unethical, and manipulative corporations. However, for this to be successful, the anti-smoking norm would have to become ingroup defining.

Beyond these specific scenarios, the self-categorization analysis has the potential to be a truly unifying theory in this arena. Variations in the third-person perception by gender, age, and education level are readily interpretable. The normative associations that people have for any given media will be predictive of first- and third-person effects.

Pluralistic Ignorance

Pluralistic ignorance is the situation where the majority of group members privately reject the group norm, yet believe that the majority accepts the norm (Allport, 1924). For example, Prentice and Miller (1993) asked Princeton undergraduates to indicate their comfort with drinking practices on campus and to estimate the comfort level of "the average undergraduate." The result was that many people reported feeling less comfortable than the average undergraduate. Prentice and Miller (and indeed others) assume that such effects are strong evidence for the misperception of group norms; there is a paradoxical divergence between private attitudes and the norm, and yet most people engage in the normative behavior. This seems to suggest that if people would only communicate their private attitudes, the group norm would change (cf. Katz & Schanck, 1938). It has been argued (e.g., Hines, Saris, & Throckmorton-Belzer, 2002) that the media are a particularly strong source for such pluralistic ignorance. People get information about group standards—such as drug use, sexual behavior, violence, and crime—that are biased and, yet, perceive such information to be accurate.

However, Allport (1924), Prentice and Miller (1993), and others assume that the aggregate of individual opinion should equal the group norm, and they assume that they have measured individual opinion. Both are questionable assumptions. Our contention is that pluralistic ignorance is an artifact of (1) equating individual opinion with group norms and (2) measurement procedures that encourage people to consider how prototypical they are of their group, and then make social comparisons between themselves and the prototypical (i.e., most normative) group position. If this is the case, then the relative prototypicality of group members should moderate the size of the self-other distinction found by researchers like Prentice and Miller (1993).

Reid and Cropley (2004) tested the self-categorization predictions in three studies. In two surveys, we measured relative group prototypicality by asking participants "how similar are you to the average undergraduate in terms of attitudes, aspirations, and outlook on life." To encourage our participants to think about themselves with respect to the prototype, we asked them to make this same judgment with reference to different student groups (undergraduates, graduates, and engineering, communication, & mathematics students). We then asked participants to estimate how comfortable they and the average undergraduate were with the amount of drinking that occurs near campus on an average weekend. First, we replicated Prentice and Miller's main effect—people rated themselves as less comfortable than the average undergraduate. However, this main effect was moderated by relative prototypicality. Participants who considered themselves highly prototypical did not evidence the pluralistic ignorance effect, whereas participants low on prototypicality showed an amplified pluralistic ignorance effect. Further, we asked participants to rate how typical it was for themselves and for the average undergraduate to drink alcohol on the weekend, and replicated the pattern. This latter finding, in particular, suggests that people's attitudes and behaviors are actually quite consistent. When people consider themselves prototypical, they report that drinking is as typical for themselves as for the average undergraduate, and to the degree that people do not see themselves as prototypical, they report a difference between themselves and the average undergraduate. Further support for consistency was provided by evidence that self-reported comfort with drinking mediated the effect of similarity to undergraduates on self-reported drinking typicality. Contrary to Prentice and Miller's assertions, our data suggest that people's comfort level is determined by their similarity to the normative group position, which, in turn, determines behavior.

Further, Reid and Cropley (2004) manipulated the content of the salient ingroup norm. In an academic standing condition, participants were given a list of 10 universities, were told that a magazine had recently ranked them in terms of academic standing, and were asked to rank them as they believe they would have been by the magazine. In a "party school" condition, the cover story was altered so that the magazine had ostensibly ranked the same schools in terms of how good they are for partying. We then measured the degree of prototypicality as an undergraduate (as in study 1), and participant gender. As expected, for female participants, there were no differences between the experimental conditions when it came to predicting the self-reported number of standard drinks consumed per week. However, for male participants, when academic standing was the salient dimension of comparison, the number of drinks reported decreased as prototypicality increased, whereas in the party school condition, the number of drinks reported increased as prototypicality increased.

Does this mean that our participants are misperceiving the norm? No, it simply means that people see differences between themselves and others that reflect the degree to which they consider themselves prototypical. If they are prototypical, then they will engage in the prototypical group behaviors—or at least report doing so—and if they are not prototypical, they will not report behavior in accordance with the group norm.

These findings have an obvious implication for applied research on self-destructive behaviors. Depending upon how prototypical the individual social perceiver considers himself or herself within a given frame of reference determines what they will report as typical behavior, and the degree to which alternative identities are salient can even reverse self-reported behaviors. Our data suggest that any researchers who aim to measure normative behavior consider their participants' salient self-categorizations.

Conclusion

Recognition that communication has received less attention than it deserves by social identity theorists, and indeed social psychologists more generally, is easy to find. The dominant paradigm prioritizes cognition above all else and, in so doing, casts language and communication as shadow effects—language as a slave messenger to cognition (Ng & Bradac, 1993). But language is central to social life, and there are a number of ways in which its study will take our (social cognitive) theories further. While this has been amply demonstrated in this volume, these are early days, and there is much work to be done. Indeed, there are some markers of this upturn in interest: a new Intergroup Communication Interest Group at the International Communication Association has come to life (with inaugural panels October 2004 in New Orleans), a forthcoming special issue in *Group Processes and Intergroup Relations* on communication and intergroup relations (Reid & Giles, in press), and the continued attention devoted to intergroup issues at the *International Conferences on Language and Social Psychology*.

But, communicative phenomena in the intergroup realm are more important than trifling social cognitive artifacts. Era defining moments in the past few years have shifted our collective attention from relatively benign intranational events and politics to the wider international stage of terrorism, state failure, globalization, zero-sum conflict, and propaganda. It takes little more than a moment's reflection to appreciate that the effects will resonate for a generation or more to come—the international scene has not been so sharpened by intergroup conflict since World War II. Along with this shift, we should expect a renaissance in the study of intergroup relations. There are a great many forms that this can, and will, take. Sociologists, political scientists, and historians will have their day. However, if social psychology is going to claim any continued relevance to understanding the social issues of our time, it will have to embrace the communicative dimension of intergroup relations.

References

Abrams, D., & Hogg, M. A. (1987). Language attitudes, frames of reference, and social identity: A Scottish dimension. *Journal of Language and Social Psychology, 6,* 201–213.

Abrams, D., & Hogg, M. A. (1990a). The context of discourse: Let's not throw out the baby with the bathwater. *Philosophical Psychology, 3,* 219–225.

Abrams, D., & Hogg, M. A. (1990b). Social identification, self-categorization, and social influence. *European Review of Social Psychology, 1,* 195–228.

Allport, F. H. (1924). *Social psychology.* Boston: Houghton Mifflin.

Arnett, J. J. (2000). Emerging adulthood: A theory of development from the late teens through the twenties. *American Psychologist, 55,* 469–480.

Aronson, E. (1992). The return of the repressed: Dissonance theory makes a comeback. *Psychological Inquiry, 3,* 303–311.

Bales, R. F. (1956). Task status and likeability as a function of talking and listening in decision-making groups. In L. D. White (Ed.), *The state of the social sciences* (pp. 148–161). Chicago: University of Chicago Press.

Berger, C. R., & Bradac, J. J. (1982). *Language and social knowledge.* London: Edward Arnold.

Billig, M. (1996). Nationalism as an international ideology: Imagining the nation, others and the world of nations. In G. M. Breakwell & E. Lyons (Eds.), *Changing European identities: Social psychological analyses of social change* (pp. 181–194). Woburn, MA: Butterworth-Heinemann.

Blumler J. G., & Katz, E. (Eds.). (1974). *The uses of mass communications: Current perspectives on gratifications research.* Beverly Hills, CA: Sage.

Campbell, D. T. (1958). Common fate, similarity and other indices of the status of aggregates of persons as social entities. *Behavioral Science, 3,* 14–25.

Castells, E. (1997). *The power of identity*. Malden, MA: Blackwell.

Cohen, J., & Davis, R. G. (1991). Third-person effects and the differential impact on negative political advertising. *Journalism Quarterly, 68*, 680–688.

Cohen, J., Mutz, D., Price, V., & Gunther, A. (1988). Perceived impact of defamation. *Public Opinion Quarterly, 52*, 161–173.

Davison, W. P. (1983). The third-person effect in communication. *Public Opinion Quarterly, 47*, 1–15.

Driscoll, P. D., & Salwen, M. B. (1997). Self-perceived knowledge of the O. J. Simpson trial: Third-person perception and perceptions of guilt. *Journalism and Mass Communication Quarterly, 74*, 541–556.

Duck, J. M., Hogg, M. A., & Terry, D. J. (1998). Perceived self-other differences in persuasibility: The effects of interpersonal and group-based similarity. *European Journal of Social Psychology, 28*, 1–22.

Duck, J. M., Terry, D. J., & Hogg, M. A. (1998). Perceptions of a media campaign: The role of social identity and the changing intergroup context. *Personality and Social Psychology Bulletin, 24*, 3–16.

Eveland, W. P. Jr. (2002). The impact of news and entertainment media on perceptions of social reality. In J. P. Dillard & M. Pfau (Eds.), *The persuasion handbook: Developments in theory and practice* (pp. 691–727). Newbury Park, CA: Sage.

Eveland, W. P. Jr., & McLeod, D. M. (1999). The effect of social desirability on perceived media impact: Implications for third-person perceptions. *International Journal of Public Opinion Research, 11*, 315–333.

Eveland, W. P. Jr., Nathanson, A. I., Detenber, B. H., & McLeod, D. M. (1999). Rethinking the social distance corollary: Perceived likelihood of exposure and the third-person perception. *Communication Research, 26*, 275–302.

Festinger, L. (1950). Informal social communication. *Psychological Review, 57*, 271–282.

Gallois, C., & Callan, V. J. (1988). Communication accommodation and the prototypical speaker: Predicting of status and solidarity. *Language and Communication, 8*, 271–283.

Gerbner, G., & Gross, L. (1976). Living with television: The violence profile. *Journal of Communication, 26*, 173–199.

Giles, H., & Coupland, N. (1991). *Language: Context and consequences*. Milton Keynes, UK: Open University Press.

Giles, H., & Johnson, P. (1981). The role of language in ethnic group relations. In J. C. Turner & H. Giles (Eds.), *Intergroup behavior* (pp. 199–243). Oxford, UK: Blackwell.

Giles, H., & Johnson, P. (1987). Ethnolinguistic identity theory: A social psychological approach to language maintenance. *International Journal of the Sociology of Language, 68*, 66–99.

Giles, H., & Reid, S. A. (in press). Ageism across the lifespan: Towards a self-categorization model of ageing. *Journal of Social Issues*.

Green, D. (1989). *Thucydides' History of the Peloponnesian War: The complete Hobbes translation*. Chicago: University of Chicago Press.

Gudykunst, W. B. (1995). Anxiety/uncertainty management (AUM) theory: Current status. In R. L. Wiseman (Ed.), *Intercultural communication theory* (pp. 8–58).

Thousand Oaks, CA: Sage.

Gudykunst, W. B., & Ting-Toomey, S. (1990). Ethnic identity, language and communication breakdowns. In H. Giles & W. P. Robinson (Eds.), *Handbook of language and social psychology* (pp. 309–327). Chichester, UK: Wiley.

Gunther, A. C., & Thorson, E. (1992). Perceived persuasive effects of product commercials and public service announcements: Third-person effects in new domains. *Communication Research, 19,* 574–596.

Haslam, S. A. (2000). *Psychology in organizations: A social identity approach.* London: Sage.

Haslam, S. A., & Turner, J. C. (1992). Context-dependent variation in social stereotyping 2: The relationship between frame of reference, self-categorization and accentuation. *European Journal of Social Psychology, 22,* 251–277.

Hines, D., Saris, R. N., & Throckmorton-Belzer, L. (2002). Pluralistic ignorance and health risk behaviors: Do college students misperceive social approval for risky behaviors on campus and in media? *Journal of Applied Social Psychology, 32,* 2621–2640.

Hogg, M. A. (2001). A social identity model of leadership. *Personality and Social Psychology Review, 5,* 184–200.

Hogg, M. A., & Terry, D. J. (2000). Social identity and self-categorization processes in organizational contexts. *Academy of Management Review, 25,* 121–140.

Hummert, M. L., Garstka, T. A., Ryan, E. B., & Bonnesen, J. L. (2004). The role of age stereotypes in interpersonal communication. In J. F. Nussbaum & J. Coupland (Eds.), *Handbook of communication and aging research* (pp. 91–121). Mahwah, NJ: Erlbaum.

Israel, J., & Tajfel, H. (1972). *The context of social psychology: A critical assessment.* London: Academic Press.

Kanazawa, S. (2003). Why productivity fades with age: The crime-genius connection. *Journal of Research in Personality, 37,* 257–272.

Katz, D., & Schanck, R. L. (1938). *Social psychology.* New York: Wiley.

Lasorsa, D. L. (1989). Real and perceived effects of "Amerika." *Journalism Quarterly, 66,* 373–378.

Marques, J. M., & Páez, D. (1994). The "black sheep effect": Social categorization, rejection of ingroup deviates, and perception of group variability. *European Review of Social Psychology, 5,* 37–68.

Marris (1996). *The politics of uncertainty: Attachment in public and private life.* London: Routledge.

Ng, S. H., & Bradac, J. J. (1993). *Power in language.* Thousand Oaks, CA: Sage.

Noelle-Neumann, E. (1984). *The spiral of silence: Public opinion and our social skin.* Chicago: The University of Chicago Press.

Oakes, P. J., Haslam, S. A., & Turner, J. C. (1994). *Stereotyping and social reality.* Oxford, UK: Blackwell.

Perloff, R. M. (1989). Ego-involvement and the third-person effect of televised news coverage. *Communication Research, 16,* 236–262.

Perloff, R. M. (1993). Third-person effect research 1983–1992: A review and synthesis. *International Journal of Public Opinion Research, 5,* 167–184.

Perloff, R. M. (2002). The third-person effect. In B. Jennings & D. Zillman (Eds.), *Media effects: Advances in theory and research* (2nd ed., pp. 489–506). Mahwah, NJ: Erlbaum.

Prentice, D. A., & Miller, D. T. (1993). Pluralistic ignorance and alcohol use on campus: Some consequences of misperceiving the social norm. *Journal of Personality and Social Psychology, 64*, 243–256.

Price, V., Tewksbury, D., & Huang, L. N. (1998). Third-person effects on publication of a Holocaust-denial advertisement. *Journal of Communication, 48*, 3–26.

Reicher, S. D. (1984). The St. Paul's riot: An explanation of the limits of crowd action in terms of a social identity model. *European Journal of Social Psychology, 14*, 1–21.

Reicher, S. D., & Hopkins, N. (1996). Seeking influence through characterizing self-categories: An analysis of anti-abortionist rhetoric. *British Journal of Social Psychology, 35*, 297–311.

Reicher, S. D., & Hopkins, N. (2004). On the science of the art of leadership. In D. van Knippenberg & M. A. Hogg (Eds.), *Leadership and Power: Identity Processes in Groups and Organizations* (pp. 197–209). London: Sage.

Reicher, S. D., Spears, R., & Postmes, T. (1995). A social identity model of deindividuation phenomena. *European Review of Social Psychology, 6*, 161–198.

Reid, S. A., & Cropley, C. J. (2004). *A self-categorization explanation of pluralistic ignorance.* Unpublished manuscript, University of California, Santa Barbara.

Reid, S., & Giles, H. (Eds.). (in press). Communication and intergroup contact [Special issue]. *Group Processes and Intergroup Relations.*

Reid, S. A., & Hogg, M. A. (in press). A self-categorization explanation of the third-person effect. *Human Communication Research.*

Reid, S. A., Keerie, N., & Palomares, N. A. (2003). Language, gender salience, and social influence. *Journal of Language and Social Psychology, 22*, 210–233.

Reid, S. A., & Ng, S. H. (2004). Identity, power, and strategic social categorizations: Theorizing the language of leadership. In D. van Knippenberg & M. A. Hogg (Eds.), *Leadership and power: Identity processes in groups and organizations* (pp. 210–223). London: Sage.

Rojas, H., Shah, D. V., & Faber, R. J. (1996). For the good of others: Censorship and the third-person effect. *International Journal of Public Opinion Research, 8*, 162–185.

Rosch, E. (1978). Principles of categorization. In E. Rosch & B. B. Lloyd (Eds.), *Cognition and categorization* (pp. 27–48). Hillsdale, NJ: Erlbaum.

Sedikides, C., & Strube, M. J. (1995). The multiply motivated self. *Personality and Social Psychology Bulletin, 21*, 1330–1335.

Semin, G. R. (2000). Agenda 2000—Communication: Language as an implementational device for cognition. *European Journal of Social Psychology, 30*, 595–612.

Semin, G., & Fiedler, K. (Eds.). (1992). *Language, interaction and social cognition.* London: Sage.

Shepard, C. A., Giles, H., & Le Poire, B. A. (2001). Communication accommodation theory. In W. P. Robinson & H. Giles (Eds.), *The new handbook of language and social psychology* (pp. 33–56). Chichester, UK: Wiley.

Sternberg, R. J., & Lubart, T. I. (2001). Wisdom and creativity. In J. E. Birren & K. W. Schaie (Eds.), *Handbook of the psychology of aging* (5th ed., pp. 500–522). San Diego:

Academic Press.

Swann, W. B. (1990). To be adored or to be known? The interplay of self-enhancement and self-verification. In E. T. Higgins & R. M. Sorrentino (Eds.), *Handbook of motivation and cognition: Foundations of social behavior* (Vol. 2, pp. 408–448). New York: Guilford.

Tajfel, H. (1969). Cognitive aspects of prejudice. *Journal of Social Issues, 25*, 79–97.

Tiedge, J. T., Silverblatt, A., Havice, M. J., & Rosenfeld, R. (1991). Discrepancy between perceived first-person and perceived third-person mass media effects. *Journalism Quarterly, 68*, 141–154.

Turner, J. C. (1987). A self-categorization theory. In J. C. Turner, M. A. Hogg, P. J. Oakes, S. D. Reicher, & M. S. Wetherell, *Rediscovering the social group: A self-categorization theory* (pp. 42–67). Oxford, UK: Basil Blackwell.

Turner, J. C. (1991). *Social influence*. Pacific Grove, CA: Brooks/Cole.

Turner, J. C. (1999). Some current issues in research on social identity and self-categorization theories. In N. Ellemers, R. Spears, & B. Doosje (Eds.), *Social identity: Context, commitment, content* (pp. 6–34). Oxford, UK: Blackwell.

Vallone, R. P., Ross, L., & Lepper, M. R. (1985) The hostile media phenomenon: Biased perception and perceptions of media bias in coverage of the Beirut massacre, *Journal of Personality and Social Psychology, 49*, 577–585.

van Dijk, T. A. (1987). *Communicating racism: Ethnic prejudice in thought and talk*. Newbury Park, CA: Sage.

Contributors

Jessica R. Abrams received her PhD in communication from the University of California, Santa Barbara. She is assistant professor in speech communication at California Polytechnic State University, San Luis Obispo. She studies intergroup communication. Her specific areas of interest include understanding the role of mass media in shaping perceptions of social group memberships, the relationship between communication and identity, and intergenerational communication. Abrams recently published articles in *Communication Yearbook* and the *Handbook of International and Intercultural Communication*.

Ann P. Anas is research coordinator in communication and aging at McMaster University in Hamilton, Ontario, Canada. Along with Ellen Ryan, she has studied intergenerational communication, computer applications, story writing, and life management of older adults. For the past 10 years, she has been the coordinator of S.H.A.R.E. (Seniors Helping Advance Research Excellence), a group of approximately 300 adults, 60 years and older, who volunteer to participate in various communication and aging research projects at McMaster University.

Selina Bajorek has a background in nursing and social work. Her writing focuses on the impact of visual impairment from the perspective of personal, interpersonal, and societal factors. Her recent article in *Educational Gerontology* addresses coping with age-related vision loss in everyday reading activities. She has considerable experience volunteering with the Canadian National Institute for the Blind.

Nancy Baym is associate professor of communication studies at the University of Kansas. She is a founding member and president of the Association of Internet Researchers (2003–2005). Her research on online community and personal relationships can be found in her book *Tune In, Log On: Soaps, Fandom, and Online Community* (Sage Publications). Her work has also appeared in journals, including *New Media & Society*, *The Journal of Computer-Mediated Communication*, and *Research on Language and Social Interaction*.

Amanda Beaman is a doctoral student in clinical psychology at the Centre for Research in Human Development at Concordia University, Montreal, Quebec. Her research explores the relationships between autobiographical memory, cognitive ability and interpersonal problem solving in older adults, and the predictors of adjustment and satisfaction in retirement. In collaboration with Ellen Ryan, she has written about person-centered communication with cognitively impaired older adults.

Richard Y. Bourhis was educated in the French and English school system in Montreal, and obtained a B.Sc. in psychology at McGill University in 1971. He pursued his graduate studies in social psychology at the University of Bristol, England, where he obtained a PhD in 1977. As associate professor, Bourhis taught social psychology at McMaster University in Ontario and then joined the psychology department at the Université du Québec à Montréal (UQAM), where he is now full professor. Richard Bourhis published extensively in English and French on topics such as language planning, bilingual communication, discrimination and intergroup relations, immigration, and acculturation. He has served as consultant on language policy issues for various governments including Canada, Québec, the Basque Autonomous Community, and Catalonia in Spain. Bourhis was elected fellow of the Canadian Psychological Association in 1988 and member of the Society for Experimental Social Psychology (SESP) in 1991. In 1996, he was elected director of the Concordia-UQAM Chair in Ethnic Studies at UQAM and is also a member of the Immigration et Métropole research group at the Université de Montréal.

Victor J. Callan is professor of management at the University of Queensland Business School, Brisbane, Australia. His latest research examines the impact of IT-driven change upon employee status and identity, and he is working with large mining companies to explore the links between building sustainable mining communities and place and social identities. His long-standing research interests examine the links between communication, organizational change, and employee adjustment. Callan is widely published in a variety of international journals in psychology, management and communication.

Cindy Gallois is professor of psychology and director of the Centre for Social Research in Communication at the University of Queensland. Her research focuses on intergroup communication in intercultural, organizational, and health contexts. Particular foci include social identity and communication accommodation, communication between health professionals and patients, and communication accommodation in adjustment to organizational change. She is a past president of the International Communication Association and International Association of Language and Social Psychology.

Peter Garrett is senior lecturer at the Centre for Language and Communication Research, Cardiff University, Wales. His primary research is on subjective factors in language and communication, such as awareness, attitudes, evaluations, ideology and values. His current focus is on issues of globalization, language attitudes and use, social identity, and on evaluations of intergenerational communication across the lifespan. He teaches sociolinguistics, attitudes to language, persuasive communication, and communication research methods. He is editor of the journal *Language Awareness* (published by Multilingual Matters).

Howard Giles (PhD, DSc: University of Bristol, 1971 & 1996) is assistant dean of undergraduate studies and professor (and previous chair) of communication (with affiliated positions in psychology and linguistics) at the University of California, Santa Barbara (UCSB). Previously, he was professor of Social Psychology, as well as head of psychology, at the University of Bristol, England. His research explores different areas of applied intergroup communication research and theory, with a longstanding focus on intergenerational communication and more recently, police-civilian relations; he is executive director of the new interdisciplinary research Center on Police Practices and Community at UCSB.

Phil Graham is Canada research chair in communication and technology at the University of Waterloo and senior lecturer in communication at the University of Queensland Business School, Australia. He has written numerous articles and chapters in his areas of research and is a co-editor of *Critical Discourse Studies*. Graham is special issues editor for *Cultural Politics* and is on the editorial boards of *New Media & Society* and *Critical Perspectives on International Business*. He is currently completing two books for Peter Lang, *Hypercapitalism* and *The Digital Dark Ages*.

Christopher Hajek is assistant professor of communication at the University of Texas, San Antonio. His research interests include intercultural and intergroup communication, and he is particularly interested in the effects of social stigmatization on communication behavior and health in a variety of contexts. He received his PhD from the University of California, Santa Barbara, and his MA from the University of Hawaii.

Jake Harwood is associate professor of communication and chair of the gerontology program at the University of Arizona. He received his PhD in communication from the University of California at Santa Barbara. His research focuses on intergroup communication, with a focus on age groups and the grandparent-grandchild relationship. He examines how cognitive and societal representations of groups relate to communication processes. His research draws on theories of social identity, intergroup behavior, and communication accommodation. He has published more than 50 articles in professional journals (e.g., *Personality and Social Psychology Bulletin, Journal of Communication, Journal of Applied Communication Research*). Harwood is book review editor for the *Journal of Language and Social Psychology*.

Michael L. Hecht is professor of communication arts and sciences at the Pennsylvania State University. He has published widely on culture, identity, and intergroup communication, including two recent books (*African American Communication; Communicating Prejudice*) and numerous articles and chapters. His communication theory of identity grew out of these studies. His National Institute of Drug Abuse funded Drug Resistance Strategies project applied this interest to examine cultural factors in adolescent substance use, and developed a successful, multicultural school-based intervention for high school and middle school students. Hecht also has helped design and evaluate culture-based drug treatment programs.

268 • *Contributors*

Michael A. Hogg is professor of social psychology and an Australian professorial fellow at the University of Queensland. He is also a fellow of the Society for the Psychological Study of Social Issues, and a fellow of the Academy of the Social Sciences in Australia. He is co-editor of *Group Processes and Intergroup Relations* and series editor of Sage's *Key Texts in Social Psychology*. His primary research interests are in social identity, group processes, and intergroup relations, with a current focus on leadership, group differentiation, and uncertainty and extremism. He has published more than 200 books, chapters, and articles on these topics.

Ronald L. Jackson II is associate professor of culture and communication theory in the Department of Communication Arts and Sciences at the Pennsylvania State University. He is associate editor of the *Howard Journal of Communications* and first vice president of the Eastern Communication Association. Additionally, he is author of *The Negotiation of Cultural Identity; African American Communication: Identity and Culture* (with Michael Hecht and Sidney Ribeau); *African American Rhetoric(s): Interdisciplinary Perspectives* (with Elaine Richardson); *Scripting the Black Body: Intersections of Communication, Culture and Identity; African American Communication and Identities: Essential Readings;* and *Understanding African American Rhetoric* (with Elaine Richardson). Jackson's theory work includes the development of two paradigms coined "cultural contracts theory" and "black masculine identity theory."

Elizabeth Jones is senior lecturer in organizational psychology at Griffith University, Brisbane, Australia. Her key research areas are organizational communication, intergroup communication, work stress, and organizational change. Her most recent publications have included a review of organizational communication for *Communication Research*.

Tamar Murachver is a senior lecturer in psychology at the University of Otago, New Zealand. She obtained her PhD from the University of California, San Diego, where she received training in cognitive and developmental psychology. Her research and teaching focus on issues in language use and child development. Her research interests include the interplay between language and memory, how language is used to create and maintain social categories (such as gender and ethnicity), and how opportunities to communicate help children learn about the thoughts and feelings of others.

Nicholas A. Palomares (PhD, University of California, Santa Barbara) is assistant professor in the Department of Communication at the University of California, Davis. His research focuses on conversational behavior and language use. Specifically, he is concerned with how individuals detect others' goals during social interaction and what consequences individuals' inferences of others' goals have on both goal detectors and goal pursuers. His other research includes understanding why and how gendered communicative behavior occurs and how such communication affects social influence and judgments.

Neil Paulsen is lecturer in organization and communication at the University of Queensland Business School, Brisbane, Australia. His research interests and publications explore intergroup perspectives on organizational behavior, change, and communication. A current project investigates the role of place identity in organizational community engagement processes. Paulsen is on the editorial board of *Intervention Research: An International Journal for Culture, Organization and Management*. His most recent work includes an edited volume on *Managing Boundaries in Organizations* (Palgrave Macmillan).

Margaret J. Pitts is a PhD candidate in the Department of Communication Arts and Sciences at the Pennsylvania State University. Her dissertation research is in the area of sojourner experiences and identities. She was recently awarded a semester teaching release from the Research and Graduate Studies Office to conduct ethnographic research in Paris, France, among US American students studying abroad. Her future research will center upon identity transitions across the lifespan from an intergroup perspective, looking specifically at significant life course events and their impact on socio-personal identities.

Tom Postmes is professor of communication and social psychology at the University of Exeter, and a research fellow of the Economic and Social Research Council. He was associate editor of the British Journal of Social Psychology (2001–2003). His research interests are group processes and communication, focusing on processes of social identity, influence, norms, collective action, intergroup conflict, perceptions of discrimination and oppression, and on the domain of online groups and computer-mediated communication. He co-edits two forthcoming books: *Individuality and the Group* with Jolanda Jetten (Sage) and the *Oxford Handbook of Internet Psychology* with Joinson, McKenna, & Reips (OUP).

Scott A. Reid is an assistant professor in the Department of Communication at the University of California, Santa Barbara. His research interests are in intergroup relations, particularly as framed by social identity, language use, and power. He has published work on leadership, language, and power, third-person perceptions, and gender. Reid is a founding member (along with Howard Giles) and current chair of the intergroup communication interest group at the International Communication Association.

Abhik Roy is associate professor in the Department of Communication and Culture at Howard University. His primary teaching and research interests are in intercultural communication, communication theory, and qualitative research methods. He is the author of the book *Selling Stereotypes: Images of Women in Indian Television Commercials*. In addition, Roy's research has appeared in several important communication journals, such as the *Western Journal of Communication, International and Intercultural Annual, Journal of Popular Culture, Journal of Language and Intercultural Communication, Journal of Applied Communication Research*, and *The Howard Journal of Communications*, among others.

Ellen Bouchard Ryan is professor in the Department of Psychiatry and Behavioral Neurosciences and in gerontology at McMaster University in Hamilton, Canada. She is former director of the McMaster Centre for Gerontological Studies and former chair of the Department of Psychology at the University of Notre Dame in Indiana. She has edited three special journal issues on aging and communication (*International Journal of Aging and Human Development; Health Communication; Language and Communication*). Her current research concerns communication predicaments experienced by older adults with sensory, cognitive, and physical impairments and the role of empowering communication in fostering successful aging with a disability.

Itesh Sachdev was born and raised in Kenya, did his training in psychology at the University of Bristol (UK, undergraduate) and McMaster University (Canada, doctoral). He is a reader in the Social Psychology of Language and Groups at Birkbeck College, University of London. He has published widely in the social psychology of intergroup relations and worked with diverse sets of participants from many parts of the world including Bolivia, Canada, France, Hong Kong, India, Taiwan, Thailand, Tunisia, and the UK. He is the current president of the British Association of Canadian Studies and the editor of the London Journal of Canadian Studies.

R. Scott Tindale is professor and chairperson of psychology at Loyola University Chicago. His major areas of research include small group performance, socially shared cognitions, individual and group decision-making, and social influence in groups. He is an associate editor at the *Journal of Personality and Social Psychology: Interpersonal Relations and Group Processes* and *Group Processes and Intergroup Relations* and has co-edited six books on various aspects of applied social psychology or group processes.

Angie Williams's research centers around social psychological approaches to language and communication. She has published more than 40 book chapters and articles dealing with the communication of ageism, communication accommodation, intergroup theory, perceptions of elder and teenage communicators, Eastern and Western perspectives on intergenerational communication, language attitudes, and media images of elders. She is a contributor to *Communication Yearbook, The Handbook of Communication and Aging* as well as *The Handbook of Perceptual Dialectology*. She has co-edited special issues of the *Journal of Communication* and the *International Journal of Applied Linguistics*. She is co-author of *Intergenerational Communication Across the Lifespan* (with Jon Nussbaum: LEA) and *Investigating Language Attitudes: Social Meanings of Dialect, Ethnicity and Performance* (with Peter Garrett and Nikolas Coupland: University of Wales Press). Williams is currently preparing an edited book on language, communication and adolescence with Crispin Thurlow.

INDEX

Howard Giles,
GENERAL EDITOR

This series explores new and exciting advances in the ways in which language both reflects and fashions social reality—and thereby constitutes critical means of social action. As well as these being central foci in face-to-face interactions across different cultures, they also assume significance in the ways that language functions in the mass media, new technologies, organizations, and social institutions. Language as Social Action does not uphold apartheid against any particular methodological and/or ideological position, but, rather, promotes (wherever possible) cross-fertilization of ideas and empirical data across the many, all-too-contrastive, social scientific approaches to language and communication. Contributors to the series will also accord due attention to the historical, political, and economic forces that contextually bound the ways in which language patterns are analyzed, produced, and received. The series will also provide an important platform for theory-driven works that have profound, and often times provocative, implications for social policy.

For further information about the series and submitting manuscripts, please contact:

Howard Giles
Dept of Communication
University of California at Santa Barbara
Santa Barbara, CA 93106-4020
HowieGiles@aol.com

To order other books in this series, please contact our Customer Service Department at:

(800) 770-LANG (within the U.S.)
(212) 647-7706 (outside the U.S.)
(212) 647-7707 FAX

Or browse online by series at:

www.peterlangusa.com